DATE DUE			

CREATIVE ACADEMIC BARGAINING
Managing Conflict in the Unionized College and University

Robert Birnbaum

Professor of Higher Education and Chairman
Department of Higher and Adult Education
Teachers College, Columbia University

Foreword by

Clark Kerr

President Emeritus
University of California

Teachers College, Columbia University
New York and London   1980

To my wife Doris
and to my children Steven, Matthew, and Ann

Copyright © 1980 Teachers College, Columbia University. Published by Teachers College, 1234 Amsterdam Avenue, New York, New York 10027.

Library of Congress Cataloging in Publication Data

Birnbaum, Robert.
  Creative academic bargaining.

  Includes bibliographical references and index.
    1.   Collective bargaining—College teachers—
United States.   I.   Title.
LB2335.885.U6B57   331.89'04137812   80-18806

ISBN: 0-8077-2631-1

Manufactured in the United States of America

1   2   3   4   5   6   7   8   9   88   87   86   85   84   83   82   81   80

87846

Contents

Foreword

Collective bargaining, in nearly all situations, has its origins more in antagonism than in affection, in hate than in love. Some persons or groups of persons have grievances, dissatisfactions, unmet aspirations. This results in unionization and unionization in collective bargaining.

But collective bargaining has a life history. It may remain, where it started, based on hostility. Hostility may even turn to enduring enmity. Or, and more commonly, it may move in the other direction toward "armed truce," and perhaps, on from there to "working harmony" and to "union-management cooperation,"* and then beyond that even to collusion.

This volume is concerned with the evolution of collective bargaining in academic life, and with a particular form of evolution from conflict to cooperation.

An excellent time to survey the experience with and the possibilities for collective bargaining in American colleges is 1980. There has now been a decade of experience, beginning with the City University of New York in 1969. At the moment (1977 to 1980) there is a lull on new extensions of bargaining; and thus a time for retrospective and prospective examination. The growth period was 1969 to 1976, with the greatest activity from 1969 to 1971 with the inclusion of the CUNY and SUNY systems, both in New York state.

A new period may lie ahead. How it will be defined is still unknown. The Yeshiva decision, depending on its further applications, may dampen the extension of collective bargaining in the private sector. In the public sector, much depends on whether the remaining half of the states protect academic collective bargaining and on what happens in a few key states that now do provide such protection, particularly Minnesota and California. Will the University of Minnesota and the California State College faculties opt for unionization?

*Frederick H. Harbison and John R. Coleman, *Goals and Strategy in Collective Bargaining* (New York: Harper and Brothers, 1951).

Currently, higher education is 30% organized at the two-year college level and 20% at the four-year level in terms of coverage of faculty members. Deteriorating levels of real salaries for faculty members and increasing intrusion of public authorities into the governance of academic life argue for a renewal of successful unionization efforts. But collective bargaining to date has a mixed record in arresting these two developments, and in its impact on on-campus relations.

It is with this latter area, on-campus relations, that this study concerns itself. The central theme is the possible and desirable movement of collective bargaining from destructive to constructive approaches— the strategies and tactics for achieving *Creative Academic Bargaining*. Bargaining need not be a zero-sum game where the gain of one party is a loss to the other, but may explore ways in which both sides can benefit.

Birnbaum places his discussion within a very broad framework of social science research. He draws on all of the social sciences for theories and insights that illuminate the process of bargaining and the opportunities that lie within it. His is a most sophisticated analysis of the roles of the internal parties and of external forces and participants. I know of no study that better draws together historical experience, social analysis, and detailed knowledge of the peculiarities of academic life around the dramatic event of the introduction of collective bargaining.

Birnbaum is not primarily concerned with whether there should or should not be collective bargaining in academic life but rather with how it can be made to work best once it is in place. And yet, showing how it can work best may affect attitudes on whether it should be permitted or encouraged or opposed.

The author has at least two major goals. One is to expand understanding of the totality of the process and its many variations. At this he is superb. The second is to persuade the parties of the benefits of "creative academic bargaining" and to indicate how the "relations between the parties" may be changed to realize these benefits. I am sure there are such benefits, and I am sure that changes can be made that will help assure them. I am less sure than Birnbaum seems to be that these steps will so frequently be taken. Experience in American industry seems to indicate that sometimes they are and that sometimes they are not.

Whether or not many or all follow the preferred path, it is still most helpful to have a guide for those who do or are considering so doing. For those who wish to follow Plato's precept that "knowledge should be his guide," here is found much useful knowledge on how to increase "problem-solving potential," on how to find "mutually acceptable solutions."

The axis of development of any human and institutional interrelationship is subject to some control. Concern with the tilt of the axis requires a historical perspective about where you want to be as much as with where you are at the present moment. Too often, parties to collective bargaining, particularly novices, concentrate on the moment and not on the more distant goal. Birnbaum dramatically highlights the importance of managing the direction of movement as well as manipulating the current situation—of longer-term strategies as well as short-term tactics. As a guide to *strategic* collective bargaining, I highly recommend *Creative Academic Bargaining*.

Clark Kerr

President Emeritus
University of California

Preface

In the vast majority of the bargaining relationships in this country, contracts are negotiated in an unimaginative and inflexible manner which is generally unsatisfactory to both parties. . . . Bargaining at its worst finds the contract itself drawn up in a series of prolonged and painful meetings in which compromises are made just before a strike deadline is reached. Enmities are formed and wounds opened which are not soon forgotten (Healy, 1965, p. 41).

THIS VIEW OF collective bargaining was written before academic unionization began developing into the significant force that it represents today in American higher education, but it is probably no less true of colleges and universities now than it was of the industrial sector about which it was written 15 years ago. The implementation of bargaining in institutions of higher education poses unusual problems, because it introduces a previously unknown structure with potentially major effects upon the ways in which faculty and administration interact. In some cases, the results of academic bargaining have been beneficial and constructive. In others, bargaining has promoted open warfare between various campus groups and has caused divisiveness and hostility, which, if unchecked, can destroy the delicate fabric of communications, authority, and interpersonal relationships that uniquely defines the academy. Where bargaining exists, its processes may be among the most important determinants of the campus environment. Little has been written about academic bargaining as a process, or about why the individuals and groups involved in bargaining behave as they do. This book is a first attempt to analyze the causes of bargaining behavior in the unionized college and university.

The book is basically concerned with two questions: What are the factors that tend to lead academic bargaining toward destructive conflict? and What can participants in the bargaining process do to make it creative, constructive, and supportive of institutional goals? Proper consideration of these two critical questions requires an interdisciplinary orientation, and the book draws widely upon a number of scholarly and professional fields. While the literature of academic bargaining provides useful descriptive and analytic material, for the most part it ignores the interpersonal and intergroup dynamics with which we shall be concerned. A significant body of work in such fields as the social psychology of bargaining and negotiation, conflict resolution, organization behavior, and creative problem solving provides critical insights into how individuals and groups in situations similar to academic bargaining are likely to behave. Specialists in such applied areas as industrial relations, organization development, and diplomacy have described the correlates of individual and group behavior in other situations involving conflicting interests or ideologies. Material from these and other fields have been drawn together in an attempt to better understand, and consequently change, the academic bargaining process.

There are a number of perspectives from which academic bargaining can be viewed. Institutionally or legally, collective bargaining can be considered as a process by which "management" and "labor" interact within certain legal guidelines to mutually determine terms and conditions of employment. The major issues considered from such a perspective include such matters as the legislative and legal context, unit determination and identification of the employer and the scope of bargaining, the effect of bargaining upon organizational patterns and existing governance units such as senates, and the impact of bargaining upon the conditions of academic work. In general, these are the approaches taken by the major works in the existing literature of academic bargaining (see, for example, Angell, Kelley, & Associates, 1977; Carnegie Council on Policy Studies, 1977; Carr & VanEyck, 1973; Duryea, Fisk, & Associates, 1973; Garbarino, 1975; Kemerer & Baldridge, 1975; Mortimer, 1976; Lee, 1978; Mortimer & Richardson, 1977; Ladd & Lipset, 1973; Tice, 1975; Vladeck & Vladeck, 1975). For the most part, the issues considered in these works will be considered only peripherally in this book.

Alternatively, collective bargaining can be seen as representing the activities of groups in conflict. Rapoport (1974) has suggested three such conflict orientations: fights, games, and debates. Fights are irrational activities designed to defeat or harm an opponent, games can be considered as rational activities that have as their purpose the outwitting of an opponent, and debates are arguments that attempt to convince an opponent to see things as you do. Games involve strategy, and Rapoport has stated that games of strategy offer a good model of rational behavior of people in situations where 1) there are conflicts of interest; 2) a number of alternatives are open at each phase of the situation; 3) people are in a position to estimate consequences of their choices, taking into consideration the very important circumstance that outcomes are determined not only by one's own choices but also by the choices of others over whom one has no control (p. 108).

In this context, academic bargaining can at least theoretically be viewed as a "game," played by rational people, aware of the consequences of various offers and responses, mixing cooperative and competitive moves depending on the perceived value to each side of certain outcomes, and leading to outcomes favorable to one's side. The strategies of the parties can be analyzed on the basis of game theory and the payoffs determined by mathematical formula.

But bargaining is a specific kind of game. While some games can be identified as "zero-sum," in which whatever one side wins another side loses, bargaining is more often a "non-zero-sum" game in which it is possible for the parties to jointly win more through cooperation than they can separately through competition. Bargaining in this context is thus a "mixed-motive" game, in which elements of both competition and cooperation are present. Moreover, it is a recurring game, so that the parties must consider outcomes not only in terms of immediate winning and losing, but also with the knowledge that the results of one game will be an important factor in the conduct of the next. This suggests to the rational bargainer that outwitting a rival by too great a margin may be dysfunctional to a continuing and profitable relationship (Rubin & Brown, 1975, p. 197). The bargainer must therefore consider the interdependence of the parties as part of the bargaining environment and refrain from taking those actions that could change the bargaining relationship from that of a game to that of a fight. While this book will not focus attention upon game theory, it will be concerned with the differences between fights, games, and debates, and we will seek to discover tactics and strategies that bargainers can employ to prevent the bargaining relationship from degenerating into irrational conflict concerned with harming or defeating one's opponents.

A third orientation to bargaining, which is almost completely unrepresented in the literature of college and university unionization, is that of the social-psychological perspective. This perspective suggests that bargaining be viewed in terms of "actors and interaction, power, and interests, and that the explanation of outcomes are found in parties and process, structure and communication" (Druckman, 1977, p. 42). It considers issues such as the personal characteristics of bargainers, the roles that bargainers are expected to fill, the effects in bargaining of negotiators who speak for constituencies, the situation in which the bargaining occurs and the antecedents of the situation, the competitive and cooperative orientations of the parties, the structural aspects of bargaining, the effects of threats and promises, and similar matters. Viewed in this context, academic bargaining can be seen as similar to any other bargaining relationship that may exist between two parties, differing only in the legal framework that establishes certain rules within which it operates, and the institutional context in which it occurs. Deutsch (1973) gives these essential features of a bargaining situation, and therefore of academic collective bargaining as well:

1. Both parties perceive that there is a possibility of reaching an agreement in which each party would be better off, or no worse off, than if no agreement is reached.
2. Both parties perceive that there is more than one such agreement which could be reached, and
3. Each party perceives the other to have conflicting preferences or opposed interests with regard to the different agreements that might be reached. (p. 216).

The focus of this book is upon the processes by which unions and administrations develop their own positions, assess the positions of the other, and interact with the purpose of reaching agreement. It is based on the premise that bargaining, as it is currently understood and practiced in many academic settings, sets the stage for destructive conflict. This conflict may not be related to differences in the goals or interests of faculty and administration, although clearly such differences often exist. Nor does it necessarily reflect a lack of rationality, or concern for the enterprise, or academic commitment, or integrity on one side or the other, although occasionally such defects in a bargainer or a negotiating team may exacerbate existing tensions and make bargaining more difficult. Rather, it suggests that the structure of bargaining itself, and the perceptions of the participants about the nature of the bargaining process, lead to predictable behavioral consequences that are typical of intergroup competition in situations in which one or both groups believe that it can achieve its goals only at the expense of the other.

The book has no white hats or black hats, defenders of the collegial faith or academic visigoths. It does not argue that unionization and collective bargaining is good or bad for higher education, that its consequences over the long term will be harmful or beneficial to the achievement of the academic mission, or that through bargaining students or society will be better or less well served. It suggests instead that bargaining itself is a powerful process in which dedicated and concerned professionals may gradually, and without knowing quite why, find themselves in an escalating spiral of destructive confrontation that they do not support, and that they feel helpless to control.

The book attempts to assist bargainers in beginning to understand why their opponents behave as they do, and in doing so to become more sensitive to their own behavior and its effect on the bargaining process. It is also meant for trustees, presidents, union leaders, and faculty and staff who believe that groups within the institution may be locked into competitive and destructive bargaining processes that are neither satisfying to the participants nor yielding the benefits inherent in bargaining, and who want to explore new ideas for changing existing relationships. The book should also be of interest to students of industrial relations and related fields, as well as to bargainers in nonacademic settings who will find the conceptual orientations, and the tactical and strategic suggestions, to be widely applicable to conflict management and negotiation in groups of all kinds.

In calling for more creative approaches in industrial bargaining, Healy (1965, p. 42) has stated:

> It is easy to say that the parties should bargain imaginatively and exhort them to take advantage of the freedom which collective bargaining can provide if used "correctly" or imaginatively. However, it is much more difficult to know how to start such an approach. Old prejudices and fears on both sides of the table must be overcome, and in most cases, a fundamental change of attitude is required on the part of both parties. . . . Perhaps more widespread is the frustration of being trapped by the traditional methods of bargaining. The parties may desire a more sensible and rational approach to their problems but do not know where to start, how to proceed, or what the eventual outcome might be.

The aim of this book is to offer suggestions about where to start, how to proceed, and what the eventual outcome might be in the academic environment. It is not meant to be a cookbook containing formulas that, if followed, will lead to more constructive bargaining, but rather a source book providing a conceptual orientation and alternative hypotheses that participants in the process can consider, modify, or build upon in an effort to construct that unique bargaining relationship meeting their needs. In this way, perhaps the often called-for alternative to the "industrial bargaining model" (Carr & Van Eyck, 1973; Ping, 1973; Boyd, 1971; AAUP, 1973) that more closely meets the needs of academic institutions can be developed.

There is good reason to believe that over the next decade changes in the environment of higher education will increase on many campuses the forces leading to or intensifying disruptive conflict. In public institutions, declining enrollment, reduced levels of budget support, and increasing demands for accountability may create a competitive climate in which defensiveness and concern for personal security erode levels of trust, openness, and commitment to the purposes of the academic enterprise. Private institutions will face the same problems, but in addition some will find another source of stress and conflict in the aftermath of the Supreme Court's 1980 decision in *National Labor Relations Board* v. *Yeshiva University*. This finding calls into question the rights of faculty in private institutions to bargain collectively under the National Labor Relations Act and affects institutions in which bargaining has not yet been established as well as those currently functioning with ratified contracts. It is clear from the decision that faculties exercising at least as much managerial authority as found by the Court to be the case at Yeshiva University do not have the right to bargain. Determining whether the faculty of any specific campus meets the test of exercising a requisite (but at present still not clearly defined) level of managerial authority will depend on a case-by-case examination of the factual situation on each campus on which the right to bargain is challenged. The disruptive conflict likely to arise from such a challenge may be seen by some as so great that the maintenance or establishment of bargaining might be considered as a preferred option if more constructive and creative ways of implementing the bargaining relationship could be found.

The book is divided into two main sections. Part I develops the conceptual orientations supporting the specific recommendations that follow. Although some readers may be tempted to "skip the theory" and go directly to the implications for professional practice in Part II, they should eventually return to chapters 1 through 4. This will not only equip them to make more critical assessments of the tactics and strategies presented, but of even greater importance, may offer insights enabling them to develop new approaches to meet the special needs of their own situation.

Chapter 1 presents academic bargaining as a form of shared authority, but one with unusual institutional and organizational problems that may lead toward destructive, rather than constructive conflict. Chapter 2 describes the specific nature of the context, situation, and persons involved in bargaining, and their effect upon the nature of conflict. When groups are locked into competitive relationships, such as those typified by traditional bargaining structures, certain perceptions, behaviors, and communication patterns are likely to result. A description of these changes is the subject of chapter 3. Chapter 4 discusses two quite different conceptual orientations to bargaining and suggests that one of these models, which is generally not well understood, may offer unique opportunities for creative negotiations in the academic environment.

While the chapters in Part I present the nature and causes of destructive conflict as they relate to the structures and processes of academic bargaining, Part II suggests behaviors and programs that may assist in conflict management and lead the parties toward more creative and constructive bargaining. Chapter 5 describes a number of dispute resolution techniques that have been developed in industrial bargaining and their application in academic settings. In general, these techniques are implemented toward the end of the bargaining interaction when the parties have reached impasse and ignore the earlier stages in their relationship when changes are both more possible and more effective.

Chapters 6 through 9 discuss the changes in the traditional bargaining relationship that can be made prior to the initiation of bargaining, or during the bargaining interaction itself. Chapter 6 presents tactical considerations in creative bargaining. These approaches presume that, even though the structure of bargaining remains essentially unchanged, behaviors of the parties can change unilaterally to promote creative bargaining relationships.

The more powerful strategic considerations in the following three chapters suggest ways in which the parties can bilaterally change the bargaining structure itself to make it more consistent with traditional academic norms and values. The suggestions in chapter 7 dealing with ways of increasing the problem-solving potential in the bargaining institution, the uses of third parties described in chapter 8, and the changes in bargaining structure presented in chapter 9 are all supported by principles developed in the applied behavioral sciences and drawn from the experiences of negotiators and organizational consultants in diverse settings.

A major purpose of this volume is to provide bargainers with a new conceptual orientation that has practical applications for college and university administrators and faculty. Organizational change is not easy, particularly when dealing with a process that can be as highly institutionalized as collective bargaining. If readers come away with a changed perception that alternatives to current practice are possible and desirable, even if they reject the specific suggestions contained here, a significant first step will have been taken toward the goal of constructive academic bargaining.

ACKNOWLEDGMENTS

We wish to acknowledge permission to reprint the following:

Blake, R. R., Shepard, H. A., & Mouton, J. A. *Managing intergroup conflict in industry,* table 1, p. 1960, and p. 194. Houston: Gulf Publishing, 1964. Permission granted by Foundation for Research on Human Behavior, Ann Arbor, Michigan.

Deutsch, M. *The resolution of conflict: constructive and destructive processes.* New Haven, Conn.: Yale University Press, 1973.

Garbarino, J. W. *Faculty bargaining: change and conflict.* New York: McGraw-Hill, 1975.

Golden, C. S., & Parker, V. D. (Eds.). *Causes of industrial peace under collective bargaining.* New York: Harper & Row, 1955.

Healy, J. J. (Ed.). *Creative collective bargaining.* Copyright (c) 1965, pp. 22, 41, 42, 142, 221, 227, 280. Reprinted by permission of Prentice-Hall, Englewood Cliffs, N.J.

Hildebrand, G. The use of neutrals in collective bargaining. Reprinted by permission from Pollard, S. D. (Ed.). *Arbitration and public policy.* Copyright (c) 1961 by The Bureau of National Affairs, Washington, D.C.

Ikle, F. C. *How nations negotiate.* Millwood, N.Y.: Kraus, 1964.

Maier, N. R. F. *Problem solving and creativity in individuals and groups.* Copyright (c) 1970 by Wadsworth, Inc. This and all other quotations from this source are reprinted by permission of the publisher, Brooks/Cole Publishing Company, Monterey, California.

Morris, W. C., & Sashkin, M. Phases of integrated problem solving (PIPS), p. 106. In Pfeiffer, J. W., & Jones, J. E. (Eds.). *The 1978 annual handbook for group facilitators.* San Diego, Calif.: University Associates, 1978.

Mortimer, K. P., & Richardson, R. C., Jr. *Governance in institutions with faculty unions: six case studies.* University Park, Pa.: Center for the Study of Higher Education, The Pennsylvania State University, May 1977.

Rapoport, A. *Fights, games, and debates* (5th Ed.). Ann Arbor: The University of Michigan Press, 1974.

Stevens, C. M. *Strategy and collective bargaining negotiation.* New York: McGraw-Hill, 1963.

Thomas, K. Conflict and conflict management. In Dunnette, M. D. (Ed.). *Handbook of industrial and organizational psychology*, Figure 4, p. 900. Copyright (c) 1976 by Rand McNally Publishing Company, Chicago.

Walton, R. E. *Interpersonal peacemaking: confrontation and third-party consultation*, (c) 1969, pages 108 and 148. Reprinted by permission of Addison-Wesley Publishing Company, Reading, Mass.

Walton, R. E., & McKersie, R. B. *A behavioral theory of labor negotiation.* New York: McGraw-Hill, 1965.

Part I

CONCEPTUAL ORIENTATIONS

1

The Consequences of Academic Bargaining

Conflict can be devastating; it can also be creative. Out of the cauldrons of conflict have been distilled many of the institutions and forms of behavior that we characterize as achievement and progress (Simkin, 1971, p. 356).

There is, however, a constant tendency for unmanaged conflict to get out of hand and to become bad for all parties concerned (Boulding, 1965, p. 1).

BARGAINING AND SHARED AUTHORITY

Conflict is a natural process of human life. It exists whenever individuals, groups, organizations, or nations believe that the activities or goals of another will prevent the achievement of their own. Conflict can be found in the most loving relationships, as well as in the most hateful. Conflict exists in families, in churches, in businesses, and, of course, in colleges and universities.

In the academy, there is a tendency to think of conflict as dysfunctional and contrary to expected norms of collegiality. But as Coser (1964) has pointed out, conflict has extremely positive elements as well. Conflict assists in balancing and maintaining a social system; it provides a means of venting hostile and aggressive sentiments, it increases group cohesion and identity, and it serves as a stimulus for establishing new rules, norms, and institutions. Of particular interest to an academic institution, conflict also prevents stagnation, stimulates interest and curiosity, increases the total energy in a system to enable it to do its work, stimulates innovation, and is the basis for personal and social change (Deutsch, 1969; Walton, 1969).

3

Conflict exists when individuals or groups have rival claims to resources, prestige, or power positions that are, or that are perceived to be, in scarce supply. In academic institutions, these rival claims manifest themselves in every area of organizational functioning, including such matters as the courses to be offered, the approval of curriculums, the selection and promotion of personnel, the allocation of budgets, and similar issues. The processes by which colleges and universities make decisions to resolve these rival claims, and to manage the resultant conflict, are called "governance."

The governance arrangements of every institution define the relationships between the various institutional constituencies, usually including trustees, administration, faculty, and students, and indicate the degree to which they exercise legitimate influence over certain kinds of decisions. The normative relationships in academic institutions have come, over the past decade, to be understood as one of "shared authority" (American Association of University Professors, 1966; AAHE, 1967), in which groups exercise their primary authority over specified areas of decision making only after appropriate involvement and consultation with the other groups.

Orientations to Shared Authority

There are three orientations to shared authority (AAHE, 1967). The first, and most highly preferred, utilizes the structure of a legislative body with representatives of different constituencies, but dominated by faculty, to consider and recommend matters of policy. The processes used to develop consensus on these issues focus upon information sharing and appeals to reason. The second orientation establishes guidelines for the area of authority for various groups and suggests the use of neutral third parties such as the American Association of University Professors (AAUP) as the means through which conflicts arising between the groups can be fairly reviewed and resolved.

The third form of shared authority is that of collective bargaining. In this form, faculty unions negotiate with administrators to reach agreement on specific matters that then become codified through the agency of a written agreement. In this form, as in the other two, authority is "shared" because neither faculty nor administration can impose its will unilaterally upon the other.

Collective bargaining is thus a process of shared authority used in some institutions to manage conflict that at least one of the parties does not believe can be resolved through more traditional academic structures. The identification of academic governance processes as a form of conflict management does not necessarily suggest its outcomes, however, and indeed conflict can take at least two different orientations (Deutsch, 1969). Conflict can be "constructive," solving the problems of the participants and leaving both satisfied with the outcome and feeling they have gained as a result. Conflict can also be "destructive," resulting in dissatisfaction by both parties and the feeling that each has lost as a consequence. A specific characteristic of destructive conflict is its tendency to escalate, to increase in size and intensity, to become independent of the processes that caused the initial conflict, and to increasingly rely upon the use of power, and upon "the tactics of threat, coercion, and deception" (Deutsch, 1969, p. 27). Under such conditions, academic bargaining can assume the characteristics of an arms race between belligerent nations, with each provocation reinforcing the determination and belligerence of the other until the spiral is terminated by war, capitulation, or the intervention of a third party.

Although academic bargaining can lead to either constructive or destructive conflict, a central thesis of this book is that it is more likely than other forms of shared authority to result in escalation in the destructive use of belligerent tactics and strategies. This in turn may change the goals of the participants from the achievement of certain ends to the defeat of the other side. The reasons for this contention, and the processes that move bargaining toward destructive conflict, will be discussed in chapters 2 through 4. This chapter will explore the institutional and organizational consequences of destructive bargaining relationships.

Development of Adversarial Relationships

It has been suggested that at least to some degree the development of destructive conflict may be related to the unmodified adoption of what has been called "the industrial model of bargaining." Although it is true that the range of bargaining practices that have developed in thousands of varied industrial settings is immense, the common elements that in general (although not in all cases) describe this approach include

the recognition of one organization as the exclusive representative of the members of the bargaining unit; explicit adversary relationships; exclusion of administrators from membership; formal bargaining over issues; detailed, legally binding written contracts; formal grievance procedures with binding arbitration of disputes by outside arbitrators; and the use of strikes or other economic pressures to resolve impasses. Unions do not deny the existence of a substantial element of community of interest

between administrators and faculty, but they regard conflict of interest as
not only inevitable but potentially dominant in the relationship. They
believe, therefore, in developing a decision-making system that accepts the
possibility, if not the probability, of conflict and is organized to deal with it
as the natural state of affairs (Garbarino, 1975, pp. 47-48).

The adversary principle is part of the ideology of American industrial
relations (Barbash, 1979). Academic organizations do not fully share
the basic division between labor and management and the irrevocable
conflict of interest that shaped the conduct of bargaining relationships
in the industrial sector. Nevertheless, "the most common approach to
collegiate collective bargaining builds an entire negotiating strategy on
the central presumption that the parties at the bargaining table are
adversaries. The tools, the weapons, and rhetoric are chosen accord-
ingly" (Graham & Walters, 1973, p. 61).

The adversarial element of academic bargaining has been acknowledged both by supporters and critics of the process (Ladd & Lipsett,
1973; Finkin, 1971; Ping, 1973; Mortimer & Richardson, 1977; Baldridge et al., 1978; Corson, 1975). This orientation toward the bargaining relationship has two immediate potential consequences. First, the
identification of the process as adversarial establishes norms legitimat-
ing conflict that might otherwise be repressed. For that reason, entering into relationships defined a priori as adversarial is likely to lead to a
self-fulfilling prophecy. Second, the identification of the opposing
bargainer as an enemy justifies the use of tactics that would not be
contemplated in dealing with a member of one's own group (Deutsch,
1973, p. 353). For this reason, academic bargainers often exhibit
behaviors that are completely different from those typically expected
in faculty senates or administrative councils.

One observer has described this development of adversarial relationships resulting from bargaining on a specific campus as follows
(Hedgepeth, 1974):

> Collective bargaining has also led to the development of adversary
> relations between the faculty/staff and the administration. There seems to
> be a cyclical effect at this level. The administrators perceive themselves as
> adversaries and use the formal rules and the contract to make more
> independent decisions to the detriment of personal relations and program
> development. As this occurs, the faculty feel more cut off and/or alienated,
> which enhances their feeling of employer-employee divisiveness, which
> posits the administrator as the adversary. The cycle then seems to renew
> itself and, as some stated it, makes the campus certainly a less pleasant
> place and reduces everyone's effectiveness somewhat (pp. 698-99).

It is probable that collective bargaining does not have the same immediate potential for destructive conflict at all institutions. It has been suggested, for example, that institutions with different levels of faculty involvement in governance may enter into collective bargaining for significantly different reasons, and this in turn may be related to the course conflict will take. "Aggressive bargaining" may occur when faculties in institutions without meaningful processes of shared governance attempt to gain authority; "defensive bargaining" may take place when faculty operating under a system of shared authority unionize in an attempt to protect their current power, usually from the reduction caused by increased centralization and interference from state level agencies and boards. It may be that these two bargaining orientations are related to specific governance styles, with aggressive bargaining representing the movement of the bureaucratized institution into bargaining, and defensive bargaining the more gradual shift to bargaining of the institution operating with a political governance system.

For many institutions functioning as bureaucratic organizations, the concept of shared governance is a polite fiction, honored in the breach more than in the observance. That is not to say that faculty have no influence on institutional policies and goals, but rather that this influence is usually indirect and informal, and that major decisions are made through a rational structure in which authority is allocated hierarchically. Both internal and external pressures prompt the institution to increasingly involve faculty in meaningful roles in decision making, but the structure and norms of such institutions inhibit the development of effective shared governance mechanisms. For such institutions, collective bargaining offers a means of unfreezing current organizational systems, readjusting authority and decision-making patterns, testing new modes of participation, and moving toward shared authority. Whenever changes of authority structures occur, however, conflict intensifies within an organization. The change from bureaucratic decision making to collective bargaining is just such an abrupt, discontinuous change in organizational form and structure, and it may be expected that the more bureaucratized the institution before bargaining, the greater the discontinuity and therefore the greater the conflict after unionization. At least in part because the initiation of bargaining is known to alter the control systems of the organization, bargaining is accompanied by a new set of rigorous controls embedded in statute and legal processes operating to limit the conflict likely to occur. These processes function by prescribing specific relationships and communications systems between the parties involved in negotiation and by establishing controlling mechanisms limiting the damage the parties can do to each other, or to the public. However, they cannot influence the attitudes and perceptions that the parties bring to the bargaining relationship and that often control their interaction.

Faculties functioning under reasonable conditions of shared authority that unionize as a defensive measure are likely to find the transition to bargaining to be much more tranquil. Previous governance mechanisms exist as before, with such changes made as necessary to accommodate the union's activities in very limited areas of authority under a dual governance approach.

For the bureaucratic institution, therefore, collective bargaining has the potential to be a valuable mechanism for institutional change and development because of its ability to unfreeze organizational behaviors and systems, create new processes and structures, and then refreeze into new patterns through the institutionalization of these new structures. At the same time, the very structure of bargaining itself is such that the conflict generated by the initiation of bargaining can be highly destructive. In such situations, the refreezing of an organization can institutionalize, not some stage in the process of organization development and shared authority, but rather the bitter and self-reinforcing antagonism that represents the worst aspects of an adversarial approach.

The probability of this type of conflict is not as high in the newly unionized institution with a history of shared authority that has functioned in the past with political decision-making processes. The transition to bargaining can be made more gradually, and the resultant conflict may not be as severe. However, even in these systems there may be a natural tendency to increase the bargaining arena (Kemerer & Baldridge, 1975; Carnegie Council, 1977; Simkin, 1971), and in doing so to increase over time the potential for destructive conflict.

Destructive conflict is nonproductive in any setting, but it is particularly dysfunctional in an institution of higher education for both institutional and organizational reasons. Institutional factors are perhaps the most immediately obvious, and several commonly cited consequences of bargaining, each of which is exacerbated by the incidence of destructive conflict in the relationship, can be briefly mentioned. They include the loss of autonomy related to centralization, limiting communication, clarifying ambiguity, failure to honor commitments, and increased legalism and rigidity. Less obvious, but more insidious and even more critical than the institutional effects of bargaining and destructive conflict are the potential organizational consequences, which are analyzed in the last section of this chapter.

INSTITUTIONAL CONSEQUENCES OF BARGAINING

Centralization

Collective bargaining is in many ways a consequence of the centralization in decision making that developed during the past 15 years with the establishment of state coordinating agencies and multicampus systems (Mortimer, 1976; Garbarino, 1977). It has also been noted that one of the effects of bargaining is itself to increase centralization (Mortimer & Richardson, 1977; Garbarino, 1977; Kemerer & Baldridge, 1975) so that bargaining and centralization are mutually reinforcing phenomena. In noting the conflict potential of bargaining, the Carnegie Foundation (1975) stated that "Collective bargaining is, in effect, a faculty-induced centralization of authority in a context of confrontation. Authority is seldom given up readily or seized without a struggle" (p. 14).

As a consequence of bargaining, decisions once made on local campuses now are made at higher levels of organization, not only leading to feelings of powerlessness on the part of campus constituencies (faculty and administration alike), but also to decreased autonomy of the campus itself. When conflict related to bargaining becomes more destructive, the process of centralization is accelerated as state-level officers attempt to correct "deficiencies" on the local campus and restore the political tranquility that is a major objective of systems administrations.

Moreover, and perhaps of even greater importance, bargaining is likely to accelerate the politicization of higher education and to bring elected government officials into the university governance process (Duryea & Fisk, 1975). Bargaining is primarily a phenomenon of public institutions, and bargaining often involves institutions more deeply in the political process for several reasons. First, the initiation of bargaining is often accompanied either by legislation or judicial ruling that identifies the governor or other elected official, rather than the board of trustees, as the "employer" for the purposes of collective bargaining. It is the governor's representatives, not academic administrators, who face the faculty unions across the table, and they are less likely to clearly understand the difference between the personnel policies of the university and the state police. Precedents set in one setting are often used to establish strategy or tactics in the other. As the level of destructive conflict increases, the judgment of state officers that all unions are alike and can be treated in the same way is confirmed by their own experience.

Conflict related to bargaining often has a visibility and immediacy that brings it into the political arena. While governance squabbles seldom arouse the interest of external parties, bitter contract negotiations and the recriminations that often accompany them arouse considerable public interest and invite legislative or executive interference. The institution is particularly vulnerable when strikes are threatened or actually take place. The settlement of a strike in New Jersey through direct negotiations between the governor and the union, without consultation with the administration's leadership or bargaining representatives, is an example of the inherent dangers of political interference in unmanaged conflict (Begin, Settle, & Alexander, 1975). Participation in destructive conflict often so distorts the orientation of the participants that they may engage in behavior that invites the involvement of politicians in institutional affairs, which would have been unthinkable outside the bargaining context.

It is ironic, but indisputable, that the process often adopted by faculty, at least in part as a political response to the problems of centralization, in fact strengthens it. As bargaining relationships move toward destructive conflict, they may contribute toward the further erosion of campus autonomy by inviting political interference in governance and permitting authorities in off-campus state-level offices to use bargaining as a "management tool" (Garbarino, 1977) to bypass institutional processes and directly influence or establish individual campus policies.

The political consequences of increased centralization are primarily the problems of public institutions bargaining under state law and subject to the authority of state officials and labor boards. However, even private institutions bargaining under the National Labor Relations Act may also find external agencies making academically related decisions without fully understanding the structures and processes of higher education. One means of avoiding both forms of interference is to permit faculty to bargain under trustee policy, rather than under state or federal law (Hanley, 1971). Nine four-year institutions are successfully bargaining under such provisions (Angell & Kelley, 1979), and further consideration of this bargaining alternative has been urged by the Carnegie Council (1977, p. 7).

Limiting Communication

Groups entering into conflict situations reduce their communications in many ways. As the group itself becomes more cohesive in response to external threat, internal communications challenging the majority opinion are ignored or punished, thereby limiting intragroup communication. In addition, contacts between the in-group and the other party are likely to become restricted in number, highly structured, and to involve only group leaders. Each of these effects limits the flow of information within a group, and between the group and other groups in its environment. This makes it increasingly probable that negative stereotypes will develop about each other's behaviors and intentions, and that disconfirming data such as an offer to engage in collaborative activity will not be accepted or utilized.

This limitation in communication is a natural consequence of forming groups that are, or are seen to have the potential to be, competitive. But the problem is made even more difficult in academic bargaining because of the concept of "exclusive representation" accompanying the selection of a bargaining agent. Exclusive representation is the right and obligation of an employee organization designated as majority representative to negotiate collectively for all employees: "When the agent has exclusive bargaining rights, the institution must negotiate only with him" (Gee, 1973, p. 246). The administration is constrained from discussing with any other faculty group, without the agreement of the union, any matter that is properly a subject of bargaining. The extent to which this is challenged in any specific situation is at the discretion of the union, which can bring action against the employer charging an unfair labor practice. The problems this can pose in an organization that has traditionally done much of its business through informal consultation, expressions of consensus, and interaction between departments and deans, for example in dealing with specific issues, is potentially enormous. At the very least, it assists in the bureaucratization of the institution, and reduces feelings of collegiality between faculty and administration (Ladd & Lipsett, 1976).

As communications become impoverished as a consequence of developing adversary relationships and moving toward destructive bargaining tactics and strategies, the increasing inability of the parties to clearly understand each other leads to the likelihood that they will engage in behaviors that will further intensify the conflict. Healy (1965) points out, for example, that the use of traditional bargaining processes often leads to strikes even though the respective bargaining positions of the parties are such that agreement is possible

> because the process itself prevents the parties from communicating sufficiently to ascertain that [their positions] do overlap. These are "senseless" strikes, which need not occur. As an example, emotions can be easily stirred to the point where intransigence, or harassment on the part of one side (perhaps only a bluff), may cause the other to stiffen, become angry, and refuse to "give" or "settle for" the limits originally intended. Such an

outcome is the result of the tendency of both sides to think in terms of victory or defeat. (p. 22)

Clarification of Ambiguities Related to Authority

It is perhaps strange to think of clarifying ambiguous relationships as being potentially harmful. However, in institutions that may control their activities through collegial interaction if they are small enough to do so, or through the interaction of semiautonomous subgroups if they are complex and functioning through decentralized political systems, it is often not only unnecessary to determine the locus of specific authority, but also often dysfunctional. The nature of authority in such institutions is highly situational, and shifts as actors and issues change. These institutions "muddle through," and potential conflicts related to matters of organizational prerogative are often resolved by a tacit agreement to ignore the issue altogether, or to form a committee whose report will be phrased in inconclusive and diplomatic language.

The bargaining institution, however, often finds itself in a position in which relationships that were acceptable, albeit unclear, suddenly become matters of contention. Collective bargaining is likely to produce such situations because of the need to reduce agreements to writing, and because external agencies may ultimately decide what the contractual language really means. The rulings of these external agencies do not necessarily create new relationships between the parties, but they do clarify and make explicit existing relationships that previously had been ambiguous and implicit. And when this occurs in an environment of winning and losing, in which the trust of both parties in each other is diminished by the action of one of them in calling in an external agency to adjudicate a dispute, and thereby accentuating the legalistic aspects of what had previously been commonly accepted assumptions, the results are potentially of great significance.

Carr and VanEyck (1973) have spoken to the problems of asking the unanswerable questions of institutional authority in the context of collective bargaining.

In practice, trustees, administrators, and faculty members refrain from pushing for final answers and are content to settle, under the most favorable conditions, for a state of equilibrium in their relationships—a state difficult to describe and impossible to define. But collective bargaining statutes were not written with this equilibrium in mind. "Labor" and "management," "employer" and "employees" are the terms used in labor relations statutes, labor board rulings, and collective bargaining contracts. If faculties elect to make use of the formal processes of collective bargaining and are permitted to do so by labor boards, it is impossible to avoid the use of these terms, even though the realities of educational life are thereby obscured and even distorted. There are inescapable difficulties, then, in applying to the world of higher education the terms and concepts originally intended to cover labor relations in private industry. (p. 31)

Two recent cases illustrate the possible dangers. In one (Board of Higher Education, 1974), a faculty union challenged the right of the governing board to add students to college personnel and budget committees. In the other (Rutgers University, 1976), a union fought against a board's decision not to negotiate certain matters including the appointment of departmental chairpersons, membership on administrative search committees, and physical facilities planning. In both cases, the respective state public employment relations agency found that the issues were not mandatory subjects of bargaining. The rationale in both cases was that these activities were *management prerogatives* that they could discharge unilaterally or delegate to faculty functioning in their nonunion roles, *at their discretion.*

By calling attention to the fact that faculty membership on presidential search and screen committees, for example, was a right delegated to them by the board, attention was also called to the fact that it could be removed or altered at any time by the same board. This would not be a serious possibility in an institution in which faculty participation was traditionally accepted and unquestioned. It becomes more likely in situations in which destructive bargaining relationships have made the parties vindictive, motivated them to punish each other, and prompted them to husband as much authority as possible in the erroneous belief that by doing so they reduce the influence of the opposing bargainer. It is this possibility that likely caused the Carnegie Commission (1973) to suggest that "Faculty members now have a certain amount of influence because of the ignorance, or the lack of interest, or the inadvertance of boards, all of which may erode with more formal and explicit arrangements. Collective bargaining could come to look like a management plot" (p. 44).

Evidence that adversarial relationships may result in assaults on faculty power as ambiguities become clarified in bargaining is already available. During the early days of bargaining at the City University of New York, for example, the Board of Higher Education attempted to replace the traditional election of departmental chairpersons with administrative appointees, on the grounds that under bargaining the administration had the right to select all persons with administrative responsibilities (Ladd & Lipsett, 1973). The development of adversarial relationships at another institution reportedly led its board to exclude the faculty entirely from decisions, such as the selection of administrators, in which they had been previously involved, and in a different institution the board has used its "management rights" clause to deny faculty involvement in governance (Mortimer & Richardson, 1977, p. 88).

As Feller and Finkin (1977) have pointed out, clarification of ambiguity may have the effect of placing the entire governance system at the discretion of the trustees; under certain conditions this would "allow the governing board to eviscerate the system entirely" (p. 136).

It is unlikely that this has occurred so far in any existing setting. However, in today's climate of decreasing resources, increased calls for accountability, and continued conflict related to adversarial relationships, trustees in some institutions and systems may give increasing heed to Corson's (1975) warning: "When the faculty organizes to advance its economic interests, it is questionable whether it can continue to claim the right to participate in decisions as to the allocation of resources as between faculty compensation and other purposes of expenditures, and in decisions as to the rank and compensation of individuals. . . . Straws now in the wind suggest . . . the faculties and the administrator-trustees will be polarized in firm, adversarial positions" (pp. 201-202).

Failure to Honor Commitments

When adversaries engage in destructive conflict, a contract may ultimately be agreed to that is not fully supported by one or both parties. Because of lack of commitment, they may be unwilling to carry out its provisions in good faith. This situation in likely to lead to grievances and further escalation of conflict. Under these conditions, the contract does not represent a resolution of conflict, but rather its codification in an ongoing and escalating war. The parties become angry, not only because the contract itself is not satisfactory, but also because the other party is not living up to it. Grievances are likely to be treated mechanically and "by the book," rather than as symptoms of problems that should themselves be addressed by the parties.

Faced with the perception that an adversary will not administer contract provisions in good faith, the parties must ask for "more in writing to be certain of getting even less in practice" (Walton & McKersie, 1965, p. 204). The same phenomenon operates in industry and on occasion has led unions with superior contracts to attempt to move toward more constructive bargaining relationships since the "gains" they made were not being realized in practice (Walton & McKersie, 1965, p. 366).

Legalism and Rigidity

Creeping legalism is a disease that affects unionized and nonunion universities alike (and virtually all other American institutions), but the union is a carrier that introduces legalism in a virulent form to the campus as a whole in a remarkably effective way (Garbarino, 1975, p. 152).

Surveys of both union officials and college presidents indicate agreement that where bargaining occurs it is likely to formalize the relationships between faculty and administration (Baldridge et al., 1978, p. 118)). This is an understandable phenomenon, since one of the purposes of bargaining is to establish rules that limit administrative discretion, and administrators in turn must establish procedures to assure that the contract is properly administered. As bargaining relationships become adversarial in nature, and trust between the parties decreases, growing attention is given by each party to more formal language, the creation of rules and clauses that will respond to hypothetical and often highly improbable "worst case" situations, and the specification of obligations and constraints in great detail to avoid later questions of interpretation.

Increasing formality and legalism promotes rigidity of institutional processes and structures and may make it more difficult for the unionized institution to engage in experimentation and change. Although there is perhaps no evidence to either support or refute the idea, it has been proposed that the work-rule mentality, which can be a consequence of destructive conflict, may inhibit institutions from attempting to implement bold, new ideas (Carr & VanEyck, 1973, p. 289). Aside from stifling innovation, the developing rigidity imposed by increased bureaucracy may tend to make unions defenders of the status quo, and their institutions able to change only in response to external threats (Mortimer & Richardson, 1977, pp. 45, 179).

Rigidity is dysfunctional to the purposes of higher educational institutions in any situation but can be particularly damaging when resources become increasingly scarce and environments hostile. More than ever, during such periods institutional survival may be dependent upon the ability to develop new missions, exploit opportunities, and increase responsiveness to the needs of their student constituencies.

These five institutional consequences of bargaining have been identified because each poses difficult problems for institutions in their quest for excellence and educational effectiveness. These consequences do not necessarily follow from the adoption of academic bargaining processes on a campus, but, for reasons which will be discussed in the next chapter, bargaining increases the likelihood that they will occur. As the bargaining environment becomes more adversarial in nature, and bargaining increasingly reflects the orientations of destructive conflict, each of these consequences also becomes more probable.

ORGANIZATIONAL CONSEQUENCES OF BARGAINING

Bargaining is a powerful determinant of the structure of an institution, and it would be expected that the implementation of bargaining on a campus would have significant effects upon every other major area of operation. The major impact of bargaining, however, is not institutional but organizational and concerns the development of relationships between individuals and groups within the institution.

Collegiality

From an institutional perspective, this relationship is often referred to as "collegiality," a term which is so integral to the culture of higher education that its meaning is reasonably well understood even though it is seldom clearly defined. At the very least, collegiality refers to the establishment of interpersonal and intergroup relationships based upon a mutual commitment to professional values, civility in interactions, and faculty influence in the decision-making process. In institutions with more mature shared governance processes, it has referred to the presumptive authority of members of academic subgroups to evaluate and recommend personnel actions concerning colleagues. There are those who confuse the concept of collegiality with that of the collegial governance model, and insist that the faculty should have the authority to make certain decisions that should then be implemented by the administration. This is clearly not a requisite to a collegial environment, however.

From a sociological perspective, collegiality can be related to Clark's (1971) analysis of social bonding in academic organizations. When individuals in an organization share beliefs, values, and attitudes, conflicts can be worked out through the collegial interaction of its members who see differences between them as of only secondary importance to their relationships and commitment to their institution. The strongest bonding of this type occurs in organizations that have developed what Clark identifies as an "organizational saga," due in large part to the establishment of a strong self-belief of individuals in their identification as members of the group. Members of such groups have little need for due process and adjudicating procedures because of the high levels of trust reflected in the interpersonal relationships of the group. In contrast, Clark argues

the weaker normative bonding in institutions of weak self-belief gives greater play to the factionalism and fragmentation inherent in the specialized commitments and orientations of the academic disciplines, and the normal division of work into "administrative" and "faculty" and "academic" and "business." As belief in the part ascends over belief in the whole, loyalty attaches to the part rather than the whole. Governance then calls for more mediation among the parts, with a tendency to explicate the mediation in quasi-formal and formal rules of procedure. As normative bonding weakens, even in systems of small scope, one or more internal groups will develop a self-interest in having informal relations replaced by a more discernable structure. Surely almost all of us at one time or another have been agents of this bureaucratic tendency. We seek to insure through rules what we feel is no longer reasonably provided through ties of sentiment and unified belief. (p. 512)

Normative bonding does not only affect the way in which individuals in the institution interact; it also determines the means by which the activities of organizational members are controlled and coordinated. And it is with this issue that the most critical potential effect of bargaining upon higher education can be seen.

Ways of Controlling Participants

Every organization has a need to control the activities of its members. The typology of Etzioni (1961, 1964) is an extremely useful means by which the control of participants in colleges and universities can be analyzed. Organizations can control the behavior of members through three kinds of power. *Coercive power* is based on the use of physical sanctions; *utilitarian power* upon the use of material means, such as money; and *normative power* upon the manipulation of symbolic rewards, such as the allocation of esteem and prestige symbols.

Etzioni also suggests three ways in which participants in an organization can be involved and oriented. *Alienative involvement* refers to an intense, negative orientation, typical, for example, of inmates in a prison. *Calculative involvement* is defined by an essentially neutral orientation, with low intensity, that might characterize the relationships of employees in a large business firm. *Moral involvement* indicates a positive relationship of high intensity, based either upon the internalization of norms and identification with authority, or sensitivity to the pressures of primary groups and their members (1961, pp. 4-11). An example might be the relationship of a parishioner to a church.

Although different organizations may use various kinds of power in various settings, organizations are most effective when the power they use is consistent with the involvement of its members. Institutions are congruent when they use coercive power with alienated members, utilitarian power with calculative members, and normative power with moral members. However, if, for example, a normative organization attempted to use coercive or utilitarian power as a primary means of influencing the behavior of its members, it would become less effective than if it controlled them through the application of symbolic sanctions. This is so at least in part because moving from normative to utilitarian to coercive control increases the alienation of the organizations' members, and thus makes the use of normative controls less effective.

Etzioni further states as a hypothesis that because of the pressure to be effective, organizations, to the extent the environment allows, will tend to shift their compliance structures from incongruent to congruent types (1971, p. 14).

Applications of Power

Based upon this typology and hypothesis, we can now consider what its applications might be to a college or university involved in bargaining. First, they are archetypical normative organizations that control their members through the manipulation of symbolic rewards, such as academic rank and the various privileges that accompany it. This concept of normative control is not necessarily related to the degree of power faculty have in institutional decision making but is rather related to the normative bonding referred to as collegiality, and to the concept of professional service commonly supported by both faculty and administration, transcending any differences between them. In defining this service orientation, Kadish (1968) has said "A professional earns his livelihood at his work, but the service he provides to other people comes first; and in any conflict between personal or commercial profit and the interests of those he serves, the latter prevails" (p. 162). It is this service orientation of participants that both provides the moral claim to professional status in higher education and permits normative controls to be effective in colleges and universities.

With the initiation of collective bargaining, there is a tendency for the organization to begin shifting its use of power from normative to utilitarian. Rather than focusing on those common values and attitudes that bind together various organizational units, such as faculty and administration, bargaining tends to accentuate their differences. Bargaining also raises to prominence issues related to salary, fringe benefits, and similar concerns that are the basis for utilitarian control. It leads to increased use of formal rules and explicit regulations in lieu of common understandings and sanctions based upon acceptance of professional norms. In some cases, as for example in the use of court orders to obtain injunctions against a strike, the university may even employ coercive sanctions through the threat of imprisonment or other legal action.

Each of these activities weakens the effectiveness of normative controls, and increases the level of alienation of the faculty. The response of the faculty to this change in the control patterns of the organization is a tendency to shift their level of involvement from moral to calculative so that the relationship between compliance and power becomes congruent.

The consequences of this change in the bases of organizational power and participant commitment can be quite profound. It reduces the perceived legitimation of organizational leaders, thus making coordination of the organization even more difficult. It replaces the more powerful sanctions of normative control with the less powerful and more contingent sanctions of utilitarian control, and in doing so increases the alienation of participants and changes their orientation from one of institutional commitment to one of calculating costs and benefits. This change erodes the distinction between higher educational organizations and business and industrial organizations.

Again, it should be pointed out that this is not a necessary consequence of collective bargaining. For reasons to be discussed at length in the following chapters, however, it is a likely consequence unless specific interventions are made into the traditional academic bargaining relationship. This extended discussion of organizational controls can be summarized as follows:

1. The initiation of bargaining may to some extent be caused by, and in turn is causally related to, the reduction of levels of social bonding, and the consequent reduction in the levels of collegiality in the organization. Bargaining has a tendency to lead the institution to institute mechanisms of control based on utilitarian power rather than normative power.
2. The use of utilitarian power creates an incongruent organizational situation, which tends to reduce levels of organizational effectiveness. In order to become congruent, the involvement of the faculty changes from moral to calculative. Faculty become less motivated by their commitment to the organization and its well-being, and more motivated by their own welfare and the degree to which their personal needs are satisfied by the organization.

3. As a consequence, participation of the faculty member in the organization changes so that the predominant relationship is that of employer and employee. In the unionized college and university, this may become institutionalized as labor and management, with all of the presumed differences in interests that this relationship traditionally implies.
4. As normative bonding decreases, increased imposition of utilitarian controls becomes necessary in order to coordinate activities no longer able to function under normative controls. This further weakens the normative structure of the organization in a mutually reinforcing cycle. In this manner, collective bargaining becomes a self-fulfilling prophecy.
5. It is in this climate of dramatic changes in organizational structure and patterns of interaction that adversary relationships can develop and flourish.

This analysis is important for several reasons. First, it indicates that the decision of an institution to adopt collective bargaining has organizational, as well as institutional consequences. The organizational consequences are by far the most profound, since they may have an impact upon the use of power within the organization and the orientation of participants. In addition, it reflects the mutually reinforcing dynamic properties of the bargaining relationship, which can realize the worst fears of the participants about each other without intending to do so, thus sowing the seeds of destructive conflict.

Protecting the Spirit of Collegiality

It also suggests that faculty influence is more fundamentally protected by the establishment of shared norms than by any codification of rules or procedures. Those committed to increasing faculty power through "tough" bargaining orientations are not only likely to find that victories won at the table are somehow lost in contract administration, but also that by engaging in interaction that creates adversaries rather than cooperative colleagues they forfeit the opportunity to develop the normative bonds that are more powerful than any contract.

In general, the differences between faculty influence in those institutions in which faculty fully participate in governance and those where they do not is not legal. In almost all institutions, administrators have legal authority for certain decisions delegated to them by the trustees who have final authority for the governance of the institution. Where faculty influence is high, therefore, it is not because administrators have no power, but because, recognizing that the degree of influence they have is inversely proportional to their use of it, administrators willingly forego it.

The statement by some union advocates that faculty governance exists at the pleasure of the administration is therefore to some extent true, but is misses an essential element. The elaborate mechanisms of faculty-administration consultation that typify the decision-making processes of institutions with high levels of faculty influence provide the means through which both groups test each other's positions so that they can avoid at almost all costs destroying the relationship between them. Administrators in such institutions, often coming from the faculty and committed to the preservation of high levels of faculty influence, are reluctant to take steps that would significantly alter the existing balance. Faculty, aware of the same problem of preserving organizational equilibrium, use the consultative mechanisms to avoid taking steps that the administration would find so difficult to accept that it would seriously contemplate the use of its power to overturn them.

Thus, the socialization of the parties and the norms of the institution effectively limit the use of administrative discretion. This limitation is far more effective than any legal interpretation by the parties, since it relies not upon the assertion by one party or the other of certain rights, but rather upon interaction by the parties to mutually assess the permissible limits of influence by both on an issue-specific basis.

A critical need is the search for alternatives to destructive bargaining and for processes through which bargaining can be used as an instrument for the development of institutional norms and values that support appropriate levels of faculty involvement in decision making. Academic institutions originally adopted the assumptions and structures of industrial bargaining because there were no other references or models to follow (Orze, 1975). In particular, its adversarial orientation has proven to be difficult to accommodate to the academic environment, because the traditional norms of the academy have been based upon trust rather than suspicion. It has been suggested that the adversarial approach to bargaining will change over time as the parties to bargaining mature in their relationship, much as the violence of the early days of industrial unionism has evolved into more accommodative processes. Likely, the more overt forms of belligerence and hostility will be transformed into less aggressive relationships as unions and administrations learn how to avoid the most destructive aspects of their new relationship. But violated trust is easier to turn into suspicion than negated suspicion is to turn to trust (Deutsch, 1973, p. 195), and it is possible that the spirit of collegiality, once destroyed, may be difficult if not impossible to create anew in an institution. Perhaps this is the meaning of the Carnegie Foundation's (1975) warning "that humane considerations that have marked internal relations may succumb before the rougher survival instincts and so change the spirit of the enterprise" (p. 136). This is the reason that discovering or creating tactics and strategies of bargaining that can lead to constructive, rather than destructive, bargaining is so imperative. Collective bargaining can be an extremely useful mechanism for institutional change, or a devastating process for destructive conflict. The following chapter analyzes in more detail the reasons why bargaining tends to lead to spiralling adversarial relationships between the parties.

2

Forces for
Constructive and
Destructive Conflict

WHETHER ACADEMIC BARGAINING leads toward constructive or destructive organizational consequences depends upon the behaviors of individuals and groups involved in the negotiation processes. The purpose of this chapter is to describe and analyze some of the societal, institutional, and personal factors that affect these behaviors and thereby affect the course of conflict in the unionized college or university. Particular emphasis will be placed upon factors related to destructive bargaining, so that the purposes of the proposals to reduce or eliminate many of them, which are presented in chapters 6 through 9, can be more clearly understood.

There are many reasons why it might be expected that, compared to other settings, collective bargaining in higher education should have constructive consequences. Some of these have been summarized by the AAUP (Finkin, Goldstein & Osborne, 1975, p. 36).

> Fortunately, the adversarial nature of industrial collective bargaining should tend to be diminished in higher education as a consequence of the professionalism of the bargaining unit, the tradition of collegial governance and peer judgment, the absence of an inevitable hostility between faculty and administration, and the reluctance of both parties to employ the common industrial weapons of the strike and lockout.

There is a long tradition of faculty participation in decision making in American colleges and universities. To be sure, the power of the faculty differs significantly in institutions of varying size, complexity, and quality, but it is the rare institution in which there is not at least consultation between the administration and faculty before important decisions are made. If shared governance and primary faculty authority in educational areas are not the norm in higher education, it is certain that the faculty in most institutions have more involvement in decision making than do professionals employed in other organizations. High levels of such participation have been found to have positive effects on negotiations in other settings. Likert (1967), for example, has noted positive changes in union-management relationships in industry as organizations move away from authoritarian management styles toward consultative and participative group processes. Although very real differences continued to characterize the two groups, there were significant increases in the ability of the parties to find acceptable solutions within the bargaining process and for effective problem solving to replace irreconcilable conflict. It might be expected, therefore, that academic bargainers would exhibit problem-solving orientations toward conflict because of the previous experiences and expectations of the parties in related decision-making processes. In addition, both faculty and administration have been socialized since student days in the academic norms of professionalism, civility, and collegiality. Academic institutions in general consider destructive conflict as symptomatic of pathology rather than effective working relationships, and it could therefore be expected that persons and groups involved in academic bargaining would attempt to engage in behaviors and interaction consistent with these norms.

It has been noted that increased levels of conflict in industrial settings is related to differences in attitudes, values, socioeconomic background, educational levels and social roles of labor and management (Eisinger & Levine, 1968), and to the inherent conflict in goals based upon their roles (Megginson & Gullett, 1970). Here too, one would expect that the unique circumstances of academic bargaining would inhibit destructive conflict. For the most part, teaching faculty and administrators have the same background and training, and have been socialized in the same environments. One would expect under such conditions that they would share similar values, and evidence indicates that indeed this is for the most part true. A large-scale study of university goals (Gross & Grambsch, 1968) indicated remarkable congruity between the rating of 47 goals by over 7,000 administrators and faculty. They concluded that

> the few differences that exist in the values and attitudes of administrators and faculty as revealed in their ratings of preferred goals are too slight to warrant any inference of deep-seated conflict. All three comparisons—of background and personal characteristics, or perceived goals, and of preferred goals — suggest that faculty and administrators are not such different breeds as they are sometimes assumed to be. They value and work towards essentially the same goals (p. 105).

The similarities of values of faculty and administrators is of great importance because research findings suggest that negotiations are more likely to lead to destructive conflict and to result in impasse when there is value dissensus (disagreement) between the parties (Druckman & Zechmeister, 1970). The presence of consensus on basic educational values (Baldridge et al., 1978, pp. 164-165) should make the establishment of constructive bargaining relationships that much more probable in the higher education arena.

Conflict is more likely to become competitive and destructive when the groups involved are internally homogeneous, but quite different from one another in many ways (Deutsch, 1973, p. 99). The overlapping membership of faculty and administrative groups, and the movement of persons between them, should reduce the homogeneity of the bargaining parties and increase the possibilities for developing more constructive bargaining orientations. Many administrators come from the faculty, and if they accept the concept of faculty participation in governance "then the psychology of negotiations may tend to be more of an integrative, problem-solving nature" (Begin, 1973, p. 23). Begin also notes that while in other settings persons move into administrative positions and assume supervisory roles, the roles of academic administrators are significantly different. Not only do many of them not have a permanent commitment to administration, but many continue to perform faculty responsibilities. "It seems reasonable to suggest that the continued identification of administrators with academic life would tend to make them receptive to increased faculty demands for participation" (Begin, 1973, p. 24).

Administrative identification with faculty concerns appears to be reciprocated and recognized in colleges and universities. In general, faculty tend to see the interests of administrators as being supportive of their own and to have reasonably high levels of trust and confidence in them (Baldridge et al., 1978, pp. 113 ff.). These high levels of trust should assist the two groups in establishing a productive orientation should they begin a bargaining relationship.

Perhaps in part because of the overlapping membership of the two groups, educational institutions are less stratified than most other organizations, and the status differentials between faculty and administrators comparably reduced. This is not to say that there are no status differentials. They exist in all social groups, and there are few institutions in which the average dean is seen as being of lower status than the average professor. But the differences are not of the same magnitude as those that exist in business and industry. Minimizing status differentials tends to make bargaining relationships more constructive (Rubin

& Brown, 1975, p. 199). As differences in status increase between the parties, the group with higher status tends to exploit the other group, and the lower-status group becomes more submissive and deferential (Rubin & Brown, 1975, p. 168). These behaviors make it impossible for the groups to work together as equals and engage in problem solving or other constructive bargaining activities.

Relatively low status differentials should be reinforced by the presumptions of legal equality established by collective bargaining statutes, further supporting the ability of the parties to engage in bargaining without domination of one party by the other (Pruitt & Lewis, 1977, p. 185). Although the parties may not have absolute equality of bargaining power at the negotiating table because of the exigencies of the situation, collective bargaining in general probably tends to increase faculty power where it has been low, and reduce administrative power where it has been unusually high. Power inequality between parties decreases the likelihood of constructive outcomes of conflict by decreasing communication and trust and inhibiting both parties from fully presenting their views (Walton, 1969, pp. 98-99). It is at least in part for this reason that imbalances in power are seen as being related to significant difficulties in collective bargaining (Simkin, 1971, p. 182). By moving the parties toward greater balance in their relationship, the implementation of bargaining in previously unbalanced situations should increase the chances that they will be able to engage in constructive interactions.

There are many ways in which organizations deal with conflict. They can attempt to ignore them or smooth them over, or they can seek resolution by the exercise of power in an effort to see which subgroup is strong enough to impose its will on the other. Effective organizations, however, tend to deal with conflict by directly confronting the issues that divide individuals or groups and to work together to seek resolutions that satisfy the participants and are consistent with organizational goals (Lawrence & Lorsch, 1969). Collective bargaining is an institutionalized process of conflict management that encourages a confrontation approach to conflict. The full expression of different viewpoints is a precondition to creative problem-solving in groups. Many organizations inhibit these expressions, and this would be most likely in academic institutions with governance systems characterized by administrative primacy or dominance. Faculty in such systems may feel insecure and therefore less likely to offer suggestions or express their opinions. Maier (1970) has proposed that one of the functions of strong labor unions is to increase the security of individuals to the point at which they are able to disagree with a person in authority. "Increasing the subordinates' commitment so that their point of view can effectively oppose that of the authority figure thus may be regarded as a way to introduce conflict and to provide the conditions for creative problem-solving" (p. 377).

There are powerful forces in colleges and universities that tend to make collective bargaining in higher education a productive and constructive process. Supporting the development of problem-solving orientations between faculty and administrations at the bargaining table are traditions of joint administrative-faculty participation in decision making, shared values and norms, orientations toward civility and collegiality, administrative participation in faculty roles and faculty support for the performance of administrators, relatively low status differentials and reductions in the differences of power between the two groups, and increased willingness of faculty to confront differences and introduce new points of view because of the security of union representation. In some institutions, the initiation of bargaining has had these productive effects. In others, bargaining participants deal with each other warily, expecting to be exploited by the other side and engaging in behaviors that make the exploration of creative approaches to common problems difficult or impossible. In still others, bargaining results in open warfare, creating wounds that may not heal for extended periods and changing the essential character of the institution and the people within it. There are no data to indicate the number of institutions in which bargaining has led to constructive, suspicious, or destructive relationships between faculty and administration. However, despite the forces described, it is unlikely that a large proportion of unionized institutions have been able to fully exploit the positive potential of the academic bargaining process to strengthen their programs and develop constructive relationships between campus constituencies.

In order to understand why this is so, we must turn our attention to other behavioral aspects of the bargaining relationship that tend to move institutions toward destructive conflict. These can be divided into four categories. The first considers the social and institutional *context* within which academic bargaining takes place. Next are the *antecedents* of the bargaining relationship including the extent to which various aspects of interaction between the parties prior to bargaining itself may affect behavior at the negotiating table. The third category involves the relationship between conflict management and the personal characteristics of the bargainer. Finally, those aspects of intergroup process that tend to increase conflict and give it a destructive orientation will be considered.

THE CONTEXT OF ACADEMIC BARGAINING

Rapid Social Change

It has been said that it is not possible to unionize a contented faculty (MaCoy & Morand, 1977, p. 29). Although this may be so, it is also true that rapid changes in the environment of higher education over the past decade have significantly increased the level of faculty dissatisfaction in many institutions. Actual and projected enrollment declines have limited faculty mobility, reduced promotion opportunities, and increased the difficulty of achieving tenure. At the same time that statewide public systems and coordinating boards have decreased faculty influence by interposing yet another level of external authority in the decision-making process, state and federal regulations of all kinds have proliferated and dramatically changed traditional processes in such key areas of governance as personnel selection. Inflation has eaten into faculty salary levels, states have shifted budget priorities from higher education to other pressing social service needs, and colleges and universities no longer occupy the privileged positions and high regard that had been theirs only a decade earlier. Faculty, not without reason, have felt increasingly threatened during this period of rapid social change. In many cases, they have turned toward collective bargaining in response to this sense of threat.

In addition to factors related to an increasing malevolent environment, the acceptance of bargaining has probably been accelerated on many campuses by the changing composition of the professoriate itself. The doubling of enrollments during each of the two preceding decades significantly expanded the size of faculties and overwhelmed the informal processes by which new faculty had been socialized into the profession during more placid times. On some campuses, and particularly on those such as the former teachers college and newly formed community colleges which now are the most actively involved in academic bargaining, newly recruited persons might have comprised a quarter or a third of the faculty each year during the 1960s. When bargaining initiatives were introduced on these campuses, younger faculty increasingly were occupying leadership positions, and the older faculty who might have been expected to take conservative positions supporting traditional governance processes were outnumbered.

Although in many situations faculty have unionized in response to specific and valid grievances and problems, it is possible to consider unionization at least in part as a response to an undifferentiated sense of anxiety and concern provoked by rapid change both inside and outside the institution. That unionization has tended to occur on campuses with higher-than-average levels of compensation and above-average levels of faculty participation in decision making (Garbarino, 1975, p. 79), rather than on campuses below average on these variables, may indicate that unionization may be related to general rather than specific concerns.

This analysis of factors related to the initiation of bargaining has several important implications for the course of bargaining. If bargaining on some campuses is related to general levels of faculty dissatisfaction caused by rapid social, economic, political, and demographic changes, then it is unlikely that bargaining will increase satisfaction since its roots are outside the control either of the faculty or the administration with which it bargains. Although bargaining has led to demonstrable increases in faculty power on some campuses where it was exceptionally low, evidence indicates that in general it has not changed faculty influence patterns when compared to institutions not involved in bargaining (Adler, 1977). If faculty enter bargaining to increase their level of satisfaction, and bargaining cannot control the critical forces that generate faculty concern, it may be expected that bargaining may lead to increased frustration and militancy of the bargainers, and thus move the parties toward destructive conflict.

Deutsch (1973) has described the dynamics through which increasing discontent on the part of a group seeking power can reinforce such adversarial relationships. As the group with lesser power continues to remain frustrated, it presses for even greater and quicker changes. This in turn makes the dominant group more defensive, which makes change increasingly unlikely. Under these conditions, notes Deutsch (p. 113), "the development of an escalating spiral of force and counterforce is not uncommon. Unless a neutral authority can intervene to reverse the upward spiral of violence, it will continue until one side exhausts, vanquishes, or persuades the other or until the costs of the escalating hostilities become intolerable to both sides."

Rapid social change leads to loss of consensus and the development of schisms and factions in social groups (Sherif, 1962, p. 13). Faculty dissatisfaction may be expected to increase as changes in college and university organization continue, and to the extent that the sources of that dissatisfaction remain undefined or outside the control of any of the participants in the governance process, the failure of unionization to resolve it may foster adversarial bargaining relationships.

Ideological Orientations

The most difficult conflicts to successfully resolve through negotiations are those based upon conflicting ideologies, representing value dissensus between the bargainers (Druckman & Zechmeister, 1970).

When groups compete over the allocation of resources, it is possible to find areas of compromise. But ideological differences usually cannot be compromised because they are matters of principle. It has been noted, for example, that because conflicting holders of incompatible ideologies each demand that the others surrender their beliefs, wars with strong ideological components are unusually bitter and prolonged (Frank, 1968, p. 131). Laboratory findings support the view that when conflicts of interest are linked to ideological orientations, bargaining becomes more difficult, and compromise between the parties more unlikely (Druckman & Zechmeister, 1970).

This is a critical consideration in academic bargaining. Anyone who has ever witnessed a faculty senate debate knows the importance academics attach to matters of "principle." Faculty members are more likely than persons in other professions to view the world in ideological terms and to organize diverse issues in consistent and related ways. In presenting data to support this contention, Ladd and Lipsett (1975, p. 51) state: "This ideological character of professorial thinking is of considerable conceptual importance to an effort to understand academic political life, *particularly the bitterness expressed against those of differing orientations*" (emphasis added).

There are at least two aspects of academic bargaining in which differences in ideological orientations may increase levels of destructive conflict between the parties. The first occurs when the faculty and the administration of an institution hold different ideological orientations concerning the legitimacy of bargaining itself. In a survey of college and university presidents, only half felt that there was a legitimate role for collective bargaining in higher education. Eighty-three percent thought unions had a divisive effect upon academic life, 78% believed faculty union leaders were unlikely to pursue objectives that were in the best interests of the institution, and 76% thought that faculty unions were likely to result in mediocrity in faculty performance (Spritzer & Odewahn, 1978). On the other hand, three-quarters of all faculty surveyed by Ladd and Lipsett (1978) believed that collective bargaining had a legitimate place in American higher education. When presidents express the view that bargaining processes "make a mockery out of scrupulous respect for truth, and seem entirely alien to the scholarly processes" (Kemerer & Baldridge, 1975, p. 139), and union officials argue that collective bargaining is the sole means by which the faculty can achieve academic democracy (Loewenthal & Nielson, n.d.), the parties are faced with extreme ideological differences, rather than with a mere conflict of interest. The major manifestation of this clash of ideologies is often an attempt by the union to increase the scope of bargaining as much as possible and efforts by the administration to reduce it to exclude all issues of governance and academic decision making. While matters of bargaining scope can be considered in the bargaining context, when they become related to ideological positions concerning the legitimacy of unionization itself concessions are difficult to make because they are seen by each side as surrender. "Commitment to the more abstract, and more idealized interests of a group organized along ideological lines . . . is seen as producing greater rigidity in the representative's bargaining behavior, transforming the conflict of interest into a conflict of 'truths'" (Druckman & Zechmeister, 1973). If the administration not only questions the point of view of the union, but also challenges the right of the union to have a point of view, and if it is determined to deal with the union only to the minimum extent imposed by law and the power of the union itself, a high level of hostility can be predicted to characterize the bargaining relationship (Megginson & Gullett, 1970). ·

Second, faculty not only tend to have ideological orientations linking together certain concepts in overarching, conceptual "umbrellas," but they also have an unfortunate tendency to expressly relate disagreement on issues to these underlying ideologies. In this way, disagreements at the bargaining table over faculty involvement in personnel policies, for example, which conceivably can be compromised, become confrontations over academic freedom, which cannot be.

In considering some of the literature concerning the relationship of ideology to bargaining, Summers (1968) states:

> When persons holding different views of the world are engaged in conflict, agreement by one person with the other person's beliefs or values involves a potential "loss"—where such a loss might range from power and authority to self-esteem. It might be further suggested that such a conflict between persons is often perceived as zero-sum: only one participant can win . . . Clearly, if such a view of the situation is indeed held by persons engaged in cognitive conflict, the likelihood of a mutually satisfactory resolution of their differences is decreased (p. 216).

Clearly, ideological differences among faculty as well as such differences between faculty and administration pose significant problems in the bargaining relationship and increase the potential for destructive conflict.

Inhibition of Hostility

On some campuses prior to the initiation of bargaining, the apparent spirit of collegiality and cooperative relationships between various constituencies masks hostile feelings the parties repress. Repression of hostility is probably a reality in every work situation, because we are taught that emotions such as anger or resentment reflect bad manners or immaturity, and therefore should not be expressed (Walton, 1969, p. 3). It is probably even more prevalent in colleges and universities because of the establishment of "scholarly" norms emphasizing restrained judgments and the superiority of rationality over feelings. When hostility is repressed, however, it does not disappear, but tends to go underground, to become indirect and more destructive, and to become more difficult to confront and resolve when conditions bring it into the open.

The operation of this dynamic is reflected in the development of adversarial relationships at an institution involved in academic bargaining. The majority of faculty and administrators at the institution ascribed the relationship to the "normal emergence of issues long present within the institution which now surface due to the existence of mechanisms for their consideration and to a greater sense of job security on the part of the faculty" (Mortimer and Richardson, 1977, p. 69).

Ironically, when conflict does occur in an academic institution because it has been legitimated through the adoption of collective bargaining, it is likely to be particularly intense because of the close relationships between administrators and faculty. As Coser (1964) has pointed out, closely knit groups having high levels of interaction and high levels of personality involvement by members are those most apt to repress conflict. When conflict emerges, therefore, it tends to encompass not only the immediate issues that appear to have created it, but also all of the accumulated grievances and repressed conflicts not previously expressed (p. 152).

Misunderstandings about Bargaining

Bargaining is new to higher education, and it is not surprising that both faculty and administrators are confused about its processes and outcomes. Misunderstandings can be corrected through effective programs of education, but if they are not they can lead to unrealistic expectations, frustration, and destructive conflict. Misunderstandings can exist about many facets of bargaining. Faculties commonly do not understand the roles of state employment relations boards (Pisarski & Landin, 1976), and they are unfamiliar with the impact of decisions made by such agencies concerning crucial issues such as the identification of the appropriate bargaining unit. The concept of "scope of bargaining" is often obscure, with faculty believing that the administration is obligated to bargain over every item placed on the table, and the

administration believing that bargaining requires that they make counteroffers to every faculty demand. In general, the definitions of "good
faith bargaining" are unclear to both parties, and the right of "management" to say "no" to a demand is often considered as a violation of the
bargaining relationship instead of a perfectly acceptable response that
is common in negotiations.

The confusion of many faculty members concerning the full meaning of the bargaining relationship is sometimes reflected in faculty
desires both to unionize and to have representation on the board of
trustees. These orientations toward governance are basically incompatible with one another (Carnegie Commission, 1973).

The participation of two parties in a highly structured setting for
conflict management, in which either or both are not fully aware of the
rules and processes governing their interactions, increases the probability that actions by one will be misinterpreted by the other, and that
the spiral of destructive conflict will continue and escalate.

Dual Role of Faculty

Collective bargaining in any setting is likely to lead to adversarial
relationships, but the scope of the conflict in the industrial sector is
likely to be at least partially controlled by the specific and limited roles
unions have developed. Traditionally, management has been granted
the absolute right to establish the goals of the organization, and to take
any and all steps to achieve these goals, subject only to the limitations on
managerial prerogatives contained in the contract and the right of the
union to process grievances. It is for this reason that the grievance
process is often considered the most critical clause of a bargaining
contract.

Unions in this country have not typically shown an interest in gaining
a voice in the determination of management goals (Jones, 1975, p. 89),
preferring instead to maintain a defensive posture. Not only does this
leave the union in a better position to grieve (since its grievance ability
would clearly be compromised if it had played a role in drafting the
work rules against which a member was complaining), but it also main-
tains the union's credibility with the membership when it actively
pursues a grievance on behalf of the membership (Barbash, 1976). In
the private sector, management acts, unions react.

Public sector bargaining, on the other hand, has been more concerned with matters that could be considered to be policy, and both the
courts and state legislation has broadened the scope of bargaining in
the public sector (Jones, 1975). The problem of bargaining with the
goal of co-management probably is most severe in the unionized public

college or university, where the movement toward greater union participation in management decisionmaking is accelerated by the traditional involvement of faculty in governance activities.

As the scope of bargaining increases, the potential for destructive
conflict increases with it for several reasons. First, it moves bargaining
away from areas in which the administration is less likely to challenge
its legitimacy, such as salaries, into matters such as personnel policies
where the proper union role is still questionable. In addition, by moving into areas considered previously to be management prerogatives, it
increases the defensiveness of administrators, and thus makes bargaining more difficult. But probably of greater importance, the collective
bargaining process which for the most part has been adopted by
educational institutions from the industrial sector, was designed to deal
with matters of salaries, benefits, and terms and conditions of employment; given the defensive nature of industrial unions and their unwillingness to become involved in running the enterprise, the process
was not designed to facilitate co-management processes. It will be seen
in a following chapter that in fact the tactics and strategies that are
effective in bargaining over some matters are dyfunctional in dealing
with others. The use of traditional bargaining approaches in considering governance or related policy issues, then, would tend to be ineffective and to lead to destructive bargaining between the parties.

Increasing Conflict Size

In many reasonably large and complex academic institutions without
collective bargaining, decisions are made through shifting combinations of political, bureaucratic, and collegial mechanisms. The large
number of groups that become involved in these processes change and
overlap, and the decisions themselves may not be consistent with those
reached on similar issues elsewhere on campus.

This process of fractionating conflict, which is in many ways extremely frustrating to the organizations' participants, as well as confusing to observers and those with an interest in studying the academy,
is probably one of the critical elements contributing to organizational
stability. Decisions made one at a time, in which small controversies are
treated independently of others, are much easier to resolve than large,
related conflicts. As issues become linked together into overall contests,
the merits of particular issues are lost in the single, overriding con-
troversy. Moreover, as the number of competing groups with overlapping memberships decline, issues come to be evaluated more on the
basis of their source than their content. Fisher's (1964) concept of
fractionating conflict suggests that combining issues escalates conflict,

leads to a win-lose mentality, and makes constructive conflict resolution more difficult. This thesis has been supported in laboratory research by Deutsch, Canavan, and Rubin (1971), which found that decreasing the size of a conflict made it easier for bargainers to come to a mutually rewarding agreement.

Rather than fractionating conflict, collective bargaining has the potential for combining it, thereby increasing the level of conflict and making constructive conflict resolution more difficult. It does this in several ways. First, it reduces the number of parties to the conflict to two, eliminates overlapping group membership that might mediate it, and tends to make each of the individual issues a union-administration conflict when in many instances they could be dealt with at lower organizational levels. Second, it tends to couple issues, so that one issue cannot be resolved unless another is as well. Although "packaging" can, under certain circumstances, be useful in negotiations, it has the tendency to lead to a situation in which no issue can be resolved unless all are. This shifts again the nature of the dispute "from a narrow subject matter to one in which the only common denominator is the parties involved—tends to bring up all possible issues in the relationship and may do more harm than good. It encourages the unfortunate 'over-all confrontation'" (Fisher, 1964, p. 98).

Collective bargaining can increase destructive conflict because it creates a forum (and in some cases an expectation) that establishes a single set of adversaries with no common membership, combines issues so that conceding on any single matter can be seen as capitulating to the overall orientation of the adversary, and suggests that agreement depends upon resolving all issues simultaneously. Conflict is less intense when the parties who oppose each other on one issue are potential allies on others. When structural elements make this less likely, however, so that cohesive groups with stable membership confront each other on an increasingly large number of issues, polarization between them is exaggerated, and future competition between them will become intensified (Druckman & Zechmeister, 1973).

The discussion in this section has indicated that, all other things being equal, destructive conflict in academic bargaining is likely to be intensified by the context in which it takes place. Aside from any of the substantive issues involved, conflict is increased as a consequence of rapid social change that disturbs old decision-making and communications processes, reduces the influence of older and presumably more conservative group members, and creates general feelings of anxiety and concern. Ideological orientations, which are present to an unusual degree in academic institutions, may come to color the bargaining relationship; in particular, the parties to bargaining may disagree on such basic considerations as the legitimacy of bargaining itself in the academic environment. Bargaining not only provides a forum in which previously repressed hostilities can be expressed, but because of the closeness of faculty and administration the resultant conflict may be particularly bitter.

Bargaining is also made more difficult by the confusion of many faculty and administrators concerning the process of bargaining itself and the impact of labor laws and court decisions on their institution. Since the bargaining process was developed in the private sector to cope with issues related to salaries and benefits, its use in coping with governance or other nonfiscal issues may be ineffective and frustrating. Finally, bargaining tends to create two sides discussing a large number of separate issues that are seen as related because they are considered in a single process and in doing so increases the size of the conflict and leads toward increased adversary relationships.

Each of these factors is inherent in the context in which bargaining occurs. We now turn to a consideration of factors that influence bargaining prior to the time when the parties sit down at the table to negotiate.

THE ANTECEDENTS OF
ACADEMIC BARGAINING

Carry-over of Previous Animosities

In general, the parties to bargaining have been on the campus before the initiation of unionization, and the quality of the relationships developed during this prenegotiation period may have a significant impact upon the course of conflict at the negotiation table. In a case study of a unionized institution, Mortimer and Richardson (1977) noted that the causes of the poor relationships could be traced to the dissatisfactions of the parties prior to entering into negotiations. These problems were then intensified by the bargaining process itself.

In summarizing laboratory research, Druckman (1971) has suggested that cooperative behavior between negotiating parties is enhanced if they have had previously friendly experiences. In the same way, it has been found (Megginson & Gullett, 1970) that the previous relationships of two organizations, such as a union and company management, can strongly affect conflict in their present industrial relations, and that "a management and union with a history of high conflict are more likely to remain hostile to one another even when some of the bases of this conflict no longer exist" (p. 498).

It could be expected, therefore, that if faculty-administration interaction on campus had been unsatisfactory to one or both parties, the initiation of bargaining may intensify the conflict and increase the adversarial nature of their relationship.

Expectation of Adversarial Relationships

Whenever persons develop attitudes or orientations toward specific objects or relationships, they tend to selectively consider information supportive of those attitudes and to filter out information which is not. When people expect that a relationship will be adversarial, they are likely to exhibit behaviors making the expectation a self-fulfilling prophecy. The literature of higher education is replete with examples of information leading participants in the process to expect, and themselves contribute to, an adversarial approach to bargaining.

Writing for the trustees, for example, Potter (1975) advises that

it is extremely important for the board to get in the right mood for collective bargaining. This means to recognize collective bargaining for what it is. You will not be entering into professional negotiations where the concern of all is the welfare of the college and the people it serves. At the bargaining table the sole concern of the teachers is their own interest. This is as it should be. Collective bargaining is an adversarial procedure. Consequently, the board must concern itself with the interest of the college and community in negotiations . . . . If you do your job right you will *win* at the bargaining table (emphasis added) (p. 22).

A university labor relations lawyer tells his colleagues:

Make no mistake about it, collective bargaining is an adversarial process. The faculty would not have chosen to forego their individuality unless a majority of them believed (rightly or wrongly) that they could wrest away that which the administration could not be pursuaded to give voluntarily. This is not to say that a faculty union necessarily is or should be treated as your enemy. But, to engage in negotiations or in the drafting of an agreement on any basis other than that of an adversary will likely prove to be the height of naivete (Schwartzman, 1974, p. 351).

And the faculty industrial relations expert states:

Collective bargaining maximizes conflict, with all its trappings. The major trapping is reliance upon coercion as the technique for resolving disputes (Oberer, 1969, p. 143).

In addition to the statement of experts in bargaining describing it as an adversarial relationship, individuals involved with the process receive confirming evidence from other sources. College and university administrators receive brochures offering bargaining seminars to prepare them for negotiations. "Negotiation of collective bargaining agreements is often rough . . . brutal . . . gloves-off . . . combining intellectualism and intimidation. Those who engage in it might be termed modern-day business warriors," says one. Another offers: "The course that shows you how to: put your opponent on the defensive, keep up a continual attack on the opponent's weak points, play up your strong points, divert attention from your weaknesses, bottle up your opponent and create dilemmas, and much more!"

The identification of bargaining as an adversarial process establishes certain expectations and attitudes on the part of the bargainers even before the formal interaction commences and makes it more likely that they will engage in behavior likely to generate destructive conflict. In addition to affecting attitudes, material such as this can have significant cognitive impact as well by providing "instructions" to the inexperienced bargainer on how negotiations should be conducted.

Laboratory experiments in bargaining have shown that it is possible to change the behavior of bargainers by the instructions given, even though all other aspects of the bargaining situation remain the same. Deutsch (1973), for example, gave different instructions to subjects in a bargaining game. One set of subjects was given a cooperative orientation by being instructed that "You're interested in your partner's welfare as well as your own." An individualistic orientation was provided to a second set of subjects who were told "Your only motivation should be to win as much money as you can for yourself. You are to have no interest whatsoever in whether the other person wins or loses." The third group was given a competitive orientation with the instructions to "win as much money as you can for yourself and also do better than the other person."

In all experimental conditions, those with cooperative instructions were more likely to make cooperative decisions in the game, and those with a competitive orientation to make competitive ones, even though doing so resulted in mutual loss (p. 188). If the "instructions" of academic bargaining say that it is to be an adversarial process, the actions of the bargainer are likely to conform to this definition. In the same way, when subjects in a conflict resolution game are told that it is a win-lose situation, they find it more difficult to resolve the conflict than when exactly the same game is presented as a problem-solving debate (Druckman, 1971).

Union-Administration Conflict

One of the major determinants of the level of conflict in the bargaining situation is the relationship existing between the union and administration prior to the start of negotiations. This relationship usually begins in a formal way at the time that the union is preparing to petition for a representational election. Unfortunately, just as is true in industry (Golden & Parker, 1955; Simkin, 1971), this activity is often characterized by escalating conflict and competition, which then carries over into the bargaining sessions.

In order to be selected as a bargaining representative, a faculty union must usually win a majority vote in a representational election. Unless the election takes place on a campus whose members had previous involvement in union activities, or one in which pro-union sentiment is strong and unambiguous, achieving this level of vote is not a simple matter. Numerous issues of importance to one or another group are ubiquitous on most college and university campuses, and the number of persons who participate actively in university affairs, as well as the intensity of their involvement, fluctuates widely (Baldridge, 1971). It is hard to get attention, and even more difficult to get agreement on action and the determination of next steps.

To maximize the probability of success at the polls, unions have to engage in activities that stress to the presently uninvolved faculty the great need for unionization, which increases in-group solidarity and commitment of active union members, and which solicits new recruits into union membership. There are a number of tactics that can assist in achieving these objectives.

1. Unions may emphasize the differences between the union and the administration to clearly define two separate groups.
2. Unions may focus attention upon institutional weaknesses so that participating in union activities presented as designed to correct them will be seen as rational.
3. Unions may attempt to reduce the levels of trust existing between faculty and administration (Megginson & Gullett, 1970) by increasing suspicion that administrative acts are prompted by sinister motives, incompetence, or both. "It is up to the [union] leadership to convince the members of the union that management is being extremely unfair, unreasonable, punitive, and perhaps even vindictive. This is all part of the ball game," reports a community college president (Campbell, 1974, p. 27).
4. Unions may search for enemies and create issues where none exist in order to decrease levels of satisfaction (Megginson & Gullett, 1970) and maintain unity and internal cohesion (Coser, 1954, p. 95).

When bargaining begins under these conditions, the union may be faced across the table with a monster of its own creation, and the establishment of destructive bargaining relationships is almost assured.

Union-Union Conflict

The efforts of a union to overcome the indifference of a faculty or the opposition of an administration can increase destructive conflict and effect subsequent bargaining. In many cases, however, there is more than one union interested in being selected as the bargaining representative. When this is the case, each union must not only convince the faculty that they should unionize, but must also convince them of the wisdom of selecting one organization over its opponents. These interunion conflicts can be quite bitter and can include two orientations. First, the unions can attack each other on the basis of past performance, stated policy issues, personalities of the leaders of the groups, willingness and ability to deal appropriately with the administration, and similar issues. This has the effect of raising the levels of conflict and tension within the organization, regardless of the outcome of the election, and will tend to increase the levels of conflict in the subsequent negotiations.

Second, in an effort to vie for faculty support and votes, the unions may engage in a spiralling attack against the administration in order to demonstrate their militancy. This has the same effects as seen in the case of a single union seeking a representational election, but the competitive nature of the union positions tends to make the rhetoric even harsher. As a general rule, interunion rivalry tends to increase conflict between union and management (Megginson & Gullett, 1970), and it may be suggested that the likelihood of destructive conflict in colleges and universities increases when bargaining has been preceded by a representational election in which more than one union was on the ballot.

The problem of interunion rivalry does not end when the ballots are counted. Faculty who support the losing union may continue to harass the winning one, hoping to replace it in future elections. The presence of dissidents in the union increases militancy and makes constructive bargaining more difficult. Commenting on this problem in industrial bargaining, McMurray (1955) has said:

> Whatever bargain the union officers make with the employer, the dissidents 'could have done it better.' If union officers make the slightest concessions to management, they are charged with having sold out to the company. . . . The net result is that the union is constantly faced with the imperative: produce or be replaced. It dare make only minimum concessions to the employers; it must always get more than it gives (p. 51).

The consequence of interunion rivalry in an academic institution may be to place the administration in a defensive or hostile position even before negotiations begin. In this adversarial atmosphere, in-experienced faculty and administrators may "overreact to each other's proposals and adopt unnecessarily hard-line positions from which neither can retreat comfortably" (Graham & Walters, 1973, p. 50).

Administrative Response

It would be folly in a first negotiation to underestimate the feeling of anxiety and urgency shared by a local bargaining committee and the union agent, particularly if the latter is not sophisticated and experienced. On the other side there is the apprehension of the management who feel not only deserted but actually betrayed by a lack of loyalty on the part of the members of the bargaining unit (Caples & Graney, 1967, p. 310).

The above comment, written long before academic bargaining was firmly established, is perhaps even more applicable to colleges and universities than to the industrial sector. Often coming from the facul-ty, and supportive of faculty norms, the administrator receives great satisfaction from the presumptions of collegiality that traditionally have related the administrative role to the academic mission of the institution. The onset of bargaining is thus a sorrowful and frightening experience for many presidents, who view collective bargaining as a unilateral and unwarranted repudiation of the collegial relationship by their faculty, as well as a rejection of their own leadership. They agree with the meaning of unionization described by Metzger (1976): "Usual-ly, when a faculty says that it wants a union, it is also saying that it sees the president as a crypto-adversary and would prefer to have him stand honestly and openly on the opposing side." Bargaining is thus inter-preted as an indication of a lack of trust in the administration and as an invitation to move from a cooperative to an adversarial relationship.

Presidents also react to unionization in terms of its effect upon their ability to perform their administrative and leadership functions. The same external forces that have reduced faculty influence in decision making have also reduced the influence and power of the president. Particularly in campuses that are part of state systems, they may feel their ability to act being eroded because of increased incursions into their authority by state-level offices on one hand, and the development of unionization on the campus on the other (Kemerer & Baldridge, 1975, pp. 9, 155). At the same time, their accountability to various constituencies and their responsibility for effective campus programs and operations remains unchanged. Frustration at being held account-able for activities they are less able to control is increased by the fear

that polarization accompanying bargaining may make campus administration and decison making virtually impossible (Baldridge et al.,
1978).

Some presidents respond to unionization by leaving office, unable or
unwilling to cope with a new campus structure and influence system
quite different from the one in place when they accepted the position.
Others become defensive, accepting what they see as the union challenge, and changing their behaviors to be consistent with the conflict
being provoked by the union. This behavior, of course, reinforces the
union's determination to increase their influence. Even if the initial
actions of each were based upon false impressions of the intentions of
the other side, the spiraling characteristics of destructive conflict are
likely to intensify the developing adversarial relationship.

Even before the union and administration meet at the bargaining
table, previous contacts between them have started to shape the course
of their relationship. If faculty-administrative interaction prior to bargaining had been positive, the parties may approach the table with
orientations promoting constructive conflict. If relationships had been
strained or adversarial, bargaining will intensify them. Regardless of
their initial orientation, the identification of academic bargaining as an
adversarial process is likely to lead the parties to filter out communications that might not confirm this expectation, and make it a self-fulfilling prophecy. Many of the "instructions" available to inexperienced
bargainers suggest the need or desirability of a competitive orientation,
and the lack of perceived alternatives to this orientation provokes the
mutual use of the tactics of destructive conflict.

When a union cannot be recognized without a representational
election, the organizing and campaigning tactics employed often draw
attention to campus shortcomings and criticisms of the administration.
When two or more unions are on the ballot, there is a tendency for
them to become even more militant and anti-administration as they
compete with each other for faculty allegiance. Administrators, faced
with the uncertainty of unionization and fearing that loss of administrative influence will make it increasingly difficult to perform well in
their roles, are also affected by what they interpret as the loss of
confidence by the faculty. As they become more defensive, they often
engage in behaviors that further increase the adversarial nature of the
relationship and make destructive conflict at the bargaining table
almost inevitable. We turn now to a consideration of the personal
characteristics of the bargainer.

THE PERSONS IN ACADEMIC BARGAINING

The Legitimacy of the Negotiators

Groups in conflict frequently assume that the leaders of the other group are speaking only for themselves and do not truly represent the majority feelings of their constituency. Administrators often question the legitimacy of union negotiators on this basis, believing that the union bargaining team represents some small, militant faction, but by no means speaks for most faculty. It is a pleasant delusion, but it can intensify conflict because it makes it more difficult for the union bargainers to convince their administration counterparts of the true intensity of their feelings and the degree to which the views they articulate represent those the majority of the faculty would support.

It has been said that "The belief that only the leaders of an opposing group are evil is practically universal" (Frank, 1968, p. 120). He continues, quoting White (1966), that this is similar to

> the complacent employer's conviction that his employees are contented and loyal but misled by union agitators. . . . It is a wonderfully consoling conception. It simultaneously eliminates the guilt of feeling hostile to a large number of people, creates a positive image of oneself as saving the underdog-masses from their conniving and oppressive leaders, provides a personal, visualizable devil on whom to concentrate all hostility, and sustains hope that, once the leaders have been firmly dealt with, the battle will be over (pp. 120-121).

When administrators believe that, despite the vote in a representational election, the faculty don't really want to be unionized, and the union bargainers do not really represent the faculty, the union is often backed into a posture that requires them to take dramatic action to disabuse management of this notion.

Leadership during Conflict

There is conflicting evidence concerning the characteristics of individuals who are likely to emerge in leadership positions during intergroup conflict. Sherif (1962) has suggested that when there is conflict between two groups, "it is usually the more responsible, the more talented, the more exemplary members of the group who are in control" (p. 6). It is for this reason that destructive conflict cannot be seen as being related to the personalities of a few deviant group members who are in leadership positions, but rather as a function of the antecedents, context, and structure of the bargaining relationship.

On the other hand, on many campuses the initiation of unionization appears to change the leadership of the faculty from senior scholars to younger, more militant, and lower ranked persons (Corson, 1975, p. 203). This new leadership orientation is not uncommon in emerging union-management situations. It may be that the intensity of administrative opposition to unionization during its organizing period attracts a certain type of leadership. Based upon experience in industrial settings, it has been said that in the early stages of unionization a labor leader is likely to be chosen who is "an aggressive and militant individual willing to press almost any issue if there are signs that it will increase the vulnerability of management. There also tend to be common structural attributes of labor leaders chosen during the earliest phase of labor-management relations. When the primary union task is to establish its existence, labor leaders are likely to emerge from the lower ranking, more deprived occupational groups" (Alderfer, 1977, p. 254).

It is possible that both views are correct. In a case study reported by Mortimer and Richardson (1977), for example, it was noted that faculty leaders considered by their colleagues as "radical" were selected to deal with the administration during the first contract. These persons were identified as wanting to "flex their muscles" in the union-administrative relationship, thus serving to show the strength and resolution of the union, but at the same time contributing to the adversarial relations between the parties. Several faculty on that campus stated that once the usefulness of the radicals was finished, they would be replaced by "more moderate leaders who will be far readier to reach accommodation with the administration" (p. 154). Based upon these comments, it may be that the selection of union leadership in higher education is contingent upon the stage of unionization on the campus and the antecedents of bargaining. More radical and lower-status representatives may be selected during early stages, and more moderate and higher status representatives may emerge as the relationship matures.

If true, this sequence poses significant problems for the course of conflict in the unionized institution. The ability of a negotiator to influence others is dependent upon such characteristics as expertise, status, and prestige. Negotiators who do not possess these characteristics, and who lack self-esteem and have feelings of powerlessness, are more apt than other negotiators to rely on coercive means of influence, such as aggressive tactics, threats, and similar measures at the bargaining table (Tedeschi, Gaes, & Rivera, 1977). As the negotiator uses coercion, there is a continued loss in the ability to use other, noncoercive means of influence effectively. This initiates, and contributes to, the continuation of processes of destructive conflict, which may eventually make it difficult for either party to initiate constructive interaction with the other.

The Effects of Personality upon Bargaining

As with the issue of leadership during conflict, there is disagreement upon the effects of personality upon the bargaining process. Personality has been identified as both playing a key role in the determination of intergroup relationships (Megginson & Gullett, 1970) and as having negligible effects on negotiations (Druckman, 1977, p. 245). The rationale for this latter view is that the forces acting upon the negotiator's role in the form of pressures from the constituency being represented have such a strong impact upon the negotiators' behavior that they overwhelm any behavioral predispositions that may be related to personality differences.

It is possible to reconcile these views by again considering the negotiating role as contingent upon the stages of the bargaining process. In the early stages of bargaining, the inexperienced negotiator may have few cues either from the constituency or from the other bargainer, and in this situation their personalities may have a strong influence upon their behaviors. As bargaining progresses, however, any negotiation orientations that might have been related to their personalities becomes of less and less importance as increasing feedback is received from the constituency, and the bargainer starts to respond to the perceived bargaining initiatives of the opponent. For this reason, the behavior of the opponent becomes a more significant determinant of bargaining behavior than the personality of the bargainer (Hermann & Kogan, 1977, p. 267). This is the reason why, as shall be discussed in the following chapters, it takes two cooperative bargainers to develop a constructive bargaining process, and only one competitive one to move the relationship toward destructive conflict. If either one of the parties in bargaining behaves competitively, the other party is likely to respond in kind, even though the party's personality supports cooperative bargaining.

The Psychodynamic Fallacy

This discussion of the effects of constituency pressure and the behavior of the other party on bargaining activity leads to a brief mention of the "psychodynamic fallacy" (Blake & Moulton, 1962). There is a tendency to attribute the behaviors of a bargainer to personality characteristics, and thus make them appear to be immutable and not open to change. Thus, union negotiators are often characterized by the administration as hostile, unreasonable, and nonsupportive of academic norms, while administrators may be viewed as autocratic and unconcerned with faculty interests. The statement that *"Because of personality and temperament* some presidents may be unable to accept a condition of complete equality with the union negotiators across the table" (MaCoy & Morand, 1977, p. 32, emphasis added) is an example of the psychodynamic fallacy. For the most part, the behaviors of negotiators, both union and administration, are affected by their roles, and the intergroup dynamics caused by the competitive bargaining situation. This misattribution of bargaining behavior to personality is particularly destructive because it leads toward attempts to devalue and belittle the adversary. As Blake and Mouton (1962) point out, however, "A change in attitude and action can be achieved, not by hoping for replacement or defeat of an aggressive union officer, who is mistakenly seen as an 'unreasonable' person, but by working toward changing the conditions that, in fact, do account for the behavior" (p. 113). In later chapters the processes of attribution, which affect not only the perception of the other bargainer but also have an impact upon attempts to move toward cooperative behavior, will be discussed in greater detail.

Bargainers sometimes attempt to avoid the issues in negotiations by believing that the negotiators for the other side do not truly represent their constituencies. This is likely to frustrate the other bargainer, who may resort to coercive tactics in order to prove their legitimacy.

In general, bargaining behavior is affected by the roles of the bargainers, the pressures of their constituencies, and the behavior of the other bargainer, rather than by the personalities of the bargainers themselves. During the earlier stages of unionization, however, it is possible that union representatives will be more radical and more militant than at later stages, depending upon the antecedents of the bargaining relationship. The tendency to see the bargainer as unrepresentative, and the chances that union bargainers may be unusually aggressive in early stages may lead to destructive conflict between the parties. It is also likely to lead to undue attention to the psychodynamic fallacy, in which the behaviors of the other bargainer are attributed to personality rather than role expectations.

SITUATIONAL ASPECTS OF ACADEMIC BARGAINING

Inexperienced Negotiators

Bargaining is a new process in higher education. It is therefore not surprising to find a great deal of confusion on the part of the parties concerning what can be expected of negotiations. In such a situation, it is not unusual for the union to make claims concerning the advantages of unionization that turn out not to be realistic as the parties become more familiar with the process. The raising of such false hopes, and the subsequent inability to deliver, increases the level of conflict between faculty and administration.

Not only are the parties new to bargaining, but also in many cases, so are the chief negotiators. Negotiations are extremely volatile settings for human interaction. Even experienced negotiators can inadvertently do things that lead to explosive conflict; inexperience in labor relations compounds the problem. As Jerry Wurf of AFSCE has said, "One of the major difficulties in public sector labor management relations stems from the ignorance and ineptness of the parties" (Keaton, 1972, p. 103). In order to control potential conflict, and to increase the probability of reaching agreement, negotiators have developed rules of behavior that are expected in the bargaining setting. These "rules" are passed down by tradition based upon experience in the field. An inexperienced negotiator, by breaking one of these unwritten rules, can terminate negotiations if the other party sees this as an evidence of bad faith, or an attempt to take unfair advantage (Cross, 1977). This lack of clear, accepted, and understood ground rules is a particular problem in higher education because of the recency of the phenomenon, but it is a commonly experienced situation in other settings. Cross (1977) has pointed out that "first-time negotiations with newly-formed unions are often accompanied with great bitterness, strikes, and even violence as tactics are employed which do not enjoy mutual acceptance as fair plays. It is not until after the parties have developed commonly understood (although perhaps unwritten) ground rules that the bitterness and violence subsides" (p. 585).

We would expect, therefore, that the initiation of bargaining would be accompanied by increased conflict in most institutions because the parties have unrealistic expectations of their possible gains, and because the inexperienced bargainer is likely to inadvertently choose courses of action that are destructive to the bargaining process. Angell (1973) commented that

> the greatest concerns to both parties have arisen from a lack of experience in predicting and responding diplomatically to the moves of the other party. Often one party, in trying to take advantage of its political position, creates a situation that is disasterous to both parties. Often a team, when frustrated, turns to emotional threats, name-calling, fillibustering, and withdrawal techniques that lead to intransigence and costly impasses. Often one or both parties are careless about making public statements that

advertise internal campus problems. In other words, the misuse of the
bargaining process by neophytes creates unnecessary obstacles to the
accomplishment of institutional priorities (p. 101).

When these unintentional consequences lead to polarization of the
parties, they are apt to become less willing to make concessions and
more likely to consider their proposals as minimum goals rather than
as points of departure for bargaining. An inexperienced union may
view any deviation from their demands as a sell-out to the administration, and instead of bargaining they may "demand total victory and
believe that unionization will result in the attainment of all their objectives and principles" (Byrnes, 1977).

Administrators experienced in the bargaining process, even under
these conditions, may be able to move bargaining toward more constructive relationships. It is probably more common, however, that
administration bargainers, themselves inexperienced, will feel
threatened and react in kind to destructive bargaining initiatives
(Begin, 1973).

Unrealistic Demands

Far too many college administrators tend to regard the outset of collective bargaining sessions as the issuance to faculty of a license to steal.
Faculty, in many cases, look to the same event as the opportunity to create
Heaven on earth without the necessity of the second coming. Neither
perception is realistic (Howe, 1974, p. 12).

Unions often make unrealistic demands in academic bargaining that
can lead toward destructive conflict due, at least in part, to the inexperience of the negotiators. Unrealistic demands are of two types. The first
concerns the number of demands and their relative importance to the
parties. Academic unions are political bodies subject to the expressed
interests of their members. Often, following the precedent of other
forms of faculty organization, they canvass the faculty to determine the
demands to be placed on the table. Unwilling or unable to sort out the
suggestions given to them, the union demands often resemble a
"laundry list," making it impossible for the administration to determine what the real concerns of the union are (Begin & Weinberg,
1976).

Demands can also be unrealistic because of the nature of the items
themselves, or the level of funding required to implement them. The
nature of bargaining presumes that parties will demand more than
they expect to get, but when the demands are themselves so high that

reasonable compromise appears impossible it is likely to create defensiveness and counterattack by the other party.

Some bargaining authorities have suggested that unions should not timidly submit "realistic demands," but rather should prepare its demands in the form of a contract that would support "ideal conditions" within the institution. "Such a proposal, if accepted, would mandate optimum policies and procedures and all working conditions that would be in effect if conditions permitted (Graham & Walters, 1973, p. 47).

Because excessive demands are seen by the opposing bargainer as unjust, their presentation is likely to insert intangible issues related to loss of public image into the negotiation relationship (Rubin & Brown, 1975, p. 132), provoke destructive conflict, and make agreement between the parties more difficult.

Personalization of Conflict

Inexperienced bargainers often find themselves responding personally and irrationally to proposals or demands made by the other side because they are coupled with attacks upon themselves and their bargaining positions. Since this is not an unusual tactic in industrial bargaining, it is not uncommon to find it employed in academic bargaining as well.

Experienced industrial negotiators are said to enjoy the rough-and-tumble of the bargaining table. They participate in the vigorous attacks that are made during certain stages in bargaining against their positions, their arguments, and themselves personally, and "they profess to relish the opportunity for indulging and parrying the verbal thrust, much in the same spirit as would contestants in a game" (Douglas, 1957, p. 72). However, the effective conduct of negotiations requires that negotiators be able to clearly separate the conflict of interest that divides the sides, which is commonly accentuated during the early stages of bargaining, from the maintenance of a positive interpersonal bargaining climate. While it is inherent in the process that the interparty climate become highly competitive and self-serving during bargaining, "for the people at the table it is of the gravest consequence that the fragile network of working relationships which is building up among the negotiators shall not become contaminated by negative emotional stress" (Douglas, 1957, p. 75).

Although negotiators who meet over extended periods of time may develop a subculture that inhibits idiosyncratic behavior, and thus lessens the likelihood of personalizing conflict (Druckman, 1971), when this occurs at all it is likely to be in the later, rather than the earlier stages of bargaining. It is, of course, during the earlier stages when the parties, not yet familiar with each other's style, are most likely to misinterpret each other's intentions because of the inherently competitive environment.

Being so different from the methods accepted in the common conduct of academic business, bargainers faced with attacks upon their integrity are likely to see them as unfair and as a personal challenge that cannot go unanswered. In addition, constant changes in union leadership on many campuses make it difficult to develop the informal relationships that permit bargainers to clearly separate interparty and interpersonal aspects of bargaining (Begin & Weinberg, 1976).

As long as inexperienced bargainers attempt to adopt the tactics of experienced professionals created in other organizational settings, the potential for destructive conflict will be consistently present at the table.

Use of External Negotiators

The use of inexperienced internal negotiators can lead to breakdowns in bargaining, making unnecessary concessions, agreeing on language with serious but hidden legal complications, the personalization of conflict, and other undesirable consequences. To avoid these problems, one party may secure the services of an external negotiator, and the other party may do so as well in order to protect itself. This cycle is probably often seen in centralized public systems in which the chief negotiator for management is a representative of the governor, and not in any way connected to the academic enterprise. In public school systems, and in some community college situations, both labor and management negotiators are sometimes seen traveling from institution to institution to confront each other again with only the names of the parties being different. The use of external negotiators, while having certain advantages (Naples, 1977, p. 437; Graham, 1976), can also contribute to destructive conflict between the parties. Institutions have found that leaving the negotiations to outsiders can sometimes lead to an unsatisfactory contract with which union and administration are forced to live, and which has significant problems associated both with its interpretation and its administration (Mortimer & Richardson, 1977).

Many external negotiators have been trained in the law and have their bargaining experiences outside the educational setting. Their legal backgrounds may lead them to require specificity in contractual areas that for academic reasons should remain vague, or to attempt to incorporate in the contract restrictive management rights or zipper clauses that may unduly restrict the relationship between the parties and increase mistrust between them. These negotiators, whose labor relations experiences are most usually developed either in private sector industrial bargaining, or in public sector, noneducational bargaining, are likely to be unfamiliar with academic norms, to believe that all unions and management are alike and that therefore all bargaining relationships can be treated the same way, and to perceive (and therefore to promote) bargaining as an adversarial process. The case study of one institution illustrates the point (Mortimer & Richardson, 1977):

> Federation leadership is also particularly bitter about the Board's use of lawyer-negotiators which forced the federation to use a state-level spokesman. Faculty leaders report that using lawyers in the negotiation process introduced an excessive degree of formalization and produced lengthy discussions about topics regarded by the faculty as irrelevant or unimportant. In retrospect, federation leaders believe that the use of what were regarded as professional negotiators helped to bring about a polarization between administrators and faculty. (p. 58)

As Rapoport (1974) has said, when negotiators think in terms of power, strategy, and manipulation, rather than in terms of bringing the parties together so that they can become more knowledgeable and empathetic about the position of the other, they tend to engage in fights rather than in debates. To focus on one's strengths and the other's weaknesses may be sensible in a win-lose situation, but where constructive bargaining outcomes are possible it may be more effective to at least initially emphasize the similarities rather than the differences between the parties. This assumption of similarity is difficult for an outsider who is employed to represent one of the parties to make. Rapoport's concept of a real debate is one joined and carried on by people who are not inhibited from assuming that the groups are similar in many ways, and acting as if this assumption is true (p. 309). This requires a long-term relationship between the parties—one that could never be fully understood or built upon by an external agent because it involves the admission of weakness to the other.

Unclear Goals

Colleges and universities are extremely complex organizations, with ambiguous, ill-defined, and constantly shifting goals. Many explanations have been offered for this situation, and all have some degree of plausibility. Goals are unclear because institutional subgroups have been self-selected and socialized in different ways, leading to different ideological orientations (Ladd & Lipsett, 1975); because the unusual characteristics of the organization create patterns of choice in which preferences follow rather than precede action (Cohen & March, 1974); because the multiple missions of the university have such inconsistent requirements for organization and decision making that the university is constantly at war with itself (Kerr, 1963); or because institutions embrace so many goals that it is impossible to establish meaningful priorities between them (Gross & Grambsch, 1968).

One of the reasons for most institutions having such innocuous and vapid statements of purpose in their bulletins is that divisions within the faculty make it possible to reach agreement only on statements that are so general in nature that everyone's personal preferences can be accommodated within them. Political subsystems operate within these institutions to enable individuals and groups to express their needs and to establish temporary coalitions to promote their interests.

With the implementation of collective bargaining in its traditional form, the luxury of embracing multiple and conflicting goals is no longer available to the union. It must develop bargaining positions that enjoy the support of its constituency.

One of the consequences of this dilemma is to include "laundry lists" of demands so that the union does not have to take the political responsibility for making decisions about which competing interest within the faculty it will support. The effects of this action on conflict have already been mentioned. But perhaps of even greater importance, the difficulty of developing demands supported by the membership when the membership cannot agree on a single set of priorities makes the position of the union negotiator extremely difficult. Operating at the boundary between the faculty and administrative groups, the union negotiator must bargain with both. And while it is possible to reach agreement with the administration, it is often much more difficult to find agreement within the union's membership itself since, as Baldridge et al. (1978, p. 106) has pointed out, not only are academic goals unclear, but they become highly contested once they are made clear. Since the union is internally unsure of its goals, it is difficult for it to make agreements it views as satisfying, regardless of the responsiveness of the administration. A lack of consensus in the constituency tends to lead to intransigence in bargaining, and thus to destructive conflict.

The Bargaining Table

It is common in collective bargaining for the negotiating groups to seat themselves facing each other, so that there are indeed "opposite

sides of the table." As Filley (1975, p. 80) has noted, spatial arrangements such as seating at the bargaining table often structure themselves to meet the behavioral expectations of the parties, and also have
the power to provoke or elicit the expected behavior. When groups
establish and protect their separate identities by their table positions,
they are less likely to engage in cooperative activity than if they are
seated so that there is no obvious physical barrier between them, for
example, in a random pattern. Whether seating arrangement contributes to competition or causes it, there is evidence that people
involved in cooperative activities tend to prefer to sit side by side, while
people competing with each other prefer face-to-face arrangements
(Filley, 1975, p. 83). The traditional seating structure of academic
bargaining is therefore likely to reinforce destructive conflict between
the parties.

Administrative Response

There are a number of administrative responses that can intensify
adversary relations and increase the probability of destructive bargaining relationships.

It has been suggested, for example, that having participated in
antiunion campaigns, the administration will become "captured by its
own rhetoric" and come to believe that unionization will, in fact,
destroy collegial life, undermine the university's mission, and have all
of the horrible consequences predicted by unionization's strongest
critics (MaCoy & Morand, 1977). Presumably, not only will this make it
more difficult for the administration to work cooperatively with the
union, but it leads the administration, by acting as if these consequences were probable, to engage in behaviors that help to promote it
and thereby complete a self-fulfilling prophecy.

Alternatively, it may be that faced with extreme union demands,
administrators feel forced into making counteroffers that they do not
really support in order to avoid having to settle at too high a level.
Engaging in this behavior creates an imbalance in their pro-faculty
attitudes, which gradually change in order to be consistent with adversary behaviors in which they have engaged.

Whether changes in attitude are cause or effect, they are a likely
outcome of bargaining. The Carnegie Council (1977) has warned that
one potential consequence of bargaining is that "managerial authority
may be increased and managerial authority may be more opposed to
the faculty" (p. 4). To a great extent, this change may be related to the
changed pattern of interaction between the parties. It is also possible
that at least to some extent it may be due to the expected roles of groups

identified in certain ways. The interactions expected of "faculty" and "administration" are based upon certain definitions of these roles; groups identified as "labor" and "management" imply a different kind of relationship. Faculty and administration can work together as colleagues. But under collective bargaining, "administrators . . . became responsible for a legally binding contract. The institution will be held responsible for their actions. They become, as the unions insist, representatives of management who seek to protect the management's prerogatives and rights under the contract" (Ladd & Lipsett, 1973, p. 88).

Bargaining may also change the composition of the administration. As the administrative role changes, the need for specialists becomes more apparent, and traditional faculty-related administrators are likely to be replaced by labor relations experts and lawyers who may not share faculty norms and are less able to establish collegial relationships with them (Baldridge et al., 1978, p. 171). Not only does this change in the administration further widen the gap between faculty and administration and encourage destructive conflict, but it is likely to be self-perpetuating. As the selection of specialized administrators increases tendencies toward destructive conflict, the board will search for administrators who can function effectively in such environments.

As administrative attitudes and behaviors change, administrative roles become redefined, and the composition of the administration itself changes, the implicit and restrained authority of the administration in establishing staffing patterns and related matters may become explicit and exercised. As Naples (1977) has pointed out, by adopting an adversary mode, "the union has freed management from the obligation to act collegially or paternalistically. Since the union is now — by self-proclamation and law — the protector and defender of faculty rights, management is free to act only in its own interests" (p. 18).

Once the norms of collegiality and consensus-based systems of decision making are replaced by the legitimization of adversary behavior, management for the first time might begin to seriously consider challenging traditional faculty work rules at the bargaining table. This new freedom from the constraints of previous relationships, and the acceptance of extreme demands as a normal part of the bargaining process, may lead to management not only "thinking about the unthinkable, but actually proposing 'unthinkable' changes" (Garbarino, 1975, p. 156).

Finally, just as a lack of consensus on goals may lead to union bargaining intransigence, so diffusion of authority in management can make it difficult for administrators to deal responsively and responsibly with faculty across the bargaining table. Management's negotiators are often not able to make commitments in certain areas because of the involvement of other officials or agencies in approving or funding bargaining agreements. Begin and Weinberg (1976, p. 86) have noted:

The diffusion of authority inherent in higher education structures has a major impact on the conduct of negotiations. Clearly, decision-makers at various levels may not share common values in respect to the needs of higher education, thus consensus among the different levels of management is often difficult to achieve.

In this situation, the union may perceive management's inability to quickly and definitively respond to bargaining initiatives as an indication of bad faith, further escalating the tendencies toward destructive conflict.

The Dynamics of Groups in Conflict

The most important situational variable in bargaining, and perhaps the most critical aspect of the bargaining relationship, is the dynamics of groups involved in competition over the achievement of goals they perceive as being incompatible. The factors discussed in this chapter can amplify these dynamics, but even alone they have the power to determine that the course of conflict will be destructive. The processes of group conflict that lead to this result are discussed at length in chapter 3.

Once at the bargaining table, the parties may find a number of factors that support destructive bargaining orientations. The negotiators, if selected from inside the institution, are likely to be inexperienced and to unknowingly break implicit bargaining "rules," which can be seen by the other side as evidence of bad faith. Misunderstanding the nature of the process, either side may enter the relationship with unrealistic expectations, and make unreasonable demands that it is unwilling to compromise. Unlike experienced negotiators who are able to separate their personal interests from their role as negotiator, inexperienced ones are likely to personalize conflict and to respond defensively to attacks upon their positions or themselves.

In order to avoid the problems of inexperienced, internal negotiators, parties often utilize negotiations experts from outside the institution, many with legal backgrounds. This often has the effect of leading to excessive formalization of the process and emphasizing the adversarial nature of bargaining. The desire to protect group interests often requires the other party to utilize external negotiators if one group unilaterally does so.

Unclear goals, which typify the college and university, also make it difficult for the union to establish clear priorities among its bargaining demands. Being unable to precisely formulate its position, the union can find itself unable to accept administrative responses; it thus becomes intransigent. Even the bargaining table itself, and the tendency for the bargaining teams to face each other in positions that inhibit cooperative interaction, poses problems in the bargaining situation.

The administrative response to bargaining can be a decisive factor in determining if conflict will take a destructive course. The interaction of attitudes and behavior may cause administrators to change their pro-faculty orientations. Increased use of administrative specialists may further reduce the sharing of common norms, facilitating destructive conflict and leading to the selection by boards of administrators on the basis of their ability to function in an adversarial environment.

Finally, the perception by the parties that they are competing with one another over goals that appear to be incompatible creates the dynamics of destructive conflict.

THE CAUSES OF DESTRUCTIVE CONFLICT

This chapter has presented a number of factors related to the bargaining context, the antecedents of bargaining, the persons involved in bargaining , and the bargaining situation. These factors tend to move unions and administrations in higher education toward negotiating behaviors leading to destructive conflict. Their listing is not meant to suggest that the problems of academic bargaining are so significant and intractable that they cannot be solved. Rather, as the parties become more aware of the ways in which their past and present interactions have contributed to difficulties in their bargaining relationship, they may be able to take steps that can make future bargaining more profitable for both, and more supportive of the goals of their institution.

Before moving toward the exploration of solutions, however, it is necessary to further examine factors that can affect the relationships between administration and union at the bargaining table. Thus far, attention has been given primarily, although not exclusively, to institutional considerations, such as the previous relationships between the two parties. In addition to considering faculty and administration as two parties to a collective bargaining negotiation, however, it is also possible to look at them simply as two groups in competition. As such, they share the same processes seen in between all forms of competitive groups. Understanding these processes is important as a means of providing insight into the parties' behavior at the table, and in understanding why certain kinds of behaviors in certain situations will probably elicit certain responses. With this understanding, the parties cannot only attempt to control their own behavior so that it is less likely to lead to destructive behavior on the part of the opponent, but they can also understand more clearly the behavior of the other bargaining team. The behaviors of groups in competition and cooperation is the subject of the next chapter.

3

Groups in Competition and Cooperation

Observers argue that faculty unionization has increased the sense of an adversary relationship between faculty members and administrators, as well as between faculty unions and students. It seems clear that the advent of collective bargaining does change the role and image of groups within the academic community (Ladd & Lipsett, 1976).

THERE IS A TENDENCY to think of cooperation and competition as being the two end points on a one-dimensional line representing intergroup activity. It is more useful, however, to consider these relationships as being only two of a much larger range of possibilities that depend upon the perceptions and goals of the parties. The description of these possibilities that follows is taken largely from Thomas (1974) and Thomas and Kilman (n.d.).

The orientation a group brings to bargaining depends upon the degree to which it is committed to satisfying its own concerns, and the extent to which it is concerned about the expressed needs of the other group and is willing to help meet them. Using these two dimensions, it is possible to draw a two-dimensional model of conflict and cooperation, and to use it to identify five basic orientations to conflict, as shown on the facing page.

Of these five orientations, two (neglect and accommodation) assume that a group has no strong desire to satisfy its own concerns, and it is

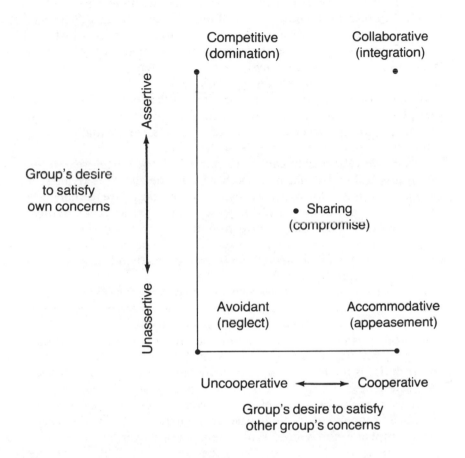

willing to either ignore an issue or to permit the other group to achieve its goals even if it means a modest sacrifice must be made. While both of these orientations certainly occur in bargaining on various issues, they shall not be discussed further since they lead to low levels of conflict because of the disinterest of at least one group in the outcome. (In passing, it should be noted that because of this low conflict level, creative opportunities for dealing with these issues will remain unrealized; reducing conflict often has costs as well as benefits.)

Because the collective bargaining orientation, for the most part, focuses upon the strong concern of the parties for satisfying their own goals at the table, major attention will be given to the conflict orientations of competition and collaboration. Competition is an orientation in which a group wishes to achieve its goals and has little or no concern for the interests of the other group. The combination of assertiveness and uncooperativeness leads to a win-lose orientation, in which the gains of one group come at the expense of the other. We will return later in the chapter to an analysis of the consequences of this orientation for the intergroup bargaining relationship.

Being strongly assertive about meeting one's needs does *not* necessarily have to lead to a competitive orientation, however. When a group combines strong concern for its own interests with equally strong interests in seeing that the needs of the other group are also met, a collaborative relationship can develop in which the parties search for integrative solutions that meet both of their needs. This requires a problem-solving approach, because such solutions are usually not obvious ones and often must be invented by the parties through their joint activities. The collaborative orientation can result in win-win solutions, since each party is able to satisfy its needs, while at the same time the relationship between them is strengthened and supportive of further cooperative activities.

When groups of equal power are involved in conflict in which they perceive that their own concerns cannot fully be met because of the interference of the other party, the result is often a compromise. Compromise is a lose-lose orientation to conflict because it ensures that neither party has its interests fully met. There are occasions when compromise is the best outcome that the parties can achieve, particularly when they are bargaining over the allocation of a limited resource. In many other cases, however, parties compromise because they are unaware of the integrative potential of a situation. Indeed, the search for a compromise may itself cause the parties to overlook alternative possibilities (Pruitt & Lewis, 1977), because they do not have the problem-solving skills to exploit it, or because, as is the case with collective bargaining, they find themselves in a situation in which compromise is expected by definition and is socially acceptable. The orientation of this book is that compromise is not a satisfying means of resolving conflict in academic bargaining, and that groups can more fully achieve their own goals, not by defeating other groups, or "splitting the difference" with them, but by working collaboratively toward mutually acceptable solutions.

GROUPS IN COMPETITION

Competing groups often behave in remarkably similar ways, whether they consist of boys engaged in "color war" competition at summer camp, union and management negotiators at the bargaining table, or nations that believe each other's interests to be incompatible. Indeed, the dynamics of intergroup conflict can be created in the laboratory by forming groups of individuals who have had no previous contact with each other and by involving them in a competitive situation. The effects of that situation can then be studied in a more controlled environment than that of the real world, but one which is, in many respects, no less realistic. One of the most interesting series of such experiments was conducted by Blake and Mouton (1961a; 1961b; 1961c; 1961d); a description of the experiments and their findings can serve as a starting point from which the issue of competitive groups can be considered.

Groups in these experiments consisted of 9 to 12 people without prior knowledge of each other who worked together over several days in workshop settings to study group formation and decision making. The workshops usually included two or four such groups, and each group was given a problem for which it was asked to prepare a group solution. The groups were told that the quality of their solution would be considered evidence of their effectiveness as a group, and that their solution would be judged against that of another group. In experiments involving four groups, none of the groups knew at this stage of the process which of the other groups would be selected as their adversary.

After completing the assignment, the solutions of all the groups were exchanged so that each group had an opportunity to study the written, two-page solutions of the other groups. At this time, groups were asked to evaluate the quality of each group's solution, to note differences and similarities among the group solutions, and to identify points needing clarification and elaboration so that the group members could increase their understanding of other solutions.

All members of the groups then met together for an extended session during which representatives whom they had selected answered questions raised by representatives of each of the other groups. Following this exchange, groups were given an opportunity to determine a "winner" and a "loser" through negotiations by their representatives, by popular vote of all members of the groups, or by some other means involving the actions of group members. If this failed, the group solutions were reviewed by several impartial judges who rendered a final decision concerning which group solution was of the highest quality.

Although these studies were not created to analyze collective bargaining, the parallels between the experimental design and the typical academic bargaining situation are striking. In both, groups are formed and asked to independently prepare their solution to a problem. The parties then meet together to exchange solutions (i.e., bargaining demands), and to question each other about aspects of their solutions that may be unclear. The parties may at this point vote to agree on the superior solution (may reach agreement on a demand), or they may disagree and have the decision made by outside judges (submit it to binding arbitration).

Naturally, these studies do not replicate every nuance of a collective bargaining relationship in higher education. Academic bargaining teams, after all, are not composed of strangers but of persons who have known each other and worked together for a period of time, and the substantive issues being negotiated obviously have some effect on the bargaining process itself. On the other hand, if significant intergroup conflict can be created among groups of people who don't know each other, it is reasonable to assume that the effects upon well-established and cohesive groups might be even stronger. In addition, while analyses of actual collective bargaining interactions in the field might be confounded by the specific issues being negotiated, laboratory settings provide an opportunity to focus attention purely on the intergroup conflict process itself. For these reasons, the Blake and Mouton studies offer a rich resource for gaining insight into some of the elements that might influence the behaviors of typical union and administration teams at the academic bargaining table.

In the initial group-forming phases, members of each group inevitably rated their group as better than average when they were asked to estimate how "good" they believe their group to be. When the same question was asked after the element of competition had been introduced, most groups tended to increase even further their evaluation of their own group. Blake and Mouton (1961d) suggest that this happened because under competition, members close ranks and become more single-minded. They now have a new objective — to win — providing them with unity of direction and increasing conformity within the group.

After each group had prepared its solution, they were given copies of the solutions of the other groups to study. When groups were then asked to evaluate the quality of all submitted solutions, every group evaluated its own solution as the best. This reflected not only the strong commitment of group members to their group's solution, but also the conformity which leads to a reduction of dissensus within each group. When academic bargainers show unanimous support for one of their demands at the bargaining table, therefore, it is probably not because a strong member of the team has forced the other members to accept it.

Rather, it is likely that, faced with competition from the other bargaining team, members have closed ranks and agreed on their solutions.

The groups were then given an opportunity to study the solutions of the other groups so that they could increase their understanding and ask questions of clarification at a future meeting. At the same time, in those workshops in which four groups were involved, each group was told for the first time the specific other group against which they would be competing.

The groups were then brought together and their representatives were permitted to question each other. Although it might be expected that questions would be directed against the group whose solution was the most complex or the most confusing, in fact questions were directed almost exclusively to the group against which they would be directly competing. Although the sessions were to be used to gain a better understanding of the other position, they were exclusively used as a means of attacking the opponent. "After studying the qualitative content of these questions, there is yet to be a question whose answer would not embarrass those who respond to it. The questions are always designed to weaken the position of the person to whom they are asked" (Blake and Mouton, 1961d, p. 425).

This period of intergroup questioning is similar in many ways to the actual negotiating interchange in academic bargaining. Having exchanged solutions to problems, generally phrased as demands, the parties attempt to clarify the intentions and meanings of the other through questioning and debate. Although superficially it may appear that bargainers use this opportunity to better understand the position of the opponent, in many cases in academic bargaining the questions of each party are not meant to clarify the position of the other, but to expose and ridicule the basic weaknesses of the other's position.

At this point in the Blake and Mouton studies, groups were given a knowledge test in which they were asked to respond to questions concerning their solution and the solution of the other groups. Analysis of the results showed that in every case individuals had more knowledge about the solution of their own team than that of the other team. Team members thought that they had complete understanding of the position of their adversary, when in fact they did not. In particular, they were unlikely to see elements of solutions that were common to both groups, and thus perceived the solutions as being more dissimilar than they actually were. Areas of commonality remained undiscovered, and inadequate understanding of each other's position made it all the more difficult for groups to view each other's position realistically (1961b).

This finding was replicated in a negotiations simulation that differed from almost all others reported in the literature because it involved the participation of actual union and management negotiators who were asked to reenact under laboratory conditions several aspects of a difficult contract negotiation that had been completed six months previously (Balke, Hammond, & Meyer, 1973). In this experiment, the researchers used scales to determine the actual weights given by each of six negotiators to four major items, the weights they believed their opponents placed on each of these items, and the weights they actually placed on them in the negotiations. Data indicated that even after months of actual negotiations, some of the bargainers were completely unable to reflect the weights and preferences of their opponents, and in fact gave the highest weights to issues considered by the other to be of least importance. The inability of a bargainer to fully understand the relative importance that the other bargainer places on the issues can be a critical factor in the bargaining relationship. Simulations of international negotiations, for example, have indicated that differences in issue emphasis can lead to misunderstanding, negative attitudes, hostile interaction, fewer concessions, and lower probability of eventual agreement (Bonham, 1971). In terms of academic bargaining, it is not only possible but perhaps probable that even after extended bargaining sessions, the parties not only do not really understand the positions of each other, but of even greater significance, they are unaware of that fact.

Returning again to the Blake and Mouton studies, representatives of the opposing groups then met to select one of the solutions as the winner. It is not surprising to learn that in one experimental series involving 33 groups, only two representatives gave up so that a decision could be reached, and there were impasses in the other 31 cases. Blake and Mouton (1961d) explain this phenomenon by suggesting that spokespersons who represent groups become committed to that group's position, and they feel responsible for winning for the group. "They elect to conform to group expectations rather than to solve the assigned problem" (p. 429). This pressure toward conformity can be more fully appreciated when the personality characteristics of the group representatives are described. Each group selected its own representatives and, compared to other group members, these representatives were unusually individualistic, procedurally skillful, and intellectually competent. Of all group members, these would be the most likely to resist conformity and to identify the other group's solution as being superior if they believed it was so. As Blake and Mouton (1961c) note, "in the negotiation situation, logical considerations may require that a representative renounce his group's prior position in order to gain a valid resolution of the intergroup problem. But acting against the exercise of a logical and factually analytical attitude are group ties that require him to gain victory and, at whatever cost, to defend a point of view that protects his membership position" (p. 177). The representative who refuses to give in to an opponent is considered a hero by the group and has increased status. The unfortunate representative who gives in or compromises his group's position is subject to being treated by the group as a traitor. In the same way, academic bargainers are subject to the pressures of their group to "win," which inhibits their ability to concede that the solution of the other group is superior to their own.

After the groups reached an impasse on identifying the best solution, a panel of impartial arbitrators examined both solutions and reached a decision that was communicated to the groups. When the groups were asked to evaluate the arbitrators, the winning group believed them to be fair-minded, impartial, competent to handle intellectual materials, and analytically skillful. The losing group identified the arbitrators as weak persons who were not competent to perform their responsibilities (Blake & Mouton, 1961d). And finally, after the issue had been decided, the winning teams, while remaining work oriented and cooperative, showed a reduction in tension and competitiveness and became "fat and happy." The losing teams became less work oriented and cooperative and initially engaged in scapegoating the judges. Following this phase, however, they began to consider the possibility that the judge was right, and they began, with increased feelings of competitiveness and tension, to plan how they would behave when another competition came along. Clearly, although the issue had been decided, the conflict between the groups had not been resolved.

The findings of Blake and Mouton support a number of generalizations that have implications for academic bargaining. These will be made more explicit in chapters 6 through 9. At this point, however, several observations can be made.

1. It is possible to create competitive groups by placing them in a situation identified and perceived as competitive. Collective bargaining is such a situation.
2. Competitive groups are likely to have a distorted view of the quality of their group and their solution to a problem.
3. Once a group creates a solution to a problem, it becomes committed to it and is unable to comprehend the elements of alternative solutions. In particular, it is able to see only the differences between its solution and that of another group and not the similarities.
4. Opportunities to gain further information about the opponent's

    solution will be used instead to attack and belittle the opponent.

5. Although groups are likely to select their most nonconforming and intellectually able members as their representatives, they will be unable or unwilling to make independent judgments of the quality of alternative proposals, and they will fight for acceptance of their group's proposal as best, resulting in impasse.

6. Judgments by impartial arbitors will be considered as fair by the winning group, and unfair by the losing group.

7. The competitiveness of the winning team will decrease, and that of the losing team will increase, after the decision is announced.

Although these outcomes have been produced in laboratory settings, the experiences of negotiators in many field settings indicate that they are commonly seen in conditions of intergroup conflict (Schein, 1969, pp. 72-73). We turn now to an examination of some of the characteristics of these settings, and a consideration of some of the conceptual approaches suggested to explain these common consequences of conflict.

Attribution

    Attribution is the process by which we infer a person's motivations from his or her actions (Kelley, 1967). In colleges and universities, as in every other social setting, we are constantly making attributions to explain behavior or events. Sometimes, attributions refer to the personality of the individual involved: ("Jones must really be a great teacher to be promoted to associate in only three years!"). This "dispositional attribution" infers that an event or behavior (Jones's promotion) was related to a personal characteristic (teaching proficiency). In other cases, attributions refer to the environment in which the event occurred: ("The dean must really have liked Jones to approve a promotion to associate after only three years."). This is "situational attribution," in which behavior or events are related to the contingencies of the environment.

    In general, individuals have a tendency to use situational attribution in accounting for their own behavior ("Given all the factors involved, I really had no choice."), and tend to attribute the actions of others to stable personality characteristics ("Well, you can't expect anything else from someone who always tried to mislead you.") (Rosenberg & Wolfsfeld, 1977).

    The process of attribution is dangerous because it tends to lead us to characterize the actions of others as being rooted in their personality and therefore not amenable to change. But of even greater importance, it leads us to believe that we understand why someone is doing something, when in fact we do not. Attributions are particularly likely in conflict situations such as bargaining in which communications are limited, and therefore information which might disprove an attribution less available. And in such conflict situations, we are likely to consider the "enemy" as untrustworthy, shrewd, aggressive, competitive, and capable of harming or destroying the cherished values of our group because of these inherent personality traits. Our reactions to this enemy are therefore purely defensive, forced upon us by the exigencies of the environment. The enemy, of course, views us in exactly the same way, so that we each view the outrageous acts of the other as evidence of our personality differences, while we each attribute our own actions to environmental pressures.

It is relatively easy to develop negative attributions of a person or group identified as an adversary, but they can be made in almost any complex and ambiguous situation, and become particularly evident when people are called upon, as they are in bargaining, to describe the reasons that they have arrived at certain policy judgments. Specialists in the processes of human judgment understand how difficult it is for a person to fully describe to another the reasons for reaching a certain decision. The nonspecialist, however, is more apt to attribute inconsistencies, inaccuracies, and incompleteness, not to an inability to be more accurate because of the inherent complexity of the situation, but to an intention to be devious (Brehmer & Hammond, 1977). This attribution is more likely to be made as communications and trust levels between the parties diminish, and of course it is most likely in competitive situations in which each party sees the other as concerned only with maximizing its own advantage.

Attributions, and the mutual and progressive distortions accompanying them, lead to what has been called "the mirror image of the enemy" (Frank, 1968, p. 117), in which the opponents attribute the same virtues to themselves and the same vices to each other.

Recent research, however, suggests that the attribution process is far more complicated than this. In their work based upon the attributions of various events in the Middle East made by persons who were associated with Israel or Arab nations, Rosenberg and Wolfsfeld (1977) examined how the need to maintain consistent interpretations of reality affect our attributions. They asked individuals with different orientations toward these competitive nations to account for certain factual activities of each of the nations, some of which were successful or moral acts, and others which were failures or immoral. Those who had a positive emotional and cognitive orientation toward the Arab nations, for example, tended to explain the successes and moral acts of these nations by references to national character, cultural traits, or similar dispositional factors. Failures and immoral acts were given situational attributions, such as the influence of outside pressures.

Attributions, therefore, seem to be made in order to permit consistent evaluations of people, groups, and their behaviors. If a group with which we have positive cognitive or affective association does something which we consider good, it can be explained as being related to the internal goals and policies of the group. If they do something with which we disagree, however, we can maintain a consistent position toward them by believing that they were forced to do it by some environmental factor over which they had no control. The same process affects the way we look at actions of groups with which we are in conflict, but in reverse, so that we attribute their evil actions to be indicative of their long-term, stable goals, and their moral actions to be caused by the pressures of outside forces.

The impact of attribution has a number of subtle, but extremely potent, effects on the bargaining process in which groups are dealing with adversaries. First, it allows us to see all of our opponent's competitive activities as hostile in intention, while ours are purely defensive. The other side, of course, has a mirror image interpretation (Frank, 1968).

Second, the dynamics of attribution make it exceptionally difficult for the parties to change their images of each other. If an opponent does something unfavorable to a group, they will attribute it to their disposition. But if the opponent makes a favorable gesture, it will be inconsistent with the group's image. They will attribute it to external pressures and therefore give it no weight in their reactions toward the opponent. Indeed, the mutual mistrust created by competitive, adversarial relationships will probably lead to questioning the motives of an advantageous offer, and eventually rejecting it as a trick to get us to drop our guard, or in some other way to harm our group's position. The same problem in international relations has been reported by Frank (1968).

> A former State Department Official stated the American attitude well: For Moscow to propose what we can accept seems to us even more sinister and dangerous than for it to propose what we cannot accept. Our instinct is to cast about for grounds on which to discredit the proposal instead of seizing it and making the most of it. Being distrustful of the Greeks bearing gifts, we were afraid of being tricked (p. 193).

Not only does attribution of the motives of an adversary tend to make groups expect hostile, aggressive, and competitive behavior (and filter and sort information so that they can ignore actions or behaviors that might tend not to confirm that belief), but it also permits them to interpret friendly and cooperative overtures in the same way so that it is impossible for the adversary to do *anything* that can change a group's attributions. Both parties, of course, find themselves in precisely the same situation.

The distortions created by attributions have other significant effects, which have been discussed in terms of nations but which have equal validity for groups involved in bargaining. The work of Rosenberg and Wolfsfeld (1977) suggest the following:

1. Each side will underestimate the limitations of its own group, and overestimate its strength. Because it incorrectly comes to see all its successes due to its own capabilities, and just as incorrectly explains its failures due to the interference of outside forces, it will tend not to see its own weaknesses and to increase its confidence in its own position.
2. Each side will underestimate the strength of the other group and overestimate its weakness. Based upon the previous logic, bargaining groups are likely to have completely erroneous views of the relative power of each side. This is likely to lead to significant errors of tactics and strategy and to increase disruptive conflict between the two groups.
3. Each group will have a distorted conception of the distribution of power and blame. As a result, each is likely to make demands that exceed what the other considers appropriate, further escalating the conflict.

Formation of Stereotypes

When groups are in conflict, and their activities are seen by each other as mutually frustrating, the processes of attribution develop, sustain, and accelerate the formation of negative stereotypes of the other. These attitudes then support the rise of feelings of power, self-righteousness, and "goodness" that the group develops toward its own positions and behavior, and the belief in the weakness of the other side, their lack of moral justification for their actions, and suspicion of their intent and their behaviors. As indicated before, these do not represent the views of group deviates, but are pervasive throughout the group. These stereotypes and hostile attitudes exist despite the objective qualities of the other group; they are resistant to change merely because of some objective change in the behavior of the other group and outlast the original group interactions which created them (Sherif, 1962).

These stereotypes may develop early in the bargaining relationship, perhaps even during the prenegotiation period if the union and the administration engage in conflict related to a representational election. Such conflict can lead to the formation of positive or negative attitudes between the parties. Positive attitudes between the groups at this early stage related to the sharing of common norms and values have the potential of permitting the formation of constructive and creative bargaining relationships, while negative attitudes and the stressing of normative disagreement is likely to lead to destructive conflict processes. One reason for this is the tendency on the part of persons to expect cooperative, trustworthy, and rewarding behavior from people they like, and to expect that disliked people will be punishing, competitive, and untrustworthy. This tendency toward stereotypes based upon previous attitudes of liking or not liking the other, as well as other processes involving perception, attitudes, and behavior, tends to be self-reinforcing. When we expect rewarding behavior from the other, we tend to overlook or downplay actions not meeting our expectations, and we make the same adjustments to our perceptions of objectively rewarding behavior from groups whom we dislike and from whom we expect punishing behavior (Tedeschi, Bonoma, & Schlenker, 1972).

The formation and hardening of stereotypical perception between groups in conflict has been called by Frank (1968) the "enemy image." The image is maintained through the restriction of communication, selective filtering, and interpretation of the evidence to fit the image. It becomes even harder and less accurate as problems in communication make interpretations of the other's intent more difficult and reduces opportunities to learn of changes in the other group's attitudes or positions. Since anxiety is increased by knowing less and less about the actual capabilities and intentions of the other group, there is a tendency for groups to reduce ambiguity by "filling in" the missing information based on their hopes, fears, and current image of the other group. The relationship increasingly assumes black-white dimensions, "with our side becoming whiter, and enemy's blacker, and the gray area progressively shrinking" (Frank, 1968, p. 129).

Conflict and Communications

Conflict develops between two individuals or groups when they *perceive* that achievement of goals by the other may frustrate achievement of their own goals. Since conflict is related to the perception of mutually incompatible goals, it can have at least two causes. It is possible in some cases that the situation is one in which there is a real conflict of interest, so that advantages gained by one side lead to disadvantages for the other. It is also possible, however, that there are no real conflicts of interest, and perceptions are related to a lack of understanding of the other side's position. To the extent that any conflict situation is related to this second possibility, conflict may be made more productive by increasing the adequacy of communications at the bargaining table, so that the parties become more fully aware of exactly what the positions of the other party are.

The work of Blake and Mouton demonstrated the typical argumentative relationship that develops when two groups each try to convince the other of the merits of "their" proposal. This form of debate not only does not convince the opponents of the error of their ways, but does not even communicate the group's position so that the adversary group is able to accurately respond to simple questions about it. Without denying the existence of real conflicts of interest in academic bargaining relationships, it can be assumed that at least some of the conflict between the parties is due to difficulties in communicating their positions to each other. If at least one or (preferably) both of the parties were able to more clearly and accurately communicate, and fully understand the responses of the other, much unnecessary and disruptive conflict could be avoided.

Because collective bargaining typically occurs in an atmosphere of threat to both parties, it commonly leads to defensive behavior. Defensive behavior caused by perceived or anticipated threat, notes Gibb (1961), means that in addition to participating in the group activity, a threatened person devotes a portion of available energy to defending himself. "Besides talking about the topic, he thinks about how he may appear to others, how he may be seen more favorably, how he may win, dominate, impress or escape punishment, and/or how he may avoid or mitigate a perceived or an anticipated attack" (p. 141).

Defensive behavior provokes defensive listening, so that the communicator is prevented from paying full attention to the message. Instead, as defensiveness increases (as it is likely to do in the bargaining environment), recipients distort what they receive, and become less able to understand the motives, values, and emotions of the sender, as well as the content of the message itself. In the same way, as defensiveness is reduced, "the receivers become better able to concentrate upon the structure, the content, and the cognitive meanings of the message" (Gibb, 1961, p. 142).

Gibb suggests that certain types of communication behavior are likely to increase defensiveness in the receiver (and thus to lead to increased distortion of the content of the message), and other kinds of behaviors are likely to lead to supportive climates in which the parties can more clearly understand each other. Examining these categories in relation to the normal communication pattern encountered in bargaining leads to an understanding of the great difficulty that parties have in the basic task of fully understanding the position of the other.

Categories of communication that Gibb believes increases defensiveness include evaluation, control, strategy, neutrality, superiority, and certainty. Those communications behaviors that lead to a more supportive climate and reduce defensiveness are description, problem orientation, spontaneity, empathy, equality, and provisionalism.

Much of the interaction at the bargaining table is evaluative and judgmental, rather than descriptive. Because of the competitive orientation of the parties, even descriptive communications (such as requests for information) are often consciously or unconsciously made to appear judgmental by the speech or mannerisms of the sender. In the Blake and Mouton studies, it will be remembered, opportunities for asking questions of the other team in order to clarify understanding of their positions, which normally would be considered a descriptive communication, was in fact done in such a way as to belittle their positions, and thus become a judgmental communication. Judgmental reactions increase insecurity in a group, and when insecure, "group members are particularly likely to place blame, to see others as fitting into categories of good or bad, to make moral judgments of their colleagues, and to question the value, motive, and affect loadings of the speech which they hear" (Gibb, 1961, p. 143). In this setting, open expressions of disagreement with the position of the other side can be interpreted as a personal attack, which calls forth similar aggressive behavior on the part of the other bargainer (Felson, 1978), and innocent remarks may be misinterpreted and lead to hostility, which, in turn is likely to reduce interaction between the parties and make the process of communication and reaching agreement more difficult (Bonham, 1971).

At the bargaining table, adversaries try to change the attitudes, behaviors, and activities of the other side, and thus use communications that attempt to control the adversary. Messages of control increase defensiveness because they imply that the opponent is inadequate and must therefore change. Defensiveness can be reduced through communications having a problem-solving orientation and indicating a desire to collaborate in studying a problem and seeking a solution. Because a problem-solving orientation implicitly indicates that the communicator does not have a preferred solution, the other party need not become defensive in the belief he or she is being asked to change.

Adversaries in collective bargaining spend a considerable period of time in developing their positions and committing their representatives and members to support it. This leads to communications phrased as demands and argumentation supporting these demands that moves both parties toward increased certainty in the justice of their positions. Certainty is associated with dogmatism, which is seen by others as "needing to be right, as wanting to win an argument rather than solve a problem, and as seeing his ideas as truths to be defended" (Gibb, 1961, p. 148). Just as certainty increases defensiveness, provisionalism, or the willingness to experiment with one's own ideas and behaviors, reduces it. The attitude of provisionalism suggests a willingness to search for solutions, rather than to debate solutions which one has already conceived and toward which one wishes to persuade the other.

Two other communications orientations that arouse defensiveness are those of superiority and neutrality. "The person who is perceived as feeling superior communicates that he is not willing to enter into a shared problem-solving relationship, that he probably does not desire feedback, that he does not require help, and/or that he will be likely to try and reduce the power, status, or the worth of the receiver" (Gibb, 1961, p. 147). The defensiveness this creates in the receiver leads to not hearing, or forgetting, the message, or to competition with the other. Defensiveness can be reduced by minimizing status or power differences between the parties and indicating a willingness to enter into the relationship with mutual trust and respect.

Neutrality supports defensiveness because it implies a lack of concern for the needs, desires, and welfare of the other. On the other hand, communications that are empathetic, and indicate to the other party that their problems and feelings are understood and respected, decreases defensive reactions.

The traditions, structures, and expectations of academic bargaining encourage the participants to engage in communications behavior that emphasizes the evaluation and denigration of the other's position, attempts to influence and control the other, develops strategy and inhibits spontaneity, lacks empathy with the other's situation and needs, attempts to increase power or status at the other's expense, and encourages dogmatic pronouncements supporting one's position and ideology. Each of these behaviors increases the defensiveness of the other group and is, therefore, likely to increase distortion, inhibit joint problem solving or collaborative behavior, and make it difficult if not impossible for either side to accurately determine what the goals of the other group really are.

Decision Making and Judgment under Stress

The process of collective negotiations in the academic environment is inherently a stressful one. When the process becomes competitive and destructive, stress increases. Groups now see that there may be a victor and a vanquished and that, therefore, their performance at the table may be related not only to how much they "win" or "lose," but perhaps to the very survival of the group itself. Threats may be exchanged between the parties, attributions lead to increasingly rigid stereotypes of evil intent and bargaining in bad faith, and inexorable deadlines motivate the parties toward closure while the parties face ambiguity on a number of key issues. All-night bargaining sessions held under approaching deadlines may tap the physical and mental resources of the participants. This increase in tension may distort the way people and groups perceive a situation, and the processes by which they analyze the alternatives and decide on a course of action. Some of these problems, which are

> relevant to bargaining and decision-making include cognitive and behavioral rigidity, a tendency to react quickly and violently, underestimation of an opponent's capability for retaliation, interpretation of a conciliatory move on the part of an opponent as a trick or a sign of weakness, a lowered tolerance for ambiguity, and a tendency, on the part of the decision-makers, to interpret messages that reinforce their preconceived view of a crisis (Druckman, 1971, pp. 532-533).

Holsti (1971) has examined the effects of stress on decision making in the context of international affairs, and his conclusions, based upon the sociopsychological literature as well as the writings of diplomats and negotiators appear relevant to any bargaining situation held in conditions of low trust and increasing tensions. They include, among others, the following.

1. Stress reduces the toleration that individuals and groups have for ambiguity. It is likely to lead them to make decisions before adequate information is available that would permit a rational consideration of its consequences.
2. Stress distorts judgment about time and inhibits the complex cognitive processes required for discovering creative alternatives to problems. Believing that there is less time than actually is available, there is a tendency to fix on a single solution or approach and to continue to use it even when it continuously proves to be ineffective. The pressure of time and the tendency toward group conformity under

stress conditions leads to early agreement, and thereby reduces the incentive to explore alternatives to policies found not to have the desired effect.

3. Stress constricts the future outlook of bargainers and leads to over-emphasis on short-term, rather than long-term goals.

4. Stress leads to an inability to perceive alternatives. Prevented by stress from exploring alternatives, a bargaining group may believe that it "has no choice" but to take a certain action, even though it understands that the action may lead to highly undesirable consequences. In doing so, the group may "resign itself to the inevitable," and psychologically absolve itself of responsibility by convincing itself that only the adversary group is able to exercise options to prevent the undesirable outcomes. Since attributions, stereotyping, and stress can all lead to a distorted view of the opponents and their motives, it is possible for the group to convince itself that their adversary is free from the very situational constraints that appear to completely limit the options of one's own group.

5. Stress and time pressures restrict the ability of bargainers to consult with their constituencies and lead them to increasingly rely for decision making on persons who share their own stereotyped impression of the adversary, and who thus tend to increase the rigidity of the stereotype. Since stress also increases the filtering of information and eliminates information that does not fit preconceived beliefs, the bargainer is in a world in which beliefs are confirmed, ambiguities simplified, and stereotypes heightened; a world that becomes further and further removed from reality.

While moderate levels of stress are necessary in order to engage in successful problem solving, the increase of stress past an optimal level decreases effectiveness and limits the range of choices bargainers see available to them. "The most probable alternatives become even more so, relatively, while the less probable become even less so" (Osgood, 1961, p. 15). And given the anxiety and fear that can be developed in the bargaining relationship, the most probable alternatives are more likely to be those that further escalate the encounter and make destructive conflict a self-fulfilling prophecy.

The Cooperative and the Competitive Bargainer

Although the antecedents to bargaining, the bargaining structure, and other environmental variables have a critical effect upon the course of a bargaining relationship, it is also true that the bargaining representatives themselves can make a significant difference. It has already been suggested that through instructions, experience, or other means, individuals can adopt a cooperative or a competitive orientation toward bargaining. It is also possible that there may be stable cooperative and competitive personality types that predispose individuals to bargain in certain ways (Kelley & Stahelski, 1970), or to have preferences for particular response patterns in conflict situations (Renwick, 1975). Bargainers may also sometimes adopt bargaining approaches for specific strategic or tactical reasons. For example, it has been noted (Tedeschi et al., 1972) that in laboratory game situations individuals who disliked the source of a threat were likely to give the threat high credibility, while individuals who liked the source of a threat were able to rationally determine the probability that the threat would actually be carried out. Tedeschi suggests the interesting possibility that one way in which bargainers can strengthen the credibility of threats, and therefore cause the other to exaggerate the opponent's power, is to cause the other to dislike them. In this situation, a weak union for example might choose to engage in a competitive bargaining strategy leading to high levels of recrimination and destructive conflict in order to increase bargaining power with the other side.

The cooperative-competitive orientation taken by bargainers is of extreme importance, because of the impact it can have on perception of issues. Judd (1978), for example, has demonstrated that subjects who were motivated to argue their positions competitively in a laboratory problem-solving exercise were more likely to focus on the differences in the positions taken by themselves and their opponents, while those with a cooperative orientation were more likely to stress the similarities. But perhaps of even greater moment is the impact cooperative and competitive orientations have on the orientation of the other party. Bargaining is a situation in which the actions of one party depend upon the perceptions of the actions of the other, which in turn depend upon the other's perception of the first party, and on and on. A series of experiments conducted by Kelley and Stahelski (1970) were based upon the assumption that a person's actions in bargaining at any time will depend upon the perceptions of the actions of the other party. This in turn was related to the perception of whether the other party was trying to satisfy joint interests (cooperate), or to satisfy his or her own interests (compete). Participants in a bargaining game were asked to indicate whether they would try to cooperate or compete in the game, and were then assigned to partners so that three different situations were created in which cooperators were paired with cooperators, cooperators were paired with competitors, and competitors were paired with competitors. When asked to identify the orientation of their opponents, cooperators were able to indicate if they were playing against a cooperator or a competitor, but competitors were not. Competitors believed that *all* of their opponents were also competitors. It is possible therefore that individuals with a competitive orientation are likely to see all potential adversaries as competitive, but that cooperators are able to discriminate between potential adversaries who are oriented toward cooperation, and those oriented toward competition.

In these studies, as would be expected, when cooperators were paired with each other they tended to cooperate, and when competitors were paired with each other they competed. When cooperators were paired with competitors, the cooperator began by cooperating. However, when the moves of the opponent were obviously competitive, the cooperator changed tactics and became competitive as well. In this way, the competitor was able to change the behavior of the cooperator, and thus *confirm the competitor's belief that people are uniformly competitive.*

Because the competitor expects everyone to compete, competitors erroneously attribute the competitive nature of a negotiating experience equally to both parties, even when the other party is cooperatively oriented. The cooperator, however, is able to correctly identify the greater role of the competitor in establishing competitive relationships. The cooperator is influenced to behave in a manner similar to that of the competitive partner, and while the cooperator is aware of this influence, the competitive partner is not.

The implication of this "triangle hypothesis" is extremely important for academic bargaining. It implies that it requires two parties, both committed to a cooperative orientation, to lead to constructive, problem-solving approaches to bargaining. If both of the parties assume a competitive, adversarial orientation, *or if either one does,* the conflict at the bargaining table is likely to be destructive in nature. The cooperative bargainer will eventually realize that the other party has adopted a competitive mode and will change tactics to bargain competitively as well. Bargainers are often heard to rationalize their participation in destructive conflict by saying that "it takes two parties to fight." This is not quite true, however. While both parties may claim that the competitive relationship is the fault of the other, the attribution by the cooperative bargainer will be accurate, and the perception of the competitive bargainer will not be.

The tendency for bargainers to reciprocate each other's styles, and for competitive bargaining to dominate in any situation in which one of the bargainers is competitive, is reflected nicely in a finding by

Mortimer and Richardson (1977) in a series of case studies of union-ized insitutions.

> There is an interesting correlation between the character of union leader-ship and the character of administrative leadership. In the two institutions which have had the most authoritarian presidents, the union leadership is the most radical and the least amenable to cooperative activities of any sort. . . . Where moderation, accessibility and openness of communication prevail, . . . the union leadership exerts (sic) similar traits (p. 173).

Conformity, Consensus, and Concessions

There is a tendency for groups in competitive conflict to "close ranks" and to develop group norms placing high value on conformity and solidarity. In such groups, bargaining representatives are ex-pected to "win" for their group, and the granting of concessions to the other side, or admission that the other's solution to a problem may be superior to that of one's own group, is considered traitorous. Since groups appear to select comparatively intelligent and nonconforming individuals as their spokespersons, it places these individuals in a difficult situation. A brief examination of the role of a bargaining representative may indicate the effects of this role upon the course of bargaining.

Competing individuals find it easier to resolve conflict than repre-sentatives of competing groups (Klimoski, 1972) because representa-tives are not free agents but are held accountable by a reference group for their performance. It has been noted, for example, that in labora-tory experiments, individuals designated as "principal bargaining agents" by their groups failed to show the typical shift toward more risky positions that has been noted after group discussion in many studies (Lamm & Kogan, 1970). Individuals designated as representa-tives appear to be more constrained by an apparent need to minimize deviations from the group's position, particularly when the group has made a specific commitment on an issue, than is true for other mem-bers of the group. For that reason, they are likely to deadlock with their counterparts, or to compromise by splitting the difference. Risk taking, such as would be implied by searching for more creative solutions, is inhibited.

Laboratory study by Wall and Adams (1974) suggests some of the dynamics affecting the negotiating leader. The bargaining representa-tive of a group is in a boundary role. The negotiator is not only a member of the in-group but is also involved in interaction with the other group as well. The representative is judged by the constituency on the basis of end results. Logically, these results can be related to two factors: the personal performance of the negotiator and the environment within which the negotiations occur, including such matters as the degree to which the opponent appears willing to concede on issues, or the political climate. Although environmental receptiveness can be important in negotiations, reference groups tend to hold the negotiator personally responsible for the outcomes of bargaining.

If the negotiator is not successful, the group's trust in the negotiator diminishes, and the group increases its desire to control the negotiator's activities and limit the negotiator's autonomy. The negotiator, recognizing the loss of trust and confidence, attempts to recoup both group support and bargaining outcomes by exploiting the opponent and engaging in "tougher" bargaining (Wall, 1975). Since tougher bargaining is unlikely to have major payoffs, trust is further diminished in what Wall and Adams call a "self-amplifying system."

The competitive nature of the bargaining situation thus establishes reinforcing feedback systems that require the bargainer to support and defend group positions, which make it increasingly difficult to perceive alternatives (Rubin & Brown, 1975), and which determine that academic bargaining becomes and remains a process of destructive conflict.

GROUPS IN COOPERATION

This chapter has described the factors helping to create and intensify conflict between groups. Chapters 6 through 9 shall examine tactics and strategies that can be considered by parties in conflict who wish to change a competitive bargaining orientation into a more collaborative and constructive one. Many of these suggestions will be directly responsive to the factors leading to competition that have been described here. Before leaving this topic, however, it will be useful to briefly comment on some general orientations to the reduction of destructive intergroup conflict.

It has already been noted that increased communication between groups is a necessary, but not a sufficient, precondition for the reduction of intergroup conflict. Increased opportunities for interaction may merely make it easier for the groups to make threats and accusations. In order for communication to assist in reducing conflict, it must take place in the presence of superordinate goals—that is, mutual goals that are urgent and compelling for the groups involved (Sherif, 1962).

A superordinate goal must be related to an objective that both groups believe is essential, but which can be achieved only if the groups work together. When such goals exist, communications channels are utilized in order to reduce conflict between the groups, favorable information about the other group that would previously have been rejected because it did not fit existing stereotypes is now accepted, and leaders are freer to delegate authority and to receive support from group members.

One traditional means of establishing superordinate goals for groups in conflict is to create, or call attention to, a common enemy. Although this is likely to lead to increased collaborative activity and more positive attitudes between the groups, these behaviors can be suddenly altered again once the enemy is vanquished, as we have seen so often in alliances formed, and just as suddenly disbanded, after a war. In searching for "common enemies" that might be useful in calling forth cooperative and constructive relationships between administration and unions in academic bargaining, one possibility stands out, at least for public institutions in which the majority of bargaining takes place: the system or statewide board. Their activities generally frustrate campus ambitions and interests, and are resented by both faculty and administration. Since the increased centralization of decision making in higher education through the establishment of such systems was one of the prime factors promoting faculty bargaining in the first place, it may be an ultimate irony that common opposition to it may provide a framework in which campus bargainers can develop cooperative relationships. It would not be surprising in the future to see interaction between campus union representatives and administrators bordering on collusion, which may increase levels of conflict between campus and central office, but in doing so prepare the way for more cohesive intergroup relation on campus.

Even more useful than a common enemy, however, is the establishment of common goals that are so important to the members of both groups that they override any special interests that might otherwise divide them. The establishment of an intellectual and interpersonal atmosphere on campus in which the business of teaching and scholarship can be most effectively pursued is such a goal.

In addition to the establishment of superordinate goals and the structures in which groups can constructively interact, the establishment of cooperative activity is fostered by the attitudes of the parties involved.

The attitudes the parties have when they enter into conflict, or develop during the course of their interaction, can have a powerful effect on whether they engage in constructive or destructive conflict (Filley, 1975).

COMPETITIVE AND COOPERATIVE BARGAINING

The general conception of bargaining identifies it as a competitive process. As seen in this chapter, groups in competition share certain characteristic behaviors. They are likely to misjudge the quality of their own group's performance and to misunderstand the essential elements of proposals or solutions created by other groups. Bargainers who represent such groups are likely to be controlled by their constituencies and cannot concede or compromise for fear of being considered traitorous. The processes of attribution that develop in conflict situations tend to confirm the negative attitudes each group has of the other, so that even friendly or cooperative overtures are received with suspicion. Reduction in communication between the groups leads to the formation of stereotypes and the creation of the "image of the enemy." Positions harden as issues become black and white, stress distorts judgment and makes it more difficult to engage in rational consideration of alternatives, and the parties become more concerned with short-term rather than the long-term consequences of their interaction. This competitive orientation dominates the bargaining relationship, even if one of the participants is cooperatively oriented. The most complete description of these interpersonal and intergroup effects of the competitive structure of collective bargaining in an actual collegiate setting is given by Sturner (1976). Participation of groups in these competitive bargaining relationships is likely to lead to destructive bargaining outcomes that do not fully satisfy the goals of either party.

Under certain conditions, bargainers can engage in cooperative activities. This is possible when the two bargaining groups have superordinate goals that are compelling for both, but which can be achieved only if they work together, and if the parties share the attitude that cooperative activity is both feasible and desirable. Cooperative activities, properly conducted, can lead to creative and constructive bargaining. "Cooperation" and "bargaining" may appear initially to be contradictory terms, because there is a tendency to think of bargaining solely as a competitive situation in which the gains of one side come at the expense of the other. But there are many areas of academic bargaining in which this is not the case, and in which the parties may jointly gain more through working together than they can by competing with each other. In the next chapter, the characteristics of such situations will be considered. Since cooperative behavior is appropriate and profitable to both sides under some circumstances, but not others, the academic bargainer should be aware of the types of bargaining behavior that are likely to have the highest payoffs under varying conditions. Various bargaining orientations are supported by specific tactics and strategies at the bargaining table, with which the academic bargainer should also become familiar. These are the subjects of chapter 4.

4

Distributive and Integrative Bargaining

The partisan, when he is engaged in a dispute, cares nothing about the rights of the question, but is anxious to convince his hearers of his own assertions. (Socrates)

The non-zero-sum game, which results in a loss to both players (who reason as if they are playing a zero-sum game) may epitomize the tragedy of man in society. If so, there is no hope. (Rapoport, 1974, p. 308)

IN THEIR CLASSIC STUDY, *A Behavioral Theory of Labor Negotiations*, Walton and McKersie (1965) identify four subprocesses of social negotiations that together describe almost all activities that occur in collective bargaining. The first of these, which they called *distributive bargaining*, includes that system of activities, group interactions, and behaviors that takes place when bargainers perceive that they have a pure conflict of interest. The second, identified as *integrative bargaining*, encompasses those activities and behaviors that are used when the parties see that their interests are not completely in conflict, and that it may be possible to develop a solution that meets the needs of both. The other two subprocesses, which include attitudinal structuring to influence the attitudes of the participants and affect their relationships, and intraorganizational bargaining, which deals with the development of consensus within each bargaining group, will not be discussed here as separate processes, although they are referred to at various points in the book.

Both distributive bargaining and integrative bargaining are joint decision-making processes (Walton & McKersie, 1965), but they require that the participants engage in quite different behaviors. Indeed, in most situations the behaviors that lead to effective distributive bargaining are precisely those that make integrative bargaining impossible, and successful integrative activities significantly weaken the ability of the parties to enter into distributive bargaining. It is important to clearly understand each of these two bargaining orientations because they operate under different systems of logic, lead to completely different ways of identifying and selecting alternatives, and have different results in terms of the relationships between the parties and consequently on the willingness of the parties to administer an agreement in good faith. They also differ in the extent to which they are consistent with traditional academic norms and values, and therefore in the type of conflict that their introduction into an academic institution is likely to engender. In terms of the five conflict orientations presented in the preceding chapter, distributive bargaining can be considered as focusing upon sharing or compromise when the parties are of roughly equal power, and competition or domination when one party is clearly stronger than the other. Integrative bargaining, in contrast, is oriented toward collaborative negotiating behaviors.

The first section of this chapter will consider the orientation, strategies, and tactics of distributive bargaining. In the second section, those elements related to integrative bargaining will be discussed. Because, as shall be seen, the concept of integrative bargaining is closely related to the issue of problem solving, approaches to problem solving in individuals and groups shall also be examined to determine the extent to which they suggest ways of strengthening the creative aspects of the bargaining process.

DISTRIBUTIVE BARGAINING

Distributive bargaining represents the kind of activity that is normally associated with the concept of "bargaining." It is based upon the assumption that the subject of bargaining, such as money or authority, exists in limited quantity, and that whatever one party wins through bargaining of this "pie" of fixed size comes at the expense of the other party. It represents what game theorists call a "zero-sum game," in which what one party gains, the other loses. In this bargaining situation, therefore, not only are interests different, but they are also inversely and perfectly related. Since each party's winnings in distributive bargaining come at the expense of the other, the primary objective of each party is to gain as much of the fixed pie as possible. But this is not their sole objective, because they are also concerned about maintaining the bargaining relationship (unless, of course, they believe that it is to their advantage to allow the relationship to be temporarily suspended, as in a strike). The game, then, is one of mixed motives.

In order to discuss the process by which negotiations occur we shall initially examine distributive bargaining in a simplified form dealing with only one issue, salaries; in an actual academic bargaining situation, of course, a large number of issues would be on the table at one time. In distributive bargaining, each party approaches the table with two goals in mind. The first is the target the negotiator desires to achieve. The second is the resistance point below which the negotiator believes it is preferable to break off interaction between the parties than to settle (Walton & McKersie, 1965). (In academic bargaining, of course, these points initially at least are not determined by the negotiator, but by the policy bodies which they represent.) Agreement can be reached between the parties if there is an overlap between the areas marked by their targets and resistance points (or if the targets or resistance points of one or both parties can be altered by negotiations so that there is overlap), *and* if the parties are able to discover this region during the negotiation process.

Hypothetical union and administration targets and resistance points on the issue of starting salaries for assistant professors as bargaining begins can be depicted this way:

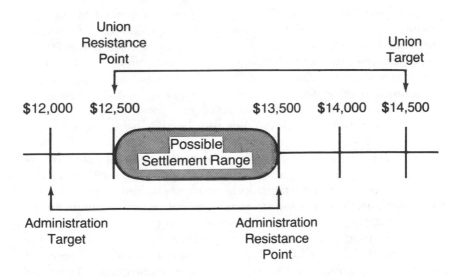

In this example, the union has a target of $14,500 as the starting salary for assistant professors (as will be discussed shortly, this is *not* the same as the demand that the union will place on the table). It would prefer to break off the bargaining relationship through a strike or some other means if the administration falls below its resistance point of $12,500. The administration has its own target of $12,000 and would be willing under certain conditions to offer up to $13,500 before it would prefer to take a strike or other action breaking off the bargaining relationship rather than settle. A settlement range is shown above, because the area from $12,500 to $13,500 is both above the union resistance point and below the administration resistance point. Of course, it is entirely possible in some situations that during the initial phases of bargaining there is no overlap between the resistance points and targets of the parties and that, therefore, no possible settlement range exists. Successful completion of an agreement in such cases will depend on one or both parties altering their aspirations.

Bargaining in this context can be seen not only as a zero-sum, mixed motive, and variable-payoff game, but also as a game of incomplete information. That is, each party begins the bargaining knowing their own aspirations, but not those of the other party, and therefore uncertain if a settlement range really exists. Minimizing this uncertainty, and maximizing one's payoff, is the purpose of distributive bargaining.

The Strategies of Distributive Bargaining

Each party approaches the bargaining table uncertain of the bargaining range of the other. A principal strategic objective of bargaining, therefore, is to determine as closely as possible the target and point of resistance of the other. Knowing the smallest amount that the other party is willing to settle for is obviously a major advantage in the bargaining process. In the same way, a party is at a disadvantage if the other knows of his or her own resistance point, and so a second strategic objective is to prevent the other from determining one's own bargaining range.

Since the bargaining range of each party is to a great extent determined by the values the parties attach to various outcomes, each party also attempts during the bargaining processes to change the values of the other and thus to change their targets and resistance points. In the above example, if the administration through various tactics can convince the union of the negative consequences of the union's goal (for example, by stating that the higher salaries demanded will result in fewer faculty positions), the union may alter its target and bring the eventual settlement closer to the administration's position. In the same way, if during the bargaining process the union convinces the administration that holding assistant professor salaries at too low a level may cause difficulties in recruiting and lead to lower faculty morale, the administration's target may alter and the contract may be settled at a salary level closer to that of the union's position.

When, as a result of the bargaining interaction, a bargainer believes that the resistance points of the other side are known, the most effective distributive strategy is to move one's own target as close to it as possible, without exceeding it. In this way, the bargainer ensures that one gets all that the other side has to give. And finally, when this point is reached, the bargainer must make a commitment to a position. If the bargainer, through various tactics, convinces the other side that this position will not be altered, and if the commitment lies within the resistance point of the other, the bargainer will likely end up with the best bargain that can be made under those circumstances. Although conventional wisdom would suggest that the strength of bargainers lies in "keeping their options open," in fact, as Schelling (1956) pursuasively argues, strength in bargaining lies in "some voluntary but irreversible sacrifice and freedom of choice. . . . The essence . . . of these tactics . . . rests . . . on the paradox that the power to constrain an adversary may depend on the power to bind oneself; that in bargaining, weakness is often strength, freedom may be freedom to capitulate, and to burn bridges behind one may suffice to undo an opponent" (p. 282). Although both parties try to gain an advantage by making an irrevocable commitment before the other, this strategy is effective only when one is certain that one's demand is less than the resistance point of the other, that it is as close as possible to one's own target, and that the commitment is communicated and understood by the other side.

The Tactics of Distributive Bargaining

Experienced negotiators have developed a number of tactics that can implement the strategies of distributive bargaining.

Since one principal objective is to keep the opponent unsure of one's real values and resistance points, the negotiator must attempt to communicate false information favorable to one's side and convince the other party that it is real, and to limit the amount of accurate information communicated to the opponent. The transmission of faulty information usually includes the presentation of demands far in excess of what the negotiator believes will be received. During the course of negotiations, the manner and timing of changes in bargaining position reflect an attempt by each side to convince the other that their maximum expectation is really their breaking-off point (Walton & McKersie, 1965, p. 87). Bargainers attempt to conceal their real priorities among items. "The union obviously would not want the employer to know that a specific bargaining demand is a low priority item among the membership, for such information would effectively eliminate that item as a 'trading piece' in the give and take of collective bargaining" (Finkin et al., 1975, p. 47). At the same time that the negotiator is trying to indicate to the other side their maximum expectation, and trying to conceal their minimum expectation (or resistance point), the bargainer is trying, through direct or indirect cues, to ascertain the actual values and resistance points of the other party. The tactics used in this process can give to the uninitiated the sense of uncontrolled conflict. For example, tactics involving personal abuse of the other side's negotiators may be used to provoke the other into revealing more information than had been planned. The use of elaborate posturing, threats, and exaggerated impatience may be used to the same effect (Walton & McKersie, 1965).

As part of the effort to obtain as much information from the opposing side as possible, while revealing as little as possible of one's own position, negotiators may adopt a tactic of a low rate of interaction and activity. Or communication may be limited to a chief spokesperson, with controls placed upon the verbal participation, and even the nonverbal behaviors of the members of one's own team (Walton & McKersie, 1965). To assist in the control of communications, academic bargainers have been advised that "Team discipline must be maintained. Only the chief negotiator should present and argue the proposal; others should not speak except with permission" (Graham, 1976, p. 19). As these examples should make clear, effective distributive bargaining requires that the parties attempt to obtain as much information from the other as possible, while withholding information and misleading the other side. In this way, as Douglas (1962) has pointed out, bargaining differs significantly from models of communication that are based upon clarity and precision. Instead, it specifically incorporates misdirection into the process by which the parties verbally interact.

During either the bargaining stage or the closing stage of negotiations, either party may engage in tactics designed to physically exhaust the other and make him or her lose sight of the objectives (Walton & McKersie, 1965). Time pressures and deadlines can also be manipulated when it appears favorable to one's position.

At the conclusion of the bargaining situation, final concessions are made and positions taken as the deadline approaches. Based upon the previous bargaining interaction, parties at this point now have a better idea of the values and resistance points of the other; they are thus in a position to seize the initiative and commit themselves to a "final" position. Once this commitment is made, rigidity rather than flexibility is the sign of strength, and reasonableness can be interpreted as meaning that concessions made now imply even further concessions later. Commitments can be underscored by relating them to threats concerning the consequences if the final demands are not acceded to, and the reputation of the bargainer is then in jeopardy if the threat is not carried out.

To one unfamiliar with the bargaining process, the interactions between parties often seem illogical and inexplicable. But Douglas' (1957) perceptive and thoughtful descriptions of collective bargaining demonstrate that the process is a reasonable and functional way of moving from antithetical to convergent positions in a relationship of low trust in which both parties must collect and analyze large amounts of fragmentary and incomplete information. Douglas believes that the process itself can be described in three stages. In the first, "establishing the bargaining range," the parties present their apparently irreconcilable positions in lengthy speeches, taking adamant postures they know will be abruptly abandoned at some point in the future, and presenting lengthy demands and counterdemands. Each side attempts to expose and discredit the opponent, and attacks on the other can be derisive and venomous. Douglas believes that this initial stage in the process is critical to the later stages, because it allows each party to demonstrate the strength with which it holds its positions and to assess the degree to which the other party may be expected to make concessions. The interpersonal communications, including the elaborate posturings and attacks, serve to expand understanding of each party by the other in ways that merely reading such demands on paper cannot do.

While the first stage of bargaining focuses upon the areas of disagreement of the parties, the second stage, which Douglas calls "reconnoitering the range," seeks out areas holding promise of agreement. Although the parties at the table exhibit many of the same behaviors as seen in the first stage, there is a subtle shift in focus from speechmaking in the role of organizational representative to "jockeying for position" within the range to obtain the most favorable position.

In this second stage, negotiators use the positions taken in the first stage as a base from which to tentatively explore modifications in position without committing themselves in any way. By virtue of these forays, each party establishes hypotheses concerning the reactions of the other, which it then tests in the arena of bargaining.

The vehemence with which the parties pursue their interests, the use of hyperbole, the pressing for special demands that later prove to be of no consequence, and all the behaviors at the table designed to place the opponent in the least favorable position are all a necessary part of this second stage. The reason is that before parties are willing to enter the third and final stage, they must be assured that everything that was available in the bargaining situation was brought to light and exploited. This cannot be done merely by having one party indicate to the other that no further concessions will be made, since both parties use this rhetoric during the process, and both know that if the other party *really* states its limits, in the language of bargaining they are really indicating that they are unwilling to offer more now, but there may be some flexibility in the future. Instead, as Douglas points out, "When a bargainer knows 'this is all' means that, it is not that the opponent has told him so but that he personally *experienced the futility* of seeking more" (p. 42).

When this occurs, parties are able to enter the third stage, "precipitating the decision-making crisis." Often, the making of final concessions or the establishment of a commitment that communicates to the other party a final take-it-or-leave-it position, is precipitated by the time pressures of the bargaining situation itself, such as the termination of the contractual period. In addition, the ambiguities created during the second stage of bargaining have a psychological impact upon the bargainers that move them toward resolving of uncertainty. When bargainers believe that all avenues have been explored, and that the potential agreement is one that provides them with as much advantage as it is possible to get, they will agree to end the negotiations.

To the naive observer, or to one whose cultural or professional orientation suggests that conflicts of interest should be resolved in more civil and intellectually oriented ways, the functioning of the processes of bargaining with a distributive orientation may appear irrational and uncivilized. Douglas's research, however, suggests that in fact it is a highly effective means of dealing with disputes over allocating resources in conditions of low trust and indeterminate values. Moreover, the histrionic and abusive behavior characterizing the process during some of its stages is an absolutely essential aspect of this form of bargaining, for it is primarily through this kind of interaction that parties assure themselves that the limits of negotiability have been fully explored. The legal environment of bargaining, on the other hand, ensures that this combative, adversarial approach stays within certain limits.

This description of distributive bargaining tactics suggests the need for utilizing experienced bargainers in the process. Not only do nonprofessionals run the risk of losing sight of the process as a "game" and allowing interparty conflict to become interpersonal conflict, but the stages of the bargaining process require adherence to a sequence of behaviors that are appropriate for each one. Douglas (1957) says that it is imperative that "the movements of two sides be synchronized to take on the phases of the bargaining sequence concurrently. A miscalculation in this respect has the effect of throwing the ratio of bargaining strengths off-balance. . . . Concessions made at the wrong time by the inexperienced bargainer can throw the entire process into chaos" (p. 81). This problem of inexperienced bargainers, or significant imbalance in the experience of the bargainers on either side of the table, has been cited as one of the major causes of breakdowns in academic bargaining (Howe, 1974; Mortimer & Richardson, 1977).

INTEGRATIVE BARGAINING

Distributive bargaining proceeds on the assumption that the parties are involved in a zero-sum game in which the gains of one are directly related to the losses of the other. Constrained in their demands only by their judgments concerning the probable resistance points of the other and their own desire to maintain the bargaining relationship, the nature of the game creates conflicts of interest that in general are temporarily reconciled through agreements based on the power each party is able to bring to the table.

There are many situations, however, in which the total resources available are not fixed, but variable. The amount of influence in a system, for example, is not a fixed "pie," but may be one in which each party can increase its own influence by increasing that of the other (Likert, 1961). In such situations, it is possible for the two parties to increase their mutual payoff through cooperative, rather than competitive, activities, and bargaining can benefit both rather than one at the expense of the other. The processes by which the parties can most effectively exploit these opportunities for increased and mutually satisfying payoffs is called "integrative bargaining."

Because the payoff structures of games defined as zero-sum and those defined as variable-sum are quite different, it would be expected that the strategies and tactics that facilitate distributive bargaining would not be suitable for integrative bargaining. They are in fact different, and these differences themselves create one of the major dilemmas of academic bargaining.

Three steps define the strategy of the integrative bargaining process. The first is to clearly understand the problem with which both parties are coping. Integrative bargaining assumes that the parties may have different perceptions about the nature of the problem, the ways in which each party feels about the problem, and how it affects their constituents, and that these perceptions may change as the parties work together to mutually define the problem and its underlying causes.

The second step is to search for alternative solutions and their consequences. Solutions may not be immediately obvious to the participants, and they may have to spend considerable time in analyzing the situation and creating new ways of considering it. The effects of possible solutions may also not be obvious and require the parties to collect and analyze data together. The final step is to mutually order the preferred solutions and to select the alternative that maximizes the joint payoff (Walton & McKersie, 1965).

The tactics of integrative bargaining are those that create an open and mutually supportive atmosphere in which problem solving can take place. Since the focus of the process is upon finding a solution maximizing the payoffs to both parties, and thus commiting them to implementing the solution, each party is motivated to work toward a solution that fully recognizes not only its own needs but those of the other as well. In order to do this, each party must be made aware of the values and targets of the other. All information and data must be made available to each party, and communication between them must be as clear and unambiguous as possible. This is critical because parties cannot expect others to propose solutions that meet their needs unless they are fully aware of what those needs are.

In order to facilitate communication between the parties, both attempt to establish a trusting and supportive climate in which they can openly communicate their reaction to various alternatives as they are discussed. This also encourages the parties to discover or create as many alternatives as possible so that the integrative potential of each may be explored. To prevent premature commitment of a party to any solution, all discussion, including the presentation of alternatives, is treated as tentative and exploratory, and parties are not bound by any suggestions they make during these exploratory phases. Because the use of time limits may inhibit problem solving, integrative bargaining works best when time constraints are set only as guidelines. The problem solving orientation of both parties makes it important that they not be distracted or confused by extraneous issues or inflated expectations, so that bargaining agendas do not contain matters that are of little or no consequence to the parties.

In the third stage, after having jointly generated as many alternatives as possible, and evaluated their consequences, the parties work together to select the preferred solution. The acceptance of a solution is not based upon the relative power of the parties, but rather on the determination by both that the solution at least meets their minimum needs and that both accept it as being better than a solution determined through other bargaining approaches. Again, open communications and concern of each party for the other ensure that the solution indeed meets the requirements of the bargainers.

DISTRIBUTIVE vs. INTEGRATIVE BARGAINING

The basic differences between the two forms of bargaining are quite obvious and powerful. "In brief, integrative bargaining is tentative and exploratory and involves open communication processes, whereas distributive bargaining involves adamant, directed and controlled information processes" (Walton & McKersie, 1965, p. 166). In general, integrative bargaining is more consistent with traditional academic norms, and faced with a choice, it is likely that most academics involved in bargaining would prefer, and feel more comfortable with, this orientation.

In addition to its basic compatibility with academic values, however, integrative bargaining has other theoretical advantages (Pruitt & Lewis, 1977). It can lead to faster settlements, because it permits the parties to reach agreements that do not require either to lower their high aspiration levels. It increases the commitment of the parties to carry out the implementation of the agreement, both because they have jointly participated in developing it and because it more fully meets their own needs. The processes inherent in integrative bargaining are also likely to lead to more satisfying intergroup relations between the union and the administration.

The outcome of a distributive bargaining interaction is likely to be a compromise between the demands and counteroffers made by the parties during the course of bargaining and are unlikely to be at the target level set by either. This compromise solution thus does not yield a fully satisfactory solution to either side, and to the extent that their interests have been frustrated, contributes to destructive conflict between them. In an integrative bargaining relationship, however, the parties are likely to have created new alternatives between them that are different from, and may be far superior to, the potential solutions that each may have considered when entering the bargaining process. Rather than the mutual dissatisfaction resulting from compromise, the creation of new alternatives opens the possibility for mutually satisfying solutions. This is likely to reduce conflict between them and lead to the use of integrative processes to deal with future matters in negotiations.

Despite the benefits inherent in integrative bargaining, and its obvious compatibility with traditional academic relationships, there are several significant problems associated with the integrative orientation. One of the most important is that not every issue on a bargaining agenda can be most effectively dealt with by using this approach. Certain issues, such as salary, are under most conditions distributive in nature. In most bargaining situations, both integrative and distributive elements are present (for example, the issue of total dollars allocated to salaries is predominantly distributive, but the question of the distribution of various fringe benefits has significant integrative potential). But when an issue is sharply and obviously distributive, dealing with it through integrative processes is unlikely to meet the needs of both parties, and may in fact disadvantage them. The reasons for this are explained further in chapter 9.

The fact that some items in a bargaining situation have integrative potential, and some do not, poses a significant dilemma for the bargainer. The tactics of both approaches are completely different, and the use of distributive tactics in bargaining on one issue virtually precludes the use of integrative processes on another. After bargainers have excoriated the other side, and questioned their intelligence, good faith, and honesty in dealing with salary increases, an immediate change toward a climate of trust and concern for the other is hardly likely, even when the next agenda item has rich integrative possibilities.

To a great extent, the integrative potential of many items is a matter of perception, rather than objective reality. Approaching each other with a competitive, distrustful orientation, parties may view an item, such as the process for the selection of departmental chairpersons, as a distributive one, in which each makes demands and counteroffers; the result is either a compromise or a trading off of one party's position for a completely unrelated item. Neither party is likely to be completely satisfied with the result, and the issue is likely to appear on future bargaining agendas.

Exactly the same issue could be approached in an integrative manner if the parties perceived the value of considering it as a problem rather than as an issue. With such an orientation, the parties would not initiate discussion with a set of demands and counteroffers concerning a selection process, but instead would begin with an indication by either that the present selection process was causing difficulties. The parties would then fully describe the nature of their dissatisfaction with the process, as well as the specific attributes that they believed would follow from a sound selection process and which they believed would have to be an essential part of an agreeable solution. Attention at this stage would be given to ends rather than means. For example, the union might contribute to an integrative bargaining process by stating that the process agreed upon must result in persons seen as responsive to departmental members' needs in certain specific ways. The administration could indicate its need for accountability in the operations of the institution. Both parties could then explore various alternative means of satisfying their requirements. These might include alternative procedures for the selection of chairpersons, but during the problem-solving phase of the process quite different possibilities may suggest themselves, such as new procedures for assuring accountability to both faculty and administration, or a change of duties. These alternatives are less likely to be considered or fully explored in distributive approaches in which the union demands "elected department chairpersons for three-year terms," and the administration demands appointed chairpersons who are considered part of the administrative hierarchy.

Although institutions of higher education may have unusual characteristics supporting an orientation toward integrative bargaining, the weaknesses of traditional distributive bargaining techniques in dealing with complex issues has also been recognized by traditional labor leaders. Almost two decades ago, Secretary of Labor Mitchell noted the emergence of new bargaining issues, and stated that the bargaining table was "an antiquated institution" for dealing with matters such as the impact of technology on work rules in the industrial setting. When the major issues are not bread and butter but involve fundamental changes, he said, they "cannot be bargained, but must be studied, thought over, and worked out with a great expense of effort, with great good will, and with great understanding over a period of time" (Hildebrand, 1961, p. 136). These conditions obviously require an orientation toward integrative bargaining approaches. In the unionized college or university, the competition and distrust that have come to typify many bargaining relationships inhibit the perception of integrative potential in many items, and confirm and continue the parties' involvement in distributive bargaining processes. Bargaining thus remains a situation in which the administration and the union see only two choices—holding firm to their own position or surrendering to the other party (Pruitt & Lewis, 1977).

The concepts of constructive and destructive conflict have been used throughout this book, defined only with the general orientation that destructive conflict leads to outcomes which do not satisfy the parties, and constructive conflict occurs when both parties believe that their goals have been achieved and are satisfied with the outcomes. Based upon the description of distributive and integrative bargaining, it is now possible to formulate the concepts of destructive and constructive conflict in the academic bargaining relationship more precisely.

Destructive conflict in academic bargaining occurs when the parties, unable to exploit the integrative potential of their relationship, utilize distributive bargaining tactics and strategies that decrease levels of trust and communication between them, create competitive win-lose orientations, and result in low-quality and unsatisfying outcomes for one or both parties. As a result of these unsatisfying outcomes, the parties further stress their adversarial relationships, thus reinforcing their reliance on distributive bargaining techniques. Parties may use distributive bargaining for problems with integrative potential because—

1. they are not aware of alternative bargaining orientations;
2. previous adversarial relationships make alternative bargaining orientations difficult to implement;
3. simultaneous involvement in bargaining over nonintegrative issues, such as salary, establishes patterns of interaction that inhibit the development of integrative approaches; or
4. the parties do not have the skills required to engage in problem-solving activities.

Constructive academic bargaining occurs when parties use problem-solving approaches to exploit the integrative potential of their relationship, based upon full communication and high levels of trust, resulting in cooperative intergroup activity and creative, jointly formulated solutions that are of high quality and meet the needs of both parties. The result of these satisfying outcomes is to confirm the utility of integrative tactics and strategies and therefore lead to their increased use in future interactions.

Tactics and strategies that can be used by the parties to academic bargaining to move toward constructive conflict and integrative approaches to bargaining are described in detail in later chapters. Since to a great extent they are based upon structures and processes known to facilitate problem solving, they can best be understood by first considering the conditions under which problem-solving activities are most effective.

PROBLEM SOLVING

Integrative bargaining is a problem-solving approach to conflict between two parties. An understanding of the process of creative problem solving can be useful, not only to explain why integrative approaches are effective under certain conditions, but also to suggest approaches that might be useful in designing new academic bargaining techniques. This section shall be limited to a summary of problem-solving techniques, with a consideration of applications in the academic bargaining context reserved for later chapters. It shall consider the bargaining session as an example of a conference group brought together for the purpose of dealing with a problem or group of problems and discuss the factors facilitating or inhibiting creative problem solving in conference groups in general. Much of the summary is based upon the work of Maier (1970).

In many situations groups are more effective in problem solving than are individuals. Not only are groups likely to solve more problems, but their solutions are likely to be better than those generated by individuals (Maier, 1970). Although there are many liabilities associated with group problem solving (for example, the tendency for social pressure to increase conformity, the possibility of domination by a strong individual, and the chance that members may align themselves with various alternatives and turn the process from solving a problem to winning an argument), the advantages appear to outweigh them. Among these are the probability that the combined information and knowledge available to the members of the group exceeds that available to any single person, and that a fully interacting group is likely to have a number of different approaches to a problem, while individuals are likely to have only one and to persist in that single approach even when it proves not to be effective. In addition, participation in the problem-solving activity is likely to increase the number of people who accept the solution, and who feel responsible for its implementation.

Although intragroup conflict can significantly enhance the group's problem-solving performance, it can be dysfunctional as well. "Disagreements among group members often lead to innovative or creative solutions to problems, but they also often lead to submission by one side or another with resulting hard feelings" (Maier, 1970, p. 405). Whether groups engage in cooperative or competitive group activity depends to some extent upon the role taken by the group leader, the processes adopted by the group, and even the nature of the problem itself. For example, competition is more likely when there are available alternative solutions that are supported by various group members, and is less likely when a solution is not immediately available at the outset of the meeting, and has to be discovered (Maier, 1970). This is one reason why distributive bargaining approaches, in which parties come to the bargaining table with their solutions (demands) already prepared, inevitably leads to competition rather than cooperation.

Problem-solving conference groups are most effective when they engage in cooperative activities and least effective when their members attempt to persuade each other of the inherent quality of their proposed solutions (Hall, 1971). It is not difficult for an observer to note the orientation of a group by its behavior. Groups involved in problem solving will keep searching for new ideas, try them out on one another, carefully listen to each other's comments to ensure complete understanding, make short speeches, and treat differences of opinion as helpful. The group will be characterized by full participation, involvement, and interest. Activities of groups that have moved from problem solving to persuasion include attempts to convince others by already formed opinions, defending positions, and listening to each other to prepare a refutation rather than to increase understanding. Group discussion is likely to be dominated by one or a few members, many members will not be involved, and disagreement among the members will be treated unfavorably. Each of these behaviors, of course, is common in traditional academic bargaining.

The mere presence of a group, therefore, does not ensure that it will engage in creative problem-solving activities. Small-group research has discovered a number of factors supporting or inhibiting group problem solving.

Factors Supporting Creative Group Problem Solving

Effectiveness of group problem solving appears to be related to the orientation of the group, the processes it follows, and the skills of the group leader.

Just as a bargainer can internalize a cooperative, competitive, or individualistic style based on the instructions given, so a group can move toward a specific problem-solving orientation if it identifies a specific situation as being appropriate. Maier (1970) reports that even having one member of a group say "let's problem-solve this issue" can often serve as a cue that alters the perceptions of the members to expect disagreement, welcome new points of view, take time to explore mutuality of interests, reduce the desire to blame, consider the nature of the problem rather than its obvious solutions, and permit the members to consider each other's perspectives as a function of their roles rather than their personalities.

"Problem solving" is an educational cliche, used so often and in so many contexts that for many it has become devoid of meaning. There is, however, a social technology of problem solving, and a generally agreed upon sequence of activities that, if followed, is most likely to permit groups to develop reasonable solutions. Each step of this sequence is important, and if not implemented in its proper order may either distort the result or inhibit the ability of the group to work together productively. A summary of the sequence has been defined in six steps by Morris and Sashkin (1978, pp. 109-110):

Phase	*Activities*
I. Problem Definition	Explaining the problem situation, generating information, clarifying, and defining the problem
II. Problem Solution Generation	Brainstorming solution alternatives; reviewing, revising, elaborating, and recombining solution ideas
III. Ideas in Action	Evaluating alternatives, examining probable effects and comparing them with desired outcomes; revising ideas, developing a list of final action alternatives and selecting one for trial
IV. Solution-Action Planning	Preparing a list of action steps with the name of the persons who will be responsible for each step; developing a coordination plan
V. Solution-Evaluation Planning	Reviewing desired outcomes and development of measures of effectiveness; creating a monitoring plan for gathering evaluation data as the solution is put into action; developing contingency plans; assigning responsibilities
VI. Evaluation of the Product and Process	Assembling evaluation data to determine the effects of actions and the effectiveness of the group's problem-solving process

Morris and Sashkin (1978) also provide an instrument that can be used by problem-solving groups to monitor their own activities and ensure that they are dealing with both the tasks and the processes of problem solving at each of the stages. Even cursory examination of these steps will indicate the extent to which traditional bargaining practice is inconsistent with some of the basic problem-solving requirements, such as spontaneity and brainstorming. The following chapters will suggest tactics and strategies to reduce or eliminate this discrepancy.

Once a group has decided to adopt a problem-solving orientation, it is important that they define exactly what the problem is. This sounds like a trivial and redundant remark, but it is true that a major reason that groups are unable to reach acceptable solutions is because different members of the group have quite different perceptions of the nature of the problem. Problem definition is probably the most difficult and critical stage of the problem-solving process, and the one given the least attention by most groups. Techniques exist, such as the STP process (Schmuck et. al., 1977), which can help groups with this essential activity. Using it, groups can develop consensus on their present situation in some specific area of interest, and the goals that the group wishes to achieve. The "problem" is then defined as the difference between the goal and the present situation. This concept of problem identification is useful because the mutual determination of current and desired levels of performance creates shared understanding of the situation, and a commitment from all group members to work toward eliminating the discrepancy. The focus is therefore on successfully overcoming any barriers that are preventing the achievement of mutually supported goals, rather than upon the means that will be used to do this. In contrast, academic bargainers begin their interaction by presenting solutions to problems, commonly referred to as "demands." Since each group is likely to perceive the nature of the problem quite differently, and to be committed to its own solution, these differences in the nature of the problem are either not explored, or else are considered in a competitive environment characterized by filtered communications and distorted perceptions.

Problem solving is more likely to be creative when certain procedures are followed by the group. One of the most important is to separate the process of generating ideas from the process of evaluating them (Filley, 1975). There is a tendency in many groups, and in academic bargaining interactions, to consider ideas in serial order, and to evaluate each new idea as it is presented. This process prevents the effective generation of ideas for two reasons. First, the creative generation of new ideas involves different mental processes from their evaluation, and jumping from one process to the other makes it difficult to establish the proper group environment to do either properly. Second, as new ideas are presented and critically evaluated, group members become defensive, and the creation of additional ideas is inhibited. The technique of "brainstorming,"in which members of the group are asked to rapidly and without evaluation present new ideas, no matter how outlandish they may sound, and in which one idea can build upon another, is one way of freeing people to think outside the boundaries of their past experience, and of temporally separating the creative and evaluative aspects of problem solving (Schmuck et al., 1977).

An additional group process leading to effective problem solving is the generation of alternative solutions. This usually must occur as part of a conscious group action, since there is a tendency for groups to discontinue the search for creative alternatives once a single satisfactory solution has been discovered. Clearly, the fact that a solution has been found does not mean that other, even more effective, solutions may not exist. Once having found a solution, therefore, groups should continue the problem-solving process to create additional ones, thus making it possible for the group to analyze and compare alternatives and select the most effective one. Research (Maier, 1970) indicates that second solutions to problems by groups tend to be superior to first solutions, and are more likely to be integrative in nature. Maier believes that this is so because groups terminate problem solving before they have achieved their best product, or because a dominant individual has superimposed his or her will on the group and prevented it from discovering the best solution.

In order to be optimally effective, problem-solving groups must have leaders, but the activities of leaders are somewhat different from those commonly assumed to be required in group settings or typified by academic bargainers. When groups exist primarily for the transmission of information, group leaders focus their activities upon persuasive techniques that attempt to gain acceptance by the group of decisions made elsewhere. The leader in this situation is at the center of the group interaction (performing those activities that are sometimes associated with "leadership"), and the leader talks more than anyone else in the group. This kind of leadership behavior is found in every formal and informal group (Homans, 1950). It is, however, not descriptive of effective leadership behavior in problem-solving groups. In this situation, the effective leader is concerned with group interaction, and therefore attempts to facilitate communication among group members. The group leader listens, rather than talks (Maier, 1970). Since this is not usual leadership behavior, persons are more effective as the leaders of problem-solving groups if they are trained to perform that function.

Since creativity arises from disagreement, one of the most critical functions of group leadership is to protect the right of members with minority opinions to be heard. In contrast, academic bargaining limits most communications to the group leaders. Almost by definition, creative solutions to problems are not obvious ones, so that minority opinions are likely to be of unusual value and deviants must be protected (Boulding, 1965). Leaders must establish a permissive discussion climate, prevent group pressure from restraining the free expression of dissenting opinions, and prevent individuals from controlling the group communications processes.

> Ordinarily persons who change opinions are influenced by the social pressure that is exerted by the majority view. It follows that when a majority opinion is wrong social pressure has an undesirable effect on the outcome of the discussion. With the presence of a discussion leader this social pressure is reduced, allowing minority opinions to exert an influence. In protecting a minority opinion from the social pressure of the majority, the leader allows the minority to have enough influence to make a possible contribution to the quality of a group's thinking. (Maier, 1970, pp. 226-227)

Factors Inhibiting Creative Group Problem Solving

Several of the factors inhibiting creative problem solving have already been discussed in the preceding section. Three specific areas are critical enough to require special mention, however.

The first is the kind of interaction that is likely to occur in groups that have not established norms in which disagreement is welcomed and protected by the group leader. In such situations, individuals who disagree with one another are likely to feel attacked by the other, to feel hurt, and to become defensive and respond with increasing competitive behavior. To avoid this kind of conflict, many group members become careful in expressing their views to avoid disagreeing. "People who get along with other participants by conforming may be good group members, but they also become poor problem solvers. Members cannot learn from one another by agreeing" (Maier, 1970, p. 269).

The second is the tendency of groups, when faced with two alternative problem solutions, to expend their energies in trying to select one of them. The most creative action under these circumstances would be to defer a choice, and turn the selection process into a problem-solving one by jointly creating some additional choices.

The third, and by far the most important factor inhibiting group problem solving, is the not-uncommon situation in which group members come to a meeting having already committed themselves to a solution. The group interaction under these conditions becomes one of competition rather than cooperation, and discussion consists of attempts to convince the other party of the superiority of one solution, and the weakness of another. In this situation, the goals for which the solutions were supposedly created are usually forgotten, and the final outcome is likely to be a compromise between the two proposed solutions. The problem is so significant that Maier (1970) has suggested that group processes are more effective when members of the group have not previously had an opportunity to think about the problem. When it has been discussed and considered beforehand, group members spend more time trying to convert each other than stimulating each other.

DISTRIBUTIVE, INTEGRATIVE, AND ACADEMIC BARGAINING

The concepts of distributive and integrative bargaining represent two completely different conceptual orientations toward academic bargaining. Distributive bargaining accepts the participants in the process as adversaries with few common interests, and establishes tactics and strategies that not only are most effective under these conditions but that lead to behavior making adoption of this model a self-fulfilling prophecy.

Integrative bargaining assumes considerable mutuality of interest between the parties, and suggests that both working together can achieve creative outcomes that can be superior to results that either could earn in a competitive environment.

A consideration of research findings concerning effective problem-solving techniques through which the concepts of integrative bargaining can be implemented suggests that they are contrary to the "principles" of academic bargaining recommended by many experts. Certainly, they are contrary to the actual practices of academic bargainers in many, if not most, unionized colleges and universities. This is unfortunate not only because it means that bargainers are engaging in processes that leave both parties with far less than could be obtained in the bargaining interaction, but also because institutions are failing to capitalize on a process through which the ties between faculty and administration could be strengthened, not torn apart.

Almost without thinking, many institutions have been swept into the destructive processes of distributive bargaining, placing in jeopardy the essential nature of goals shared by faculty and administration that traditionally have distinguished colleges and universities. The traditional bargaining structure, inevitable processes that develop when groups are placed in competitive situations, and the perceived lack of alternatives all function to move institutions toward distributive bargaining procedures even when both parties would prefer some other outcome.

Academic bargaining is inherently a process of intergroup conflict. Whether the consequences of bargaining are bitter and destructive, or constructive and creative, depends upon the attitudes, structures, and processes that the parties bring to the bargaining relationship in their effort to manage conflict. The next five chapters present three alternative orientations toward the management of intergroup conflict. Chapter 5 discusses the commonly accepted forms of conflict management in unionized settings and assesses their effectiveness in promoting creative bargaining. Chapter 6 presents alternative tactics that can be adopted by the parties within traditional bargaining structures. In the final analysis, however, creative bargaining is best facilitated by new structures and orientations. Chapters 7, 8, and 9 give a number of alternative approaches to such changes.

Part II

PRACTICAL APPLICATIONS

5

Dispute Resolution
and the
Unionized University

GROUPS IN COMPETITIVE interaction are not always able to peacefully resolve their differences. When the parties in collective bargaining are unable to agree to the provisions of a contract, they are at impasse. Impasse can be an outcome of any negotiation, but it is reasonable to assume that it is more likely when the parties have engaged in distributive bargaining leading to destructive conflict processes that make joint decision-making almost impossible.

Just as higher educational institutions for the most part have adopted negotiations processes created to deal with labor-management bargaining in other types of organizations, so they have also become involved in the use of impasse resolution practices, some of which have been developed over a considerable period of time based upon experience in industrial relations, and some of which are relatively recent creations to deal with the new phenomenon of public sector bargaining. The small number of unionized private colleges and universities fall under the jurisdiction of the National Labor Relations Board, which can provide mediation services to parties at impasse at the request of either party or at their own initiative. Should mediation fail, the parties have available to them the ultimate weapons of the union strike or the management lockout, by which the relative power of each group can be tested and coercion used as a means of forcing the parties into agreement.

The use of impasse procedures has become particularly important because of the recent growth and development of public sector collective bargaining. Nearly all legislation that establishes public sector impasse processes has been enacted since 1967 (Jones, 1975). Operating under state legislation, rather than the federal law applicable to non-public corporations, and precluded by these laws from legally using the strike as a means of forcing agreement in impasse situations, a rich and somewhat confusing array of impasse processes have been adopted in various jurisdictions. The use of such dispute management techniques, and their applicability to the particular needs of higher educational institutions, will be the focus of this chapter.

It is necessary to begin by noting that there is very little research and information available concerning dispute resolution in the unionized college or university. Those few references to the concept of conflict resolution in this setting deal for the most part with the grievance process (Leslie & Satryb, 1974; Satryb, 1976; Leslie, 1975b), which in many unionized institutions includes binding arbitration as a final step. The arbitration of grievances, however, is a completely different process than the arbitration of contract disputes, which is also called interest arbitration.

The grievance process has been called "the primary provision for conflict management between the interests of faculty and the interests of the institution" (Leslie & Satryb, 1974, p. 15). Although this contention is inconsistent with the orientation of this book, it is clearly true that grievance arbitration is an important element in academic conflict management. The functions of the grievance process have been carefully considered by Leslie (1975a) and shall not be considered further in this volume. All references to the use of arbitration, therefore, shall refer to interest arbitration used to resolve impasses in the negotiation of contracts.

Although there is not much information available concerning the use of impasse processes in colleges and universities, there is a considerable amount of material, mainly speculative or descriptive, concerning the use of various techniques in other public-sector settings. Not all states permit public employees to bargain by statute, and not all of the states that do include higher education in the authorizing legislation. Where higher education is covered, however, the general practice is to treat faculty identically with every other public employment group. Professors, therefore, have the same access to specific procedures as do the state police or office workers. An understanding of how interest arbitration, for example, has been utilized in the relationships between firefighters and municipal governments can offer insights into its possible utility in educational settings. The statutes of many states have been modeled around the provisions of the National Labor Relations Act that governs private organizations, so that the laws of some states are remarkably similar in some ways. However, since public sector bargaining is a state matter, and since in many states specific situations or orientations led to the consideration of laws with unique properties, some states have developed unusual approaches to public sector bargaining and have experimented with new and creative approaches to bargaining impasse. In some states, the impasse procedures are included in the legislation granting public employees the right to engage in bargaining. In others, the law may stipulate the processes, but also gives the parties themselves the right to negotiate their own impasse processes as a first step in negotiations (Gilroy & Lipovac, 1977).

This chapter will present some of the procedural elements of various impasse processes and describe the reactions of industrial relations experts to their use and effectiveness. Unlike most observers, however, we shall try to focus our attention upon the potential of each technique for constructive conflict management, rather than upon the degree to which it appears to "resolve conflict" by leading to the signing of a contract.

For the reader unfamiliar with the terminology employed in the labor relations field, a brief definition of some common terms, and an introduction to the ways they will be used will be useful.

Impasse is a situation in which the parties to a collective bargaining relationship are unable to come to agreement on the terms of a contract. When this occurs, federal law (for private institutions) and most state legislation for public institutions have procedures that bring a third party into the bargaining arena to assist the parties in reaching a settlement. Such persons are referred to as "neutrals."

Mediation is a process by which a third party attempts to assist the two negotiating groups to reach a mutual agreement. The processes and assumptions under which mediators operate shall be discussed below. The critical element in mediation is that the neutral has no authority whatsoever to impose a settlement on the parties; the mediator functions by persuasion only.

If mediation fails, a common second stage in the process is *fact-finding*. Fact-finding is a newer technique than mediation, and probably because of its recency exists in several forms. In general, the fact finder is empowered to meet with the parties, hear their arguments concerning the issues in disagreement, collect and analyze data, and prepare a report of the "facts" of the situation.

The third stage in some impasse processes is called *arbitration*. In all arbitration processes, a neutral, or a panel of neutrals, renders a decision concerning the terms of a contract between the parties. Occasionally, this decision is nonbinding, and the process is called "advisory arbitration." This process is identical to common forms of fact-finding, and will be included in the discussion of that process. A more recent process, and one coming into more common usage, is *binding arbitration*. In this process, the neutral issues a specific finding concerning the issues under dispute that both parties are legally bound to accept.

A fourth impasse resolution process, which is the most recent in the labor relations repertoire, is that of *mediation-arbitration,* or *med-arb.* In this process, one neutral successively performs the mediation and the arbitration phases of the process, and in so doing completely changes the communication structure of the participants.

We turn now to a description of the processes and conceptual orientations of each of these procedures, and an examination of the extent to which they can contribute to constructive conflict management and creative bargaining.

MEDIATION

Mediation is the first step in most impasse resolution processes. Since the mediator has no authority to impose any solution on the parties, impasse can only be resolved through mediation if the parties themselves are able to reach an agreement through the neutral that they were unable to reach alone. Mediators in many cases are able to do this. Their stock in trade is the manipulation of the social interactions and communication between groups and altering of the psychological environment in which they interact.

The mediator traditionally enters the bargaining situation with little or no information about the parties or the issues that have created the impasse. The purpose of the mediator is to get the parties to reach an agreement (Kochan & Jick, 1978; Byrnes, 1978; Stevens, 1963). While this appears self-evident and not worthy of further comment, in fact it is an extremely profound aspect of the mediative orientation, and its implications will be examined later in this section.

Mediators usually begin their involvement by meeting jointly with the parties to establish their trust and confidence, to determine the actual status of the negotiations, and to more clearly ascertain the reasons that impasse exists. This initial meeting also serves as a means by which the parties confirm to each other their perceptions of the reason for impasse (something which might be assumed to be clearly understood by the parties, but which in fact may be completely misunderstood by each because of the use of misleading communication as a distributive bargaining technique), and indicate to the mediator and each other their interest in finding a negotiated settlement.

After the initial meeting, the activities of an experienced mediator become highly contingent upon his or her diagnosis of the situation, including not only an understanding of the manifest issues but also the hidden agendas that become visible through individual meetings with each of the bargaining parties (Kochan & Jick, 1978). The mediator's selection of tactics and strategies is usually based upon experience with what worked or did not work in similar settings in the past. An experienced mediator, therefore, is likely to apply the learnings gleaned from working with many other, quite dissimilar groups, when faced with a college or university impasse assignment.

Although the work of the mediator is not grounded in conscious application of applied behavioral science techniques, in some ways the mediation sequence of system access, diagnosis, and intervention parallels the activities of the organization development (OD) consultant to be described in greater detail in chapter 8. The purposes and behaviors of the labor mediator are quite different, however.

Depending upon the situation, the mediator may work with the two groups together, or may separate and move between them, collecting impressions and evaluations of the relative strengths of the parties and communicating various alternatives to them. The mediator may relieve emotional tension by demanding that hostile language and posturing cease across the table, and by listening patiently and nonjudgmentally as the parties deliver themselves of tirades against the other in secret sessions. The mediator will usually gather factual information from the parties, and fashion proposed compromises at opportune times, or suggest packages that might be attractive (Byrnes, 1978). The mediator's role ends either when the parties can be convinced to mutually agree to terms of a contract, or when the mediator believes that mediation cannot resolve the impasse and a new stage in the process should be implemented.

The types of contributions that the mediator can make to the resolution of conflict between contending parties in collective bargaining have been listed by experts in the field (Simkin, 1971; Yager, 1976; Haman, Brief & Pegretter, 1978). Probably the most insightful analysis and description is that of Kerr (1954), which established five broad categories of mediator functions. Each of them can be considered related to the problems of groups in conflict discussed in chapters 3 and 4.

Reduction of Irrationality

Kerr suggests that the mediator can give bargainers an opportunity to "vent their feelings to him, by keeping personal recriminations out of joint discussions, and by drawing the attention of the parties to the objective issues in dispute and to the consequences of aggressive conflict" (p. 236). The cognitive distortions and attribution processes that are related to the initiation and cyclic reinforcement of competitive group interaction have already been noted. By allowing the parties to vent their emotions to the mediator, rather than to the opposing group, the mediator may reduce the tension and competitive irrationality that has developed between them (Kochan & Jick, 1978).

It should be noted, however, that while the mediator is able, through controlled communication, to reduce the symptoms of irrationality, this type of intervention does not necessarily affect the underlying causes of the destructive conflict between the parties. However, since the structures and processes of distributive, win-lose bargaining are likely to move the interests of the parties away from the problems with which they are confronted, and to focus their attention upon "beating" the other side, the mediator can orient them once again to the issues on the table that must be resolved. The reduction of irrationality is important, not only because it separates real from imaginary issues, but also because a high level of irrational or emotional conflict, which may have been initially caused by perceived substantive differences, may itself lead to the proliferation of issues and increased substantive conflict.

Until irrationality is reduced in the bargaining relationship, emotional issues, such as "loss of face," may be so pervasive that they swamp all consideration of the substance of the negotiations. Not only do these emotional issues make agreement between the parties more difficult, but they can become so intense in a climate of adversarial relationships that parties may persist in advocating and maintaining positions they rationally "know" will result in extremely high costs to themselves (Brown, 1977, pp. 275-276). Unless separated by mediation or some other intervention, therefore, the relationship between the rational and irrational elements of bargaining are such that parties may find themselves accepting major substantive losses in order to avoid the appearance of weakness at the bargaining table. Although there are no data that speak to this issue, it is probable that the majority of strikes in unionized colleges and universities have been the consequence of bargaining relationships with high levels of irrationality on one or both sides.

Removal of Nonrationality

While the reduction of irrationality is primarily, although not entirely, a process of altering the attitudinal climate, the removal of nonrationality is primarily, although not entirely, a process of changing the cognitive perceptions of the parties. Kerr (1954) includes in this activity the mediator's attempts to clarify to each side the intentions of the other, to move the parties toward a greater understanding of each other's positions on the issues, and to ensure that significant facts are known and appreciated by the parties. This is a difficult process, since the utilization of distributive bargaining techniques prior to the mediator's involvement has emphasized the withholding of information, the use of tactics designed to keep one's intentions secret, and the manipulation of data favorable to one's position. The parties have often reached the point where any statement of fact or intention by the other side is viewed with suspicion. Information supplied to each party by the mediator, however, is more likely to be accepted as truthful. In some cases, both parties may both be willing to support a specific resolution of their conflict, but are unable to communicate this to each other. The mediator can assess the positions of each, and propose solutions that are known in advance to be acceptable to the parties.

A second manifestation of nonrationality is presented by the inexperienced bargainer who is unable to understand the probable effects of continued conflict. Kerr (1954) says, "Quite commonly, each party, particularly when collective bargaining is new to it, underestimates the costs [of aggressive conflict] and overestimates the potential gain. The mediator can often bring a truer estimate of the strength of the opposing party and a truer expectation of the outcome than is available initially" (p. 237).

The mediator can also ensure that inexperienced bargainers know the legal consequences of continued impasse, such as the employer's right to impose new conditions of employment in the absence of a contract, and provide them with some assessment of how each party's position might fare should impasse proceed to a further stage such as arbitration.

Assistance in Graceful Retreat

Since all bargainers ask for more than they expect to get, or offer less than they know they will eventually settle for, concessions must be made on both sides in order for a settlement to be reached. Once parties reach impasse, however, the win-lose orientation of the two sides, increased group conformity, and the commitment of the negotiating representative to the group make concessions appear as defeat and label the negotiator as traitorous.

Kerr (1954) identifies three ways in which the mediator can assist the parties in the making of concessions leading toward resolution. First, the mediator can call the parties together. In some impasse situations, parties who have broken off communications may wish to continue negotiations, but are afraid to contact the other party for this purpose lest their interest be misconstrued as weakness.

Second, the mediator can act as go-between in the making of offers. Without revealing the true position of the parties, which have been assessed in separate meetings, the mediator can suggest possible rates of concession on various issues to either side, without requiring either to make a complete commitment until both parties are in agreement. Often this is done with the parties meeting separately in nearby rooms, and the mediator moving between them and "trying things on for size" (Simkin, 1971, p. 95). "The mediator," says Kerr (1954), "makes it possible for the parties to yield and thus to disclose their true positions to each other without being eternally committed to them" (p. 238).

Third, the mediator can help the parties save face. Parties can accept a neutral's recommended solution more easily than they can if the other side puts forward the same solution. This is particularly true if the suggested solution is a compromise between the positions of the parties (Pruitt & Johnson, 1970). In some situations, the proposal of a mediator allows both parties to accept what the negotiators know is a realistic solution, but one which they can sell to their constituencies only by using the mediator as a scapegoat who "forced our side" into accepting the agreement.

Raising the Cost of Conflict

On rare occasions, Kerr (1954) notes, mediators will raise the costs of conflict by bringing into the situation the involvement of external groups and thereby encourage resolution by the parties. This can include such tactics as making public statements that will bring public pressure to bear on the parties to settle or going behind the backs of the negotiators to deal directly with the principals of the two groups. Kerr suggests that this tactic is used only in dealing with cases involving extremely high levels of public concern.

Before describing the fifth function of the mediator suggested by Kerr, a comment is in order concerning the previous four. All of them are based upon an acceptance of the basic adversarial nature of bargaining and presume a distributive posture between the parties. The mediator's primary function is to change the affective or cognitive predispositions and understandings of the parties so that they can reach agreement through partially overcoming some of the effects of behaviors related to destructive conflict orientations. The mediator is not necessarily interested in the causes of their disagreement or in the relationships between the parties. The mediator is interested in resolving the dispute, which is narrowly defined as having the parties reach agreement.

Because of this orientation, the mediator faces a conflict of interest between considering the short-term and long-term consequences of any agreement between the parties and in general will provoke and support an agreement even when its terms may contribute to intensified conflict at some later stage in the parties' relationship. Concern over this short-term objective is manifested in such matters as the mediator's orientation toward the rationality of the parties. As indicated above, mediators can contribute to agreement between the parties by removing elements of nonrationality that may exist, for example, when one party underestimates the strength or bargaining position of the other and therefore holds out for a settlement that is rationally unrealistic. Providing additional information to the recalcitrant bargainer that indicates that the opponent is stronger than suspected tends to reduce unrealistic expectations. However, the mediator does *not* wish to reduce rationality when the bargainer has *overestimated* the strength of the opposition, nor where the parties have overestimated the consequences of not agreeing or underestimated the benefits, for to do so would make agreement even more difficult (Kerr, 1954). Stevens (1963) has said:

> The mediator does not have a direct interest in bringing the parties to a realistic appraisal of the situation. His objective is to induce them to agree. Bringing them to a realistic appraisal of the situation may be a means to this end. However, bringing them to a non-realistic appraisal may also be a means to this end. That is, it might be the case that a party could be brought to agreement if he overestimated the cost of a strike, underestimated the gains to be had thereby, and underestimated the cost of agreement with his opponent upon his opponent's terms. In this case a mediator might abet the agreement process by deliberate deception (p. 129).

In his discussion of mediator-generated pressure tactics, a former chief negotiator of an AAUP chapter writes of the use of deliberate deception to settle a strike during bargaining (Byrnes, 1978). In this case, the mediator falsely informed the union that the administration was planning to shut down the college if agreement was not reached immediately and assured the union that the threat was genuine. Faced with this "knowledge," the union settled immediately, but the fact of agreement on a contract probably has not contributed to a more constructive bargaining relationship between them.

Exploration of Solutions

The one function of mediation with integrative potential is that of assisting the parties in developing solutions to the issues dividing them. Kerr (1954) states, "Not only can a skilled mediator help the parties explore solutions which have occurred to them independently, but he can create new solutions around which positions have not yet become fixed" (p. 237). Simkin (1971) adds that the performance of this function requires the mediator to have a high level of imagination and experience. Unfortunately, the integrative potential inherent in this role is usually not exploited. Partially this is a function of the mediator's orientation toward closure that makes it more likely that relatively simple solutions will be offered so that the parties have a reasonable chance to appraise their consequences. Most complex issues do not have simple solutions, nor can such solutions be developed in the relatively brief period of time that a mediator typically works with the parties. To some extent it is also a function of the bargaining structure and the tendency of mediators to suggest, and the parties to adopt, compromise positions based on the prominence of certain possible solutions, such as "splitting the difference," which arise as a result of tacit bargaining (Schelling, 1960).

In addition, while the intergroup relations established by the parties can be somewhat modified by the mediator, they are probably too entrenched by the time impasse is reached to be dissipated to the extent necessary to permit the emergence of real problem-solving behaviors between them.

Finally, the unusual characteristics of the academic enterprise in terms of its structure and organization, its technology, and its norms should be noted. The differences between academic and either industrial or public sector organizations may be more of kind than degree from the "shop differences" that exist between employees in other settings. While it is probably true that an experienced and sensitive mediator can contribute to the resolution of any human dispute on the terms stated by Kerr, the unique qualities of the academic setting suggest that assisting the parties to develop innovative solutions to mutual problems requires a neutral with significant experience in the field of higher education. Mediators in any setting are expected to have "good ideas" that can assist the parties in settlement (Landsberger, 1955). But in higher education a "good idea" must not only be defined as one that appears to rationally fall within the bargaining ranges of the parties, but also as one that the parties can accept as consistent with the purposes of the academic profession. Only someone familiar with educational organizations can normally provide ideas meeting these criteria. This is not to say that the ideas of the nonacademic are always, or even usually, without merit. But laymen are more apt through ignorance to make suggestions that are at such variance with the culture of higher education that they may destroy their credibility with the parties and render less useful their participation in the process.

Is mediation effective? To some extent, that may be an unanswerable question. Kerr (1954), after stating that all industrial conflict involving mediation is finally resolved, so that no mediator is unsuccessful in the long run, also points out that the same thing can be said of conflicts that don't involve mediators. Yet it appears to be true that the skillful mediator can "speed the negotiations, reduce the likelihood of miscalculation, and generally help the parties reach a sounder agreement, an adjustment of their divergent valuations that will produce something like an optimum yield of the gains of reciprocity" (Fuller, 1971, p. 318), to the extent that the parties consider their bargaining relationship as primarily distributive in nature. There is general consensus by experts that mediation is the stage at which most impasses are resolved (Jones, 1975, p. 195; Gilroy & Sinicropi, 1972), and experimental evidence indicates that mediation tends to improve the performance of groups bargaining through representatives (Vidmar, 1971).

It is difficult to determine the extent of the use of mediation in academic bargaining. Although there are reports of its effective use in several situations (Finkin, Goldstein, & Osborne, 1975), there are few published data indicating the number of institutions engaged in mediation, or its effectiveness in colleges or universities.

FACT-FINDING

In some jurisdictions, fact-finding is the step in the impasse process that follows upon unsuccessful mediation. In fact finding, a neutral or a panel of neutrals is charged with the responsibility for hearing the arguments of both parties, collecting other relevant information, and issuing a report based on the facts discovered. Like mediation, the recommendations of a fact finder are advisory only, and not binding on either party. Unlike mediation, however, in most but not all cases, the fact finder's report is made public.

One presumption of fact-finding is that when the parties are confronted with the facts, and a neutral agency recommends how an appropriate settlement should be made, the parties will recognize the error of their ways and reach quick agreement. In this way, the fact finder in a more public way assumes some of the functions of the mediator by establishing a solution which, in the absence of clear alternatives to which the parties agree, can serve as a reference point for a settlement. It also serves, as does the mediator's recommendation, to make it possible for one side to gracefully withdraw from a position, or for the bargaining representatives to use it as the basis for an agreement they believe is reasonable but, in the absence of a fact-finding report, they would be unable to sell to their principals or constituents.

The second presumption about the fact-finding report is that when it is published (as most of them are), the public will place pressure on the parties to settle the dispute in accordance with the fact finder's recommendations. This rationale for fact-finding is well stated by the report of the New York Governor's Committee on Public Employee Relations in 1966 (cited in Wollett, 1972, p. 71).

> Fact-finding requires the parties to gather objective information and to present arguments with reference to these data. Any unsubstantiated or extreme demand from either party tends to lose its force and status in this forum. The fact-finding report and recommendation provide a basis to inform and to crystalize thoughtful public opinion and news media comment.

Although the concept that "objective" recommendations provided by a neutral and made public will assist in resolving the conflict between the parties, or at least narrow the differences between them, sounds reasonable, Wollett quotes a union lawyer's comments on why it does not work in practice:

> The notion that when the public really appreciates the ultimate facts of a dispute it will generally respond constructively and compel the solution along the lines recommended is, of course, a romantic delusion. Fact-finding reports are rarely publicized, rarely heeded by anyone other than the parties, and their intellectual quality has generally been so low that neither party is persuaded, although one or the other may accept for political or strategic reasons (pp. 71-72).

The unwillingness of competing parties to accept the recommendations of a neutral is, of course, precisely what would be expected from the Blake and Mouton experiments.

There is disagreement about the effectiveness of fact-finding as a useful impasse procedure, with different states having varying experiences and success rates (McKelvey, 1969). It has been more recently suggested that during the early years of public sector bargaining in the 1960s, fact-finding was a useful tool in resolving disputes, but that its effectiveness has been constantly diminishing with many viewing it as a way-station between the mediation that preceded it and the arbitration that often follows it (Doherty, 1976).

In some jurisdictions, fact-finding is made and the report is issued without recommendations. In general, this is not considered an effective practice because the complexity of most labor situations are such that mere recital of the "facts" does not suggest any directions for resolution (Simkin, 1970). Under these conditions, fact-finding becomes an exercise in futility.

In those cases in which the fact-finding report is accompanied by recommendations, it is commonly assumed that the recommendations "flow almost automatically from the facts." Quite clearly, however, as Simkin (1970) points out, facts by themselves can never suggest policies until they are mediated by value judgments. Because of the ambiguity of "facts" and their relevance and meaning in any particular situation, the fact finder often bases decisions upon the relative strength of the parties, in essence asking, What would the parties have been likely to get had they not engaged in fact-finding but had the authority to resort to the ultimate economic weapons of the strike and the lockout? This really means, What will the parties consider acceptable? Doherty (1976) has phrased the situation nicely:

> Because it is so difficult to determine the relative weight of these criteria (comparability, the market, ability to pay, the public interest, etc.), the fact-finder will frequently use the parties' arguments only to justify what he has wanted to achieve all along—*acceptability*. Certainly this will be the case if the factfinder sees himself as part of the conciliatory process, rather than performing a quasijudicial role. The only question the fact finder asks under these circumstances is: what will the parties accept with the least amount of bad humor? This means an acceptance based not so much on the grounds that the factfinder's recommendations were models in logical persuasion, but because he or she was smart enough to give the lion the lion's share and give the mouse what mice deserve. In other words, there is a tendency for factfinders to make their recommendations conform to relative power positions (p. 366).

In the final analysis, then, fact-finding is a process that attempts to assist the parties in reaching an agreement based upon their relative bargaining power, without any great concern for the content of the agreement, or its effects upon the future development of the relationships between the parties.

ARBITRATION

Although grievance arbitration has a long history in industrial collective bargaining, the use of arbitration in contract disputes, called "interest arbitration," is a new procedure designed to deal with negotiations disputes in the public sector. It also in many ways has offered the greatest opportunities for creative alternatives, and several interesting variants have been developed and are being utilized. In total, 17 states provide for some form of compulsory binding arbitration (Somers, 1977).

Interest arbitration is a quasijudicial process in which a neutral, or a panel of neutrals, receive arguments from the parties, take testimony under oath, and render a decision concerning the matters under dispute in a contract. In those states permitting interest arbitration of public employee disputes, the process by which it can be invoked varies, and sometimes requires only that one party request it, that both parties request it, or that the process is mandatory (McAvoy, 1972). When the arbitration process is conducted by a panel, the most common arrangement is one composed of three persons, one each selected by each side, and a chairperson selected by these two partisan members. Although this means that many arbitration awards are made on a split vote, with the chairperson casting the deciding vote, the presence of bargaining group representatives on the panel is helpful. They are more knowledgeable about their sponsors' positions on the issues than would be the chairperson, and thus able to ensure that the neutral does not make a serious error of interpretation during the preparation of the award (McAvoy, 1972).

The statutes of many, but not all, states with interest arbitration establish general criteria the arbitrator should use in determining an award. Typical criteria may include such matters as relative equities, comparisons of wage rates, conditions in the general area, the interests and welfare of the public, and occasionally, the ability to pay (McAvoy, 1972; Somers, 1977). Within these guidelines, the arbitrator or arbitration panel is free to make any award it believes proper. This award may be similar to the demands of either of the parties, or it may be different from any of them.

Interest arbitration has been criticized because of its negative impact on negotiations. It has been pointed out (Long & Feuille, 1974) that in traditional arbitration there is a tendency for the arbitrator to make awards on the principle of compromise and to give the parties more than the employer has offered, and less than the union has asked for. To the extent this is so, it has a "chilling effect" upon the negotiations process itself. It encourages the parties to enter arbitration with high demands and low offers in order to gain the maximum advantage from the compromise award. Parties, aware that the negotiations process may end in arbitration, may be reluctant to move toward settlement in the belief that they can get more from an arbitrator than they can from the bargaining table (McAvoy, 1972). In this situation, arbitration, far from having the parties incur severe costs of disagreement, may in fact encourage them to disagree and subvert the entire bargaining process.

In response to this potential problem, several variants of traditional arbitration have been developed. They include final offer by issue, final offer by total package, final offer with dual offers, and mediation-arbitration (med-arb).

Final-Offer Arbitration—By Issue and Package

In traditional arbitration, the neutral or panel is empowered to make awards that in many cases compromises the positions of the parties. Under the concept of final-offer arbitration, however, the arbitrator is restricted to making an award by accepting only the position of one of the parties. The principle behind this restriction is that the either-or character of the situation increases uncertainty on the part of the parties and thus encourages them to bargain for a settlement rather than risk losing everything in the award. One of the advantages to this process is that "there is no reason to suppose that big claims may be rewarded and concessions penalized. Indeed, expectations may tend to be the other way around, as each party may assume that the arbitrator will reject an 'exaggerated' position in favor of an opponent's more moderate claim" (Stevens, 1966, p. 46). Final offer arbitration procedures have been legislatively adopted in six states (Feuille & Dworkin, 1979).

Common practice in final-offer arbitration follows the process seen in Massachusetts (Somers, 1977). After going through mediation and fact-finding without agreement, a tripartite panel conducts hearings. At the commencement of the hearing, the parties each present a written statement of its position on each matter still under dispute. During the hearing itself, the parties are given an opportunity to alter their positions, or to reach agreement and request that arbitration be terminated. If this does not happen, however, they must submit to the arbitration panel within a stated period after the hearing a written statement containing its last, best offer on each issue.

In some states the neutral or panel at this point considers each issue individually and makes an award based upon the merits of each (Somers, 1977). This process has been attacked on the grounds that permitting the arbitrator to make an award based upon the selection of offers from both sides diminishes the risk to each party and, therefore, continues to discourage good-faith bargaining.

In other jurisdictions final offers are made, and the arbitrator's decision is based on all issues as a single package. The high risk imposed on the parties in this situation presumably discourages the inclusion of unrealistic demands in the final offer and encourages the parties to reach settlement outside of the arbitration process. The theory behind this belief is presented by Subbaro (1978):

> Since the third-party's order is of the strictly "either-or" variety, the cost of disagreement is minimized if one expects his offer to be ordered. If, however, one expects the neutral to rule in favor of the opponent, then the expected cost of disagreement is high. Negotiators reduce their respective expected costs of disagreement through concessions and compromises. They negotiate (i.e., concede and compromise) at least until their expected costs of disagreement are perceived as equal. At that point, the differences between their offers is expected to be small. (p. 84)

Some of the criticisms of package, final-offer arbitration have been summarized by Lipsky and Barocci (1978). Negotiators who do not perceive the risk of the process, or who see the risk but are unalterably convinced of the strength of their position may not have any incentive to compromise their original positions. As has already been indicated, the more destructive the conflict between the parties, and the stronger their adversarial relationship, the more likely it will be that they will overestimate the quality of their position and underestimate that of the other. This may therefore negate the effectiveness of the final offer process in promoting compromise. In addition, arbitrators may be unable to make a judgment about which of two complex offers is indeed the most reasonable, and thereby end up making an award that is not in the public interest; or the parties may include in an otherwise reasonable package a "sleeper" item that is totally unacceptable to the other side or unreasonable by the other's standards. In any of these situations, the process calls into question the ability of the arbitrator to make a fair and equitable award.

The effectiveness of final offer arbitration by package, as evaluated through analysis of its use in the field, is uncertain. Studies in Massachusetts, for example, have indicated either that it has increased the probability that the parties would reach agreement on their own (Lipsky & Barocci, 1978), or that it has had no effect in increasing incentives to bargain (Somers, 1977). Even among its supporters, however, there is concern that in the long run even package approaches to final offer arbitration too may reduce the effectiveness of bargaining itself as a means of resolving differences between the parties.

Analyses of the effectiveness of last-best-offer arbitration in higher educational institutions are not available. Reportedly, the process has been used at Oakland University, a public institution in Michigan, with what the AAUP chapter there considers to be "reasonable success" (Finkin, Goldstein, & Osborne, 1975, p. 6).

Final-Offer Arbitration with Dual Offers

An interesting variation of final-offer arbitration has been developed in Eugene, Oregon (Feuille & Long, 1974; Long and Feuille, 1974) in which each party, after reaching impasse, presents not one, but two final offer packages to a panel of arbitrators. After holding a hearing, the panel selects one of the four proposals in its entirety as being the "most reasonable." As in other "last-best-offer" arbitration situations, it is suggested that the process changes the incentives of the parties away from widening areas of disagreement in order to receive more favorable treatment in a compromise, and toward developing proposals that are more reasonable than those of the other side. A more specific advantage of submitting two rather than one offer is that it increases uncertainty on both sides of the table.

> If a party only had to present one offer, it seems reasonable to expect that this offer would approximate its final negotiating position and the other party would be aware of that. This relative certainty is substantially reduced when each side may present two offers, for even if one offer does approximate the final negotiating position, the other may not. Not only does this uncertainty put pressure on both parties to be more "reasonable" in their offers, it increases the probability that each party might have one offer so close to an offer of the other party that the two sides can reach their own agreement (Long & Feuille, 1974, p. 198).

Mediation-Arbitration

The newest dispute resolution technique in the public sector, called mediation-arbitration, or med-arb, combines some of the attributes of both processes. Although it retains the sequential characteristics of other impasse processes, with mediation preceding arbitration, it differs from them in having both procedures conducted by the same neutral.

When the neutral functions as a mediator, the parties recognize that if they are unable to come to agreement the neutral will then function as an arbitrator and make an award.

As Kagel and Kagel (1972, p. 12) state, the med-arb technique

> places the med-arbitrator in a position where he does far more than transmit messages between labor and management. He, in effect, becomes

a party to the negotiations in the sense that, while negotiating, each of the contending parties must necessarily seek to convince him that their position is reasonable and acceptable. In doing so, the parties no longer maintain the arm's length attitude normally assumed in orthodox mediation nor the semilegal stance assumed in an arbitration.

THE UTILITY OF IMPASSE PROCESSES IN HIGHER EDUCATION

Each of the procedures discussed in this chapter has been developed over a period of time by experienced professionals in labor relations for the expressed purpose of resolving conflict in the collective bargaining setting. How appropriate and useful are they to the college or university that has adopted collective bargaining? The answer to that question depends to a great extent upon the values of the parties and their perception of the purposes of collective bargaining and the unique properties of higher educational institutions. To examine these issues more closely, we must first discuss the role that these dispute resolution mechanisms play in the philosophy of collective bargaining. We will then examine the assumptions that appear to be related to the use of these impasse techniques and their relevance to constructive conflict and integrative bargaining.

Costs of Disagreement

The traditional perspective of collective bargaining is that it cannot function without the availability of the strike as a means of bringing pressure on both parties to reach agreement. Strikes fill three functions (Bowers, 1973): they provide an impetus to the processes of concession and compromise, they create a sense of urgency that fosters agreement, and they impose a cost of disagreement upon the parties.

Because of the almost universal proscription against strikes in states with enabling legislation, collective bargaining by public employees has always been problematic. Mediation has always been an accepted practice in the private sector, since it did not interfere with the ability of the parties to reach their own agreement without external interference, and because it can be helpful in situations in which the strike is an ultimate possibility and the parties therefore have an incentive to agree. Although mediation has been adopted in public sector bargaining as well, without the possibility of a strike there is no countervailing force to the right of management to either accept or reject the union offer, no sense of urgency in reaching agreement, and no cost to management of not agreeing. The usefulness of mediation in such a situation is significantly lessened.

A major principle of collective bargaining is that two parties will not agree unless there are significant costs of disagreement. The strike is the process by which those costs are imposed. Stevens (1966) has suggested that if these same costs could be exacted by some other means, a "strike-like" process could serve the same function as a strike. He recommended the adoption of compulsory, binding arbitration as a process that comes closest to imposing the same costs of disagreement that a strike would, as long as (1) resort to a strike is precluded; (2) either party can invoke arbitration; and (3) awards are based on a one-or-the-other principle. Although there has been almost no literature commenting on the utility of binding interest arbitration in higher education, a later work by Stevens (1972) arguing for its utilization in public sector bargaining appeared in the pages of the *AAUP Bulletin*, indicating at least the belief on the part of some academics that it was not entirely unrelated to the needs of colleges and universities.

Assumptions of Impasse Procedures

To various degrees, each of the accepted impasse procedures in public sector bargaining are predicated on, and in some ways intensify, the traditional view of collective bargaining as an exercise in relative power. The focus of the processes, and the basis for their presumed effectiveness, is the degree to which they have the ability to increase both the perceived and the actual costs of nonagreement. Questions related to the relationships between the negotiating parties get lost in this coercive environment.

In the final analysis, the ultimate rationale for binding arbitration of any type is that it can motivate the parties to bargain an agreement. Their failure to do so may mean the imposition of a decision by a third party, which neither supports. Laboratory evidence suggests that in fact bargainers faced with the possibility of having a binding decision made by a third party in case of impasse are more likely to make concessions and are more conciliatory than are bargainers not subject to binding arbitration (Johnson & Pruitt, 1972). Wollett (1972) has even suggested, with tongue in cheek, that the costs to each party of engaging in arbitration, and therefore their desire to reach agreement and avoid impasse, could be increased by implementation of the "klutz theory" of dispute settlement. This theory requires that arbitrators be selected from a panel of klutzes (a klutz in Yiddish is a congenital bungler), thus adding "a new dimension of fear," and making "the risks of non-agreement intolerable."

Arbitration, even last-offer, package arbitration, encourages parties to think in terms of conservative positions and adversarial relationships. One side will still win and one will lose, and the parties must engage in a guessing game to determine the probability that their offer will be selected rather than that of their opponent. To the extent that the process motivates the parties to alter their original position, it does so by suggesting the possibility of compromise rather than the establishment of creative new alternatives that might prove more suitable to each.

Mediation, except when it is combined with arbitration in med-arb, is less coercive, and therefore more agreeable to the conventional notions of academic decisionmaking. However, its greatest weakness is that it functions through the controlling and manipulating of communications by the neutral. By deciding what elements of the attitudes and orientation of each side should be communicated to the other, the mediator prevents hostile and competitive interaction from limiting the parties' willingness to make concessions. At the same time, however, the parties are never really made fully aware of the complete positions of the other, nor are there opportunities, given the structure of the arrangements, to explore integrative alternatives.

In addition, both mediation and arbitration (fact-finding is not treated separately, since it is a variant of either of the other two processes, depending upon the orientation of the neutral and the statutes under which it operates) share three major failings.

First, both are concerned with the settlement of an immediate dispute. If the long-term relationships of the parties are considered at all, which they seldom are, they are certainly of secondary significance.

Second, both processes function in higher education as they do in every other collective bargaining relationship. Neither has been altered to accommodate the distinct environment of higher education or to reflect its unusual "employer-employee" relationships.

Third, and from the perspective of this book, most important, each of these third-party neutral interventions takes place after the parties have reached impasse in their relationship, which is the point at which any intervention is least likely to be effective.

Understanding the nature of impasse procedures in collective bargaining, and their potential impact upon institutions of higher education, is important because there is evidence that where such dispute resolution procedures exist they tend to be used. A study of bargaining in the 16 public community colleges in New Jersey, for example (Begin, Settle, & Berke-Weiss, 1977), indicates that over a nine-year period the institutions negotiated a total of 62 contracts. The New Jersey collective bargaining law provides for a two-step process of mediation and fact-finding. Mediation was used a total of 28 times, or in 45% of the contracts, while fact-finding was used 12 times, or in 19% of the negotiations. Only one college did not use either process in any of its negotiations, and three used one or both of the processes in every negotiation. The report contains no indication of the effects of mediation or fact-finding on the outcomes of the negotiations, or upon the relationships between the parties, although the high rate of use suggests that it may have a chilling effect on the bargaining process.

The use of accepted impasse procedures in the bargaining college or university, then, appears to be well suited to resolving conflict *if* the institution has adopted and wishes to perpetuate a distributive bargaining orientation. If it wishes to move toward creative academic bargaining, however, it will have to reconsider constructive means of minimizing the probability of impasse, rather than relying on traditional or newly developed impasse processes to serve as the major forum for conflict management in the institution.

6

The Tactics
of Creative
Academic Bargaining

The industrial model cannot be imposed blindly on the academic world. (Syracuse University, 1973)

PREVIOUS CHAPTERS have presented concepts related to cooperation and competition, intergroup conflict, various bargaining orientations, problem solving, and dispute resolution techniques commonly used in labor relations. The purpose in doing so has been to provide background that will lead to an understanding of some of the behavioral aspects of academic bargaining. This chapter draws upon these concepts to develop a number of tactics which can be adopted by bargainers to promote creative academic bargaining and constructive approaches to the management of conflict in the unionized institution.

The basic assumptions of a tactical orientation to more creative academic bargaining are:

1. Acceptance by the parties of what are commonly understood to be the traditional relationships of collective bargaining.
2. The bargaining relationship, except perhaps at impasse, will involve only the two parties.
3. Although the effects of tactics may be intensified by reciprocation of the other side (indeed, the focus of many tactics is the eliciting of reciprocity), they can either be adopted unilaterally by one bargaining party, or require joint agreement on an activity so similar to traditional bargaining behavior that it should encounter relatively little resistance from the other.

Because the tactical suggestions presented here are modest in nature, it should not be expected that they will by themselves completely transform a bitter and contentious bargaining relationship into a constructive and mutually beneficial one. While their adoption should have a measurable effect upon the relationships between the parties, significant change will require not more effective tactics, but an alteration in the basic structure and environment in which academic bargaining takes place. In the long term, unions and administrations should consider these tactical suggestions, if successfully implemented, as serving as a foundation upon which they can more profitably explore the strategic suggestions recommended in the following chapters.

A major emphasis of the tactical suggestions made here is to improve accommodative relationships between union and administration by increasing levels of trust and facilitating cooperative activities. It assumes that at least one, and preferably both, of the parties have an interest in moving from destructive to constructive conflict, but that their relationship is not yet developed to the point where they are willing or able to take the risks related to attempts to significantly alter the environment in which they function, and thus to move from accommodation to integrative approaches to bargaining. The parties, therefore, continue the traditional labor-management format as an expected part of their interaction.

Although specific recommendations are given, it is recognized that in some settings each of them may not be appropriate, and in others not possible (for example, suggestions on administrative behavior during a representational election is of no value to a campus already negotiating its second or third contract). It is not assumed that it is necessary for a campus to adopt *all* of these ideas in order to have a positive effect on union-administration relationships. However, it is probably true that in order to be effective there must be reasonable consistency in the positions the parties take defining their relationship, and it should not be expected that engaging in cooperative behavior in one area and competitive and destructive behavior in another will have any major consequences on the developing relationship.

If the major long-term objective of tactical orientations toward academic bargaining is to prepare the parties to consider experimenting with more critical strategic change, then perhaps it is fair to categorize the short-term objective as "academic peace." Peace as an alternative to war can be an end in itself, or it can mark the point of departure for new collaborative relationships.

The concept of academic peace is similar to that of "industrial peace" defined by Golden and Parker (1955), based on a number of case studies carried out to determine factors related to the quality of union-management relationships in various industrial settings. They summarized the nine "causes of industrial peace" to include the following:

1. There is a full acceptance by management of the collective bargaining process and of unionization as an institution. The company considers a strong union an asset to management.

2. The union fully accepts private ownership and operation of the industry; it recognizes that the welfare of its members depends upon the successful operation of its business.

3. The union is strong, responsible, and democratic.

4. The company stays out of the union's internal affairs; it does not seek to alienate the workers' allegiance to their union.

5. Mutual trust and confidence exist between the parties. There have been no serious ideological incompatibilities.

6. Neither party to bargaining has adopted a legalistic approach to the solution of problems in the relationship.

7. Negotiations are problem-centered; more time is spent on day-to-day problems than on defining abstract principles.

8. There is widespread union-management consultation and highly developed information sharing.

9. Grievances are settled promptly, in the local plant whenever possible. There is flexibility and informality in the procedure. (Golden & Parker, 1955, p. 47)

The first two points are obviously the most critical, and in many higher educational institutions the most problematic aspects of the administration-union relationship. Put into terms more closely related to colleges and universities, these "causes of academic peace" could be rephrased as follows:

1. The administration recognizes the legitimacy of collective bargaining as one means by which faculty may participate in governance processes characterized by shared authority. The representatives selected by the bargaining agent to negotiate with the administration are accepted as truly representing faculty interests, and their positions considered to accurately reflect the concerns of their constituencies. Participation by faculty in the governance of their institution is essential for the maintenance of strong and effective programs. The administration thus commits itself to collaborate with the union and other legitimate representatives of faculty and institutional constituencies as they attempt to employ integrative and creative processes through which both faculty and administration interests may be satisfied.

2. The union recognizes the responsibility of the administration for managing the institution and its legitimacy in representing the interests of the public through proper utilization of authority delegated to it by the trustees. Participation by administration in the governance of their institution is essential for the maintenance

of strong and effective programs. The union thus commits itself to collaborate with the administration and other legitimate representatives of faculty and institutional constituencies as they attempt to employ integrative and creative processes through which both faculty and administrative interests may be satisfied.

These two statements reflect specific values and cannot be imposed by fiat upon any administration or union. Presenting them, however, provides an opportunity to express once again, in explicit form, the orientation of the creative bargaining approach. It does not necessarily advocate the unionization of faculties, nor does it necessarily suggest that, if unionized, the statements above reflect the most appropriate relationship between a union and the administration. Rather it presents the most effective tactics and strategies to follow *if* the parties to a collective bargaining relationship wish to change from a destructive to a constructive orientation to conflict management. In this context, the legitimacy of both parties must obviously be recognized and their roles accepted by the other. If the administration focuses its energies on reducing or eliminating union influence or the union denies the decision-making authority of the administration and attempts to undermine its credibility, both will find academic "peace" only with the defeat of the other side. They will forego any opportunities to engage in mutually rewarding constructive activities with the other.

This chapter is divided into four sections. The first discusses a number of cooperative orientations to bargaining and the context for cooperative tactics. The second section discusses tactics related to the prenegotiation experiences of the parties. Section three includes means of strengthening intergroup relations between the bargaining teams through tactics employed in preparing the proposals that each team will place on the bargaining table and engaging in negotiations itself. Finally, the last section suggests tactics for administering the contract that are likely to promote cooperation between the parties.

THE CONTEXT FOR COOPERATIVE TACTICS

The paradigm for conflict in chapter 3 included five different orientations resulting from concerns for achieving one's own goals and concerns for the goals of the other party. Two of these orientations, ignoring the conflict or engaging in win-lose competition, will not be considered in this chapter because neither includes any degree of interest by one party in meeting the needs of the other. The three remaining orientations are *appeasement,* in which one party sacrifices its own interests in order to permit the other party to achieve its goals;

compromise, in which the parties each reduce their aspirations and share available payoffs; and *collaboration*, in which parties search for alternative outcomes that fully meet their joint needs.

Appeasement

To the naive bargainer, and particularly one committed to the collegial image of colleges and universities, the concept of appeasement, or unconditional cooperation, has a certain appeal. Agreeing to the demands of the other bargainer would appear to be an effective means of convincing the other of one's intention to cooperate. Even if the other party initially takes advantage of the willingness to be forthcoming, according to the rationale of this position, the establishment of high levels of trust resulting from this approach will eventually create optimum conditions for cooperation that will be to the advantage of both parties. Both experience and laboratory experiments indicate that this outcome does not occur, however.

In the winter of 1966-67, the faculty of Chicago's two-year municipal colleges unionized and went out on two strikes at least in part caused by the uncertainty of the bargaining relationship and a number of unresolved grievances that had developed when the colleges were part of the city school system. As reported by Bowen (1977), negotiations were adversarial in nature from the beginning. The board's newly hired negotiator asked for union agreement on a number of matters as a precondition to bargaining, the board was intransigent on salary issues and secured a court injunction after the first strike, and the union instituted new demands for reduced loads when the bargaining resumed.

The board then suddenly changed its bargaining posture and agreed to the majority of union demands. The outcomes of the negotiations "exceeded the wildest dreams of the union officers," stated Bowen. "Just why the board switched from rigid intransigence to overwhelming generosity isn't clear, but it was probably because both parties were pioneers without a road map, and because the board believed that a generous settlement would erase the name calling passions of the strike" (Bowen, 1977, p. 617).

What was the long-term effect of this change from a competitive to an unconditionally cooperative strategy? Almost ten years later, after their fifth strike since the formation of the union, Bowen (1977) stated:

> The few teachers who chose to cross the picket lines are isolated. The credibility of the chancellor—and of all administrators—is at a low ebb. Administrative proposals are greeted with suspicion and negativism. Fac-

ulty members are told they have no rights except those in the written board/union agreement. There is a strong "we-they" dichotomy between administrators and teaching faculty and a seige mentality on both sides. The distinction between an adversary and an enemy is poorly understood. (p. 616)

Why should efforts to yield to an adversary's demands lead to interaction that is still more competitive rather than cooperative? An experiment dealing with the response of negotiators to pacifist strategies (Shure, Meeker, & Hansford, 1965) may provide some insights.

Shure designed a bargaining game in which individuals who were given a competitive orientation were playing against a simulated bargainer who was programed for an unconditionally cooperative strategy.

After playing the game four times, about 80% of the negotiators who originally had said that they would adopt a cooperative strategy had changed their positions and were competing and exhibiting dominating behavior.

Shure indicates that the tactics of the pacifist are meant to induce in the adversary a recognition of the unfairness of his claims and the immorality of his means, to establish his own personal resolve, and to give reassurance that he has acted and will act in good faith. Presumably, this should induce the other bargainer to be cooperative as well. What apparently actually happens, however, is that the bargainers learn early in the game that they can dominate with impunity, and rather than soften their demands they plan for increased payoffs. "The pacifist's tactics apparently invite exploitation and aggression even among those who do not begin with such intentions" (p. 116).

Similar studies (Swingle, 1970; Kuhlman & Marshello, 1975; Reychler, 1979) have confirmed these findings and indicate that unconditionally cooperative opponents in a bargaining game are more likely to be exploited, not when they are weak, but when they are perceived as strong but unwilling to use their power to punish the other. This has significant implications for the selection of tactics by an administration, particularly one which had been considered as autocratic and perceived by the union as having a great deal of power. Swingle's (1970) findings suggest that inordinate cooperation under such circumstances may cause the union to evaluate the administration negatively, and thus invite exploitation on the grounds that "a stupid opponent deserves to be exploited" (p. 131). An alternative explanation by Swingle is that "a highly cooperative strategy by an extremely powerful opponent may not be viewed as a desire to cooperate, but rather as hesitation from fear or guilt about the effects of the use of such power. An opponent perceived as hesitant may be exploited because the credibility of his use of the potent punisher is reduced" (p. 132).

Compromise

The second conflict orientation that includes as a component some concern for the goals of the other party is compromise. The impact of the compromise expectation upon inhibiting problem-solving behavior has already been noted. The basic problem of compromise is that it prevents either party from achieving its goals.

Collaboration

The most satisfactory conflict orientation, both from the perspective of avoiding exploitation as well as that of increasing integrative possibilities, is one which moves the parties toward collaboration. The most effective posture of the parties in this collaborative relationship has been described by Pruitt and Lewis (1977) as "flexible rigidity." This apparently paradoxical description is based upon considering a bargainer's position from two perspectives. On the one hand, bargainers establish certain *aspiration levels,* and they can be either rigid or flexible in the degree to which they maintain their support of these goals during the bargaining interchange. On the other, bargainers can consider the *means* by which their goals may be achieved, with adherence to a small range of possibilities indicating rigidity, and willingness to consider a number of alternatives reflecting flexibility. When bargainers have inflexible goals, and pursue them through inflexible means, they engage in distributive bargaining with win-lose orientations. Both parties wish to achieve their goals, and they have become committed to a limited, and usually incompatible, range of means for doing so. Academic bargaining often assumes this posture, with the demands placed on the table reflecting the means that a group has decided (often erroneously) will best meet their goals, and the unwillingness of the group, once committed to those means, to fully consider alternatives that would equally, or even more effectively, do so.

It is possible for both parties to enter the bargaining relationship with both flexible goals *and* flexible means. This is likely to occur when they consider the reaching of an agreement to be of greater importance than the agreement itself. The consequence of this orientation may be not only for both parties to make premature concessions, thus reducing the potential payoff to each, but also to reach agreement before other, and perhaps more integrative, alternatives can be explored.

When the parties approach each other with flexible goals, but inflexible means, they are apt to resolve their interaction by compromise, a lose-lose orientation in which neither party obtains its desired results.

The concept of "flexible rigidity" calls for the parties to establish high and inflexible aspirations and goals. Unless these goals are present, and unless the parties insist that any acceptable outcome must meet them, the incentive to search for integrative solutions will be significantly diminished. At the same time, the establishment of rigid goals must be accompanied by a willingness to consider a great variety of alternative means to reaching the goals. The parties must be flexible in their approach toward designing programs that will be consistent with their aspirations, and both parties must continue to search for an alternative that will implement not only their goal, but that of the other party as well.

This paradigm for viewing ends and means as flexible or inflexible illustrates clearly that the difference between distributive and integrative approaches to bargaining is not that one is a "hard" approach and the other is "soft." To be successful, integrative, collaborative, or problem-solving approaches demand that the parties establish high aspirations and refuse to accept unsatisfactory solutions. At the same time, they must engage in cooperative activities with the other group to search for or create new programs, or procedures which not only satisfy one's own group, but also the goals of the other as well.

MANAGING PREBARGAINING CONFLICT

The Representational Election

When a union has evidence of support from a majority of the faculty, it can go to the administration and ask to be recognized as a bargaining agent. The institution may agree to do so, and bargaining may commence.

The institution may refuse to recognize the union, however, and thereby require that a representational election be held under the auspices of the National Labor Relations Board (for private institutions), or the state public employee relations board (for public institutions). At this point, the reaction of the administration can have a significant impact upon the future course of bargaining on the campus.

The number of institutions in which bargaining has been rejected in a representational election is small, although the proportion of elections resulting in a victory for the "no agent" option has increased during the past several years. However, for the most part those institutions rejecting bargaining have been those with characteristics that typically do not engage in bargaining, such as small independent liberal arts colleges, or large prestigious multiversities. The probability of bargaining being rejected in a community college or public regional university is quite small. It may be that understated administrative opposition to bargaining may have some impact in the complex, research-oriented institution if the faculty oligarchy is also in opposition. There is no evidence to indicate that administrative opposition to bargaining in institutions of lesser prestige has any effect upon reducing the probability of unionization.

Waging, and losing, an antibargaining campaign on campus has several effects. First, the history of previous competition will make it more difficult for the groups to cooperate later in their relationship (Worchel et al., 1978; Deutsch, 1969). Their previous interaction will inhibit the relaxation of group boundaries and lower the attraction of the groups for each other. This attraction will become even less if their attempt to cooperate (as manifested by successful completion of a mutually acceptable contract, for example) results instead in failure.

In addition, when groups are engaged in active and aggressive competition, they are likely to select as their leaders highly aggressive group members. They will tend to represent the more radical elements of the adversary group and, as will be recalled, being themselves competitive will find it much more difficult to engage in cooperative activity.

In view of these effects, therefore, involvement in an antibargaining campaign is not a tactic that should be utilized by an administration wishing to develop a cooperative and creative approach to bargaining on campus. The campaign is likely to be ineffective and its consequences will be to reduce intergroup attraction and lend support to leaders who will be less likely to cooperate.

It has been recognized in the industrial sector that these first stages in the bargaining relationship may be among the most important. The same principle holds in the academic world, and advice given to support industrial peace applies as well to the academic bargainer looking toward the establishment of creative bargaining relationships.

> If [new bargaining relationships] could be started on a more constructive footing, their quality would doubtless be improved. To this end, unions would do well to consider more carefully the effects of organizing campaigns upon eventual collective bargaining. Members of management might find much to change in their initial reactions to a union campaign if they were to consider seriously the consequences of their policies for later collective bargaining (Golden & Parker, 1955, p. 28).

As a general rule, therefore, if unionization is inevitable, constructive bargaining can be facilitated by recognizing the union without the need for a representational election. This was the course taken by Rutgers University, and it is considered to be one of the reasons that the administration-union relationship at that institution has been relatively harmonious (Garbarino, 1977, p. 56). If a representational election is necessary because of the existence of more than one potential bargaining agent, the administration should not participate in the election nor make any statements that could be construed by the union to indicate an antiunion position.

Role of Department Chairpersons

The status of the chairpersons has become a major issue in determining the appropriate unit in many colleges and universities facing a representational election. In many cases, the administration has claimed that chairpersons are administrative representatives who make effective recommendations concerning personnel and should be excluded from the bargaining unit as supervisors. A common union argument is that chairpersons are faculty representatives, that the chairpersons' actions related to personnel are recommendations only with no force or effect, and, therefore, they should be included in the bargaining unit.

Labor relations boards have resolved this issue on a case by case basis, usually depending upon findings of fact related to the actual role that chairpersons play in institutional governance. It is true that there are potentially serious administrative consequences involved, since, for example, chairpersons often have responsibility for evaluating the performance of colleagues, or serve as the first grievance level—both activities that could not easily be entrusted by management to a person who was a member of the same bargaining unit. Yet despite the administrative difficulties involved, departmental chairpersons should be included in the bargaining unit as a tactic to facilitate the development of creative and constructive bargaining.

There are two related reasons for this suggestion. First, when groups are homogeneous in terms of the values of their members, or the mutuality of their interests, conflict between that group and other groups becomes more intense. As the values and interests of a group become less uniform, the creation of subgroups fractionates the major groups and lessens the intensity of conflict between them (Druckman & Zechmeister, 1973). Group flexibility, and therefore the possibility of moving toward collaboration rather than dogmatic adherence to a specific position, is likely to increase as the membership and roles of participants in the bargaining groups becomes more diversified. The mere presence of persons such as chairpersons with administrative roles and sensitivities on the union bargaining team should be helpful at least to some extent in reducing the intensity of the intergroup conflict and in mediating the we-they orientation of bargaining.

Second, as a rule department chairpersons are among the most conservative faculty, and the most supportive of administrative policies. They are likely to be selected from among the older faculty, and to represent more traditional values than the younger "locals" who are likely to compose the leadership of a new union (Ladd & Lipsett, 1973). The presence of chairpersons in the bargaining unit, therefore, may moderate what might otherwise be extreme union demands, and at the same time offer the possibility of introducing more conservative leadership into the union hierarchy. As in other group conflict situations, the moderates in the union group can serve as a link to moderates in the administration group, and thus help to bring their more extremist teammates together (Druckman & Zechmeister, 1973).

Including chairpersons in the bargaining unit, therefore, appears to be a potentially useful tactic for increasing flexibility and providing opportunities for more creative bargaining. In general, increasing the heterogeneity of both bargaining teams is helpful in negotiating situations, and additional recommendations promoting this diversity will be discussed in the following chapter. Inclusion of chairpersons in the bargaining unit has been recommended by the Carnegie Commission (1973, p. 49), although for reasons unrelated to the arguments presented here.

Preplanning Strategy

In the earlier discussion of the Blake and Mouton experiments in intergroup conflict it was noted that once competitive groups had determined their solution to a problem and were given an opportunity to plan the strategies that they would use in forthcoming negotiations, they were more likely to believe that their solution was better than the other group's, less likely to understand the other group's position after debate, and more likely to deadlock rather than mutually agree that one solution was better than the other. Many of the experimentally designed features of the Blake and Mouton settings reflect the traditional collective bargaining situation, including the preplanning by each group of its bargaining strategy. Before academic negotiators sit down at the bargaining table, it is common practice for them to hold unilateral meetings at which they plan their strategy for the forthcoming sessions. Several studies (Druckman, 1968; Bass, 1966) have evaluated the effects of such prenegotiating experiences.

Druckman's (1968) findings were based upon bargaining in a complex, zero-sum game that attempted to replicate a union-management collective bargaining situation. After participants were assigned to either union or management teams, they were given information about the unresolved issues on the table, as well as background and rationale for each union demand and company offer. Some union and management teams were given a 40-minute period during which they were to meet together and jointly discuss the issues that they would shortly be dealing with at the bargaining table. Other groups were separated, and the labor and management teams were told to spend their time planning bargaining strategy.

Compared to the bargaining results of teams that had studied the issues together, planning strategy was found to lead to hardening of positions, less agreement, and less yielding by the negotiators. Bass (1966), using a bargaining simulation with a greater number of variables and experimental conditions, reached the same conclusions concerning the likelihood of deadlocks between bargainers who had spent time unilaterally planning bargaining strategy. In one series of experiments with imposed negotiation deadlines, groups that planned strategies took an average of 163 minutes to negotiate a contract, compared to under 30 minutes for groups that did not.

One of the experimental conditions in both studies was the bilateral study of issues, in which both teams worked together prior to negotiations to freely discuss the issues without considering strategies. The desirability of bilateral study will be more fully discussed in the next chapter, since it involves the willing participation of both parties and therefore by our definition is a strategy rather than a tactic. An interesting aspect of the Bass study, however, was the incorporation into one series of experiments of a condition in which each team met separately prior to negotiations, but instead of developing strategy, discussed among themselves the positions of both parties.

This unilateral study of issues was as effective as bilateral study of issues in permitting quick agreement on contract terms and in avoiding deadlocks. While bilateral study of issues may be a more desirable process in academic bargaining because it is more consistent with academic norms, the use of unilateral study of issues might be considered as an alternative in those situations in which one of the parties is interested in making the bargaining relationship less destructive, but joint study is not yet feasible.

Training Negotiators

We have previously indicated the problems associated with hiring external negotiators to conduct bargaining either for the administration or the faculty bargaining team. Not only are such persons likely to bring with them a bargaining orientation developed in a different setting and often inappropriate to the academic environment, but they are apt to be unfamiliar with the history, relationships, and specific problems and opportunities of the individual campus. Such persons can often assist in "winning" a negotiation, but they can rarely assist the institution to strengthen its own internal operations.

The use of inexperienced internal negotiators often leads to destructive conflict as well. Having no knowledge of collective bargaining, they may make serious legal errors, lack skills to plan or implement successful tactics, and inadvertantly lead the institution down a road in which destructive conflict becomes inevitable.

This dilemma suggests two alternatives for academic bargainers: educate trained negotiators about the norms, traditions, attitudes, and purposes of colleges and universities, or take faculty and administrators already socialized in these institutions and train them to bargain. The latter appears to be the more reasonable alternative if the ultimate objective is to move toward the creation of new structures and processes in which constructive bargaining is more likely to take place.

This training can be of two types. The first type would introduce the academic negotiator to the law and processes of collective bargaining and the development of bargaining in the academic and nonacademic environment. The second type of training orientation, and the more interesting from the perspective of this book, includes team development and intergroup activities in which negotiators have an opportunity to experience the bargaining process in a supportive environment and learn for themselves the consequences of certain kinds of behaviors. An example of this kind of training activity is reported by Stern and Pearse (1968) in their work with the Amalgamated Meat Cutters and Retail Food Store Employees Union (Local 342), and summarized here in the belief that this same kind of training experience can be useful in a professional environment.

Union and supermarket employers association relationships had become so exceptionally bitter during a previous round of contract negotiations that the union decided to develop a training program for its negotiators that would assist them in moving toward problem-solving approaches to bargaining. They decided to do this by educating them in techniques of conflict resolution and bargaining, by communicating more openly with the membership about realistic possibilities in contract settlements rather than presenting unrealistic demands that could never be met, and by beginning the intraunion prebargaining activity at an early date to have time to explore and resolve any conflict existing between the union's own negotiators.

The activities designed and coordinated for them by a team of applied behavioral scientists included the use of training groups (T groups) to assist in team-building, communications workshops to assist the negotiators in developing skills in two-way communications, and collective bargaining workshops in which negotiators could experiment with new bargaining behaviors and roles.

At the conclusion of the actual negotiations, which were highly successful from the union's perspective, the union attributed a number of positive results to the training program. Among them were the greater involvement of various union constituencies in jointly setting negotiations goals, better communications between the bargaining team and rank and file members as the negotiations progressed, and better understanding by the rank and file of the union positions during bargaining and the probable outcomes as bargaining proceeded.

In calling for new and more productive approaches to collective bargaining, Stern and Pearse suggest that it would be useful for both union and management teams to learn the techniques of integrative bargaining. This is a matter that we shall discuss in the next chapters, because it suggests strategic, rather than merely tactical, approaches to bargaining. But the fascinating finding of this study is that positive results were achieved by one party acting unilaterally. It *is* possible to induce cooperation in a competitive partner and to gain more from cooperation than from competition, as this prenegotiating experience demonstrates.

A somewhat different approach to working with one bargaining team to create cooperative and constructive union-management relations in what had previously been a continuous win-lose confrontation was reported by Blake and Mouton (1962). Asking the question "What happens when one group which is dedicated to battle meets an 'adversary' which no longer acts like one?" social scientists provided laboratory training experiences to management personnel in a large corporation focusing upon issues of intergroup conflict and collaboration.

The behavioral science intervention with management's bargaining team began with norm-setting conferences in which management's bargainers confronted differences in attitudes among their own members, ranging from strong desires to cooperate as a means of encouraging reciprocity, to beliefs that all-out warfare would be necessary to get the union to "straighten out" and be responsible. As a result of these conferences, consensus developed that only collaboration offered the possibility for long-term benefits to the company, and common attitudes such as the desirability of treating the union and its officers with dignity and respect were developed as norms to support this goal. These norms were to be sorely tested in the negotiations that followed, but they managed to prevail at least in part because the behavioral scientist was able to observe the negotiations and provide corrective interventions to management behavior and attitudes at appropriate times.

While management was discussing ways in which they could establish appropriate collaborative relationships, the union was meeting unilaterally to plan its own strategy. In the belief that it had previously not spent enough time in this process, it developed its new proposals over a six-month period. The list of demands was belligerent and aggressive in tone, and contained many items known to be unacceptable to management.

Despite the preparation of management for cooperation, the delivery of the union demands to management and a subsequent analysis of the differences between them and management's position immediately reinforced the previous attitudes of some managers that the union was impossible to deal with, and that their demands were outrageous and unreasonable and should be immediately rejected. Management began to plan a campaign to seize the initiative from the union and go directly to the workers to convince them of management's good intentions and the visciousness of the union.

At this point, the behavioral scientist intervened to indicate the self-perpetuating and disastrous consequences of their reaction, and to suggest ways in which they might change the position of the union from win-lose hostility to cooperation. It was suggested that rather than look only at differences between the management and union position, an analysis also be done of similarities. While this analysis revealed significant differences, it also led to an understanding that some points in dispute were not as different as had originally been thought. Management was therefore able to approach the next bargaining session with a problem-solving rather than with a confrontation orientation.

As a result of interventions of this kind, the normal consequences of win-lose bargaining (presenting firm positions, failure to understand the position of the other side, using questions to belittle the other's position rather than to understand it, focusing attention on differences rather than similarities in positions) were averted. Although elements of destructive conflict emerged at many points during the negotiation, the application of tactics designed to elicit cooperation proved in the long run to be effective, and led to long-term collaborative relationships between the parties.

MANAGING BARGAINING CONFLICT

Establishing Fair Demands

When groups prepare to initiate their bargaining activities and prepare their demands, two tendencies are often seen. First, demands are inflated well beyond what the group expects to receive in order that it may have some "bargaining room." Second, particularly in a new bargaining relationship, bargaining teams often solicit suggestions from the membership for items to be placed on the table, and then feel compelled to include all of them in their demands for political reasons.

Both tactics are known and understood by experienced bargainers and, used properly, neither should necessarily intensify destructive conflict. However, when the use of these tactics is seen as unfair—when demands are either so unrealistically high that they give the opponent no information at all about the range within which bargaining can be conducted, or so numerous that they provide no clue as to what issues really are important to the other — then there will be a tendency to accept the demands as reflecting a challenge to enter into a highly competitive interaction. In this situation, repeated statements by the team issuing the demands that it desires to engage in constructive interaction may be considered to be duplicitous by the other team and intensify their anger.

The escalation of demands has several causes. An obvious one is the instructions given to bargainers to ask for what they think they "deserve," rather than what they believe they can reasonably get, so that the demands include "the maximum desires of the faculty" (Finkin et al., 1975, p. 49). Somewhat more sophisticated is the concept suggested by Finkin that if the faculty's demands contain their maximum positions, at least some of that language is likely to be included in the counteroffer the administration often drafts based on the union's proposal (p. 49). Demands are also inflated by the perception of the parties that they are involved in a distributive relationship and, to some extent, by the legal requirements of bargaining as seen from an adversarial perspective. The union asks for more than it expects to receive, and the administration offers less than it will eventually yield because neither knows what the best offer of the other party will be. Rationality, as defined in a distributive relationship, suggests that to do otherwise makes it possible that one could ask for less than the other was prepared to offer — a possibility that the bargainer cannot afford to overlook.

To a great extent, this orientation is supported by legal interpretations of the requirement that parties "bargain in good faith." The ability of the bargainers to demonstrate that they have made concessions from their opening positions is one factor often examined by state labor relations boards, the NLRB, and the courts in hearing charges of bad-faith bargaining. Since such accusations are not unusual given the tactics and strategies of the distributive orientation, parties may attempt to protect themselves by beginning with unreasonable demands or counteroffers so that movement away from these positions will protect them from the legal sanctions that would follow if they were found guilty of not bargaining in good faith. This rather convoluted, Alice-in-Wonderland approach to the making of offers and counteroffers, which requires bargainers to make bad-faith offers so that they can bargain in good faith, need only occur in situations of low trust in which parties believe that the other may in fact resort to external agencies to apply sanctions against them. As trust increases, the parties can reduce the discrepancy between initial offers and mutually understood probable outcomes so that their bargaining relationship is more likely to be seen as being fair.

But what does "fairness" mean in bargaining? Bartos (1977) has stated that it implies that the parties are willing to accept the midpoint of their demands and offers as a solution to their negotiation. In order to achieve this state, the parties must determine the appropriate level of their opening bid. For any bargainable issue, possible solutions have different payoffs for the parties; these payoffs may be positive, negative, or neutral. Bartos suggests that it is in each party's interest to make an opening bid that is as close as possible to having a zero payoff for the other but does not have a negative payoff since an opening offer with a negative payoff is likely to be perceived as an indication that negotiation is not yet possible. When each of the parties reluctantly accepts the offer of the other as a bona fide opening bid, then negotiations can begin and the parties can have a realistic expectation that the eventual outcome will be at the midpoint of these offers.

The Bartos theory assumes, of course, that the parties are operating in a situation in which the level of cooperation is high enough to permit negotiations, but trust is low enough so that each party will take advantage of the other if that is possible. That is why negotiators cannot quickly arrive at a settlement, even though they know once opening bids have been accepted what the settlement is likely (fairly) to be. If one negotiator should, through inexperience or miscalculation, immediately suggest that they compromise their opening positions, the other can appropriately make a counteroffer that falls halfway between the offered compromise and the bargainer's opening bid. For this reason, Bartos suggests that after opening bids are received, the negotiators must proceed by making small concessions on both sides. Each concession is considered fair by the other side as long as it does not force the bargainer to revise the original expectation of what the outcome will be.

This discussion of fairness must distinguish between the fairness of an offer and the fairness of an agreement. An offer is seen as fair when it is perceived as moving the parties toward a fair solution, even if the offer itself is quite distant from the eventual settlement point. The less experienced the bargainers, the more likely the possibility that they will confuse these two definitions. Failing to have insight into the area of probable agreement, and the process of bargaining by which the parties make offers and counteroffers allowing them to meet there, the bargainers are more likely to perceive offers as unfair to the extent they differ from their own offers, rather than to the extent they suggest the need to reassess the probable solution point.

The moral "fairness" of a bargaining result, which is derived from its relationships to standards known and appreciated by both parties, can be reinforced by the power of a "fair" result to focus attention and coordinate the expectations of the parties, even in the absence of communication between them (Schelling, 1957). Schelling's concept of tacit bargaining suggests that certain solutions become prominent in the minds of the negotiators for various reasons, such as, for example, the fact that a mediator recommended it and there is no other prominent feature in the dispute that would make another solution appear more reasonable. When this happens, a specific bargaining result may seem fair simply because it has the power "to communicate its own inevitability to the two parties in such fashion that each appreciates that they both appreciate it" (Schelling, 1957, p. 31). In some situations, "splitting the difference" would be a similar protocol ensuring "fairness."

In addition to seeing the size of the demands of the other party as being fair, the number and range of the demands must be fair as well. The presentation of a large number of demands without evaluation or control by the union team has a number of consequences that are not supportive of constructive relationships and creative bargaining. It obviously makes it more difficult for the other party to understand exactly what the real interests of the union are, and thus it frustrates a problem-solving orientation or intention. Often, such unscreened demands contain elements so blatantly inconsequential that they suggest the lack of serious intent and good faith on the part of the proposer. But perhaps the most serious consequence is in the response that such demands are likely to provoke in the administration.

The outrageous response to the outrageous demand initiates the spiraling nature of destructive conflict and reinforces the competitive and adversarial picture that each side has of the other. It is also likely to make bargaining more difficult because increasing the number of issues in a bargaining interaction is likely to also increase the time needed to reach agreement (Rubin & Brown, 1975, p. 145).

Although as indicated in an earlier chapter some bargaining "experts" recommend the inclusion of many unimportant items in the demands of the parties in order to confuse the opponent, the more effective tactic for the bargainer concerned with developing constructive relationships is that suggested by Byrnes (1977).

> From my experience as a negotiator for a faculty union, I would recommend against including too many excessive and/or throwaway demands. Not only are these extreme proposals difficult to justify to the administration at the bargaining table, but there is a strong possibility that these excessive demands will raise the expectations of the membership. Higher expectations will increase the difficulty of obtaining an acceptable compromise agreement. (p. 22)

Communicating Fair Demands

In addition to understanding the nature of a fair agreement, bargainers must use communications channels to transmit them to the other party. The legal requirement that the parties to bargaining must meet with each other provides access to such channels. However, as Deutsch (1973) has pointed out, the mere existence of communications channels does not guarantee their use, and even when bargainers are compelled by external agencies to use them, there is no guarantee that they will be used effectively.

The need to use communications channels to transmit fair proposals in order to increase joint payoffs to the parties was investigated in a laboratory experiment (Krauss & Deutsch, 1966). Subjects who were tutored in the use of communications to make fair proposals to another negotiator achieved significantly higher payoffs than did subjects who were required to communicate but who were not tutored on what should be said. The experimenters concluded that tutoring the bargainers established a norm of fairness or equity that became part of the context of the experiment. "For a subject in these circumstances to attempt to secure more than his fair share violates the cultural standard of reasonable or sportsmanlike behavior. But when no such restrictions are present, . . . the subject is free to respond to the competitive aspects of the bargaining situation, and this is reflected in his communication behavior as well as his bargaining behavior" (Krauss & Deutsch, 1966, p. 577).

A similar dynamic operates in the academic bargaining environment, and it is possible for a group to communicate to the adversary a desire to engage in constructive bargaining and maintain the credibility of that position even when it is accompanied by a high demand, *as long as it is not so high as to be seen as unfair by the other*. For example, a demand for a 20% yearly salary increase at the beginning of negotiations may be considered as a "fair" initial bargaining stand when the cost of living has gone up 10%, one other college in the area has settled for 12%, and the average settlement in the state has been for 7%, even though the parties both "know" that the settlement in this case will probably be below 10%. An initial demand for a 50% increase would likely be considered by the other party as unfair and an indication of a lack of interest in negotiating in good faith.

Issues and Problems

There are at least two ways that an item can be placed on the bargaining table   as an issue, or as a problem. An issue is usually a demand that includes specific language indicating the party's position and meant to serve as the opening bid in negotiation. A problem is a statement by a party of a felt need. The use of these two methods of presentation have significant implications for the interaction that follows and for the strategy and tactics of the bargainers.

Issues presented as demands can be considered as unilateral solutions to problems. If both parties treat an item as an issue, they will present their demands and counteroffers, and distributive bargaining orientations and tactics are almost assured as the parties attempt to compromise their positions or use power to seek reluctant agreement from the other on one's own terms. Because the problem-solving activity has occurred unilaterally within each group prior to bargaining, and the members of each group share common values and limited information, the "solution" generated by each side is likely not to be a good one, and almost certain not to be the best one available. Each party having committed itself to it, however, will find it difficult to understand the "solution" of the other side. Probably the most limiting factor, however, is the likelihood that, having created two possible solutions, the parties in a distributive bargaining relationship are likely to limit their consideration of alternatives to those two, and to refrain from exploring other alternatives that may be superior to either. Integrative bargaining is promoted when items are brought to the table as problems, rather than as solutions. In such a situation, the parties can explore their perceived needs and those of the other and can begin to establish some means by which alternative ways of solving the problem can be developed that meet the needs of both.

The preparation of opening bargaining positions by either or both parties in academic bargaining almost always takes the form of demands and solutions to problems. A more constructive tactic would be for the parties to experiment with the use of problem statements instead of demands. This could initially be done for a small number of items or it could be done in prenegotiating meetings before bargaining begins at the table. In such a situation, rather than place a demand for an agency shop on the table, the union, for example, might state that it has a problem related to union security which it wants placed on the bargaining agenda. To demand an agency shop immediately provokes arguments opposing it and minimizes the possibility that the myriad of other means by which union security problems could be dealt with, including some that might be unique to the specific setting, will be carefully considered. A collaborative bargainer is more likely to understand and listen carefully to a union express the problems that lack of union security was posing and to work with the union in attempting to find mutually advantageous solutions.

Opening Bids and Concession Rates

We have already discussed the negotiation theory of Bartos that suggests that fair solutions are those that compromise the minimum acceptable offer to each party. It will now be useful to present and discuss several other theories related to opening bids and concession rates and their implications for tactics in constructive academic bargaining.

The matter of opening bids is of critical importance in the bargaining interaction because probably more than any other bids they have a tendency to set the stage for the interaction that follows. "In a sense, a structural tone is given to the players' interactions by their first series of encounters. The early initiation of cooperative moves establishes a framework of expectations and regularities that conditions subsequent plays" (Druckman & Mahoney, 1977, p. 81). If bargainers engage in cooperative behavior early in their relationship, it is likely to lead to the development of trust and collaborative relationships. Should the parties begin by competing, mutual suspicion is the likely consequence (Rubin & Brown, 1975, p. 263).

The "Tough Bargainer."   The first theory to be presented is that of the "tough bargainer" proposed by Siegel and Fouraker (1960). They suggest that the most effective bargainer is one who "(1) opens negotiations with a high request, (2) has a small rate of concession, (3) has a high minimum level of expectation, and (4) is very persistent and quite unyielding" (p. 93). While there is some laboratory evidence to support this contention, it is probably an ineffective and ultimately self-defeating strategy for bargainers who wish ultimately to move toward a cooperative posture. Although it has been found, for example, that hard bargaining positions by one negotiator are likely to result in concessions and "softer" bargaining by the other (Druckman, Zechmeister, & Solomon, 1972), this tactic is appropriate only if the party using it wishes to maintain a competitive orientation and does not see any particular value in moving toward creative bargaining models. Komorita and Brenner (1968) have summed up the advantages and disadvantages of this approach by saying that a firm bargaining strategy increases the probability of reaching an advantageous agreement but reduces the probability of reaching a fair one. As has already been indicated, fairness is an essential element in the development of constructive bargaining.

Reciprocation Strategy.   As an alternative to the "tough bargainer" model, it has been proposed that effective bargaining depends upon reciprocating the concessions of the other party. The evidence for this position is equivocal. Some findings indicate that reciprocation, or a "tit-for-tat" strategy, produces more cooperation than a competitive one, but no more than cooperative or coaxing strategies (Wilson, 1969). In general, however, evidence appears to indicate that reciprocation strategies are effective in inducing cooperation between bargainers (Esser & Komorita, 1975); and that bargainers are responsive to the concession rates of their opponents (Druckman, Zechmeister, & Solomon, 1972).

Making an Initial "Fair" Offer.   There is a third bargaining orientation, which may be adopted by inexperienced bargainers but which is inappropriate for situations of low trust. In this orientation a bargainer makes what is sincerely meant to be a fair offer reflecting what the bargainer believes both sides could achieve were they to engage in continual bargaining. Laboratory data indicate that making an initial "fair" offer and remaining firm thereafter is an ineffective means of reaching agreement (Komorita & Brenner, 1968). This bargaining tactic has been implemented in labor relations in the past, notably at General Electric where it was called Boulewarism (McMurray, 1955). For a number of years, the company engaged in extensive research to determine the needs of its workers, and used these data to offer final package proposals to the union at the bargaining table from which management would not deviate (Healy, 1965). Despite the fact that their offers were more than "fair" by any objective measure, the practice caused considerable labor unrest, and was eventually declared to be an unfair labor practice by the NLRB. This approach, even if it was not illegal, would not be effective in academic bargaining since it is basically unilateral, deprives the union leadership of any satisfaction at the bargaining table, and flouts the union's responsibility for the employee (Healy, 1965).

Graduated Reciprocation in Tension-Reduction.

A fourth bargaining approach, which is related to reciprocal models but which provides even greater incentives to the reluctant cooperator, was developed by Osgood (1961). Called Graduated Reciprocation in Tension-Reduction (GRIT), it suggests reversing the process of incremental, aggressive moves that are reciprocated and create the escalating conflict of situations such as arms races, by introducing instead small, unilateral concessions. The process suggests that faced with a reluctant cooperator, the bargainer can induce trust in the other by making a small, unilateral conciliatory overture, while at the same time suggesting to the adversary a number of alternative steps that could be taken and that would be viewed as reciprocation. The unilateral act is carried out regardless of any statements made by the adversary concerning an intention to respond.

Osgood suggests that this process could reduce intergroup tension and lead toward spiralling levels of cooperation as long as the unilateral concessions were announced in advance, they were graduated in nature, and they spelled out the forms of reciprocity that would be considered as appropriate. The Osgood proposal has been tested in laboratory settings (Pilisuk & Skolnick, 1968) and found to be effective in reducing tension between groups, but only marginally more effective than other matching strategies.

Much of the research on concession rates has been done in artificial settings which lack the complexity, environmental pressures, and continuing relationships characterizing bargaining in the real world. For that reason, it is possible to find research results that support almost every approach as yielding the greatest payoffs to the bargainer utilizing it. In general, however, it seems reasonable to agree with the assessment of Hamner and Yukl (1977) that a hard approach to bargaining may lead to increased payoffs when the bargainer's orientation to the process is that of winning. When the continuing relationship between the parties is important, however, and there is a desire to promote constructive interaction, steady reciprocal concessions may lead to the most mutually satisfactory agreements. The tactical orientation of the constructive bargainer, therefore, should be to (1) make fair offers, and (2) reciprocate all concessions.

The Order of Negotiations

The demands of the bargaining teams will usually include items capable of easy resolution, as well as controversial ones requiring extended time and discussion to understand and to resolve. Items capable of quick resolution may include matters on which the parties agree, but which one or the other, for some reason, wishes to have codified in the contract, issues that have low- or no-cost implications, and issues that are of great importance to one party and of negligible importance to the other.

Reaching agreement on these noncontroversial items before engaging in full negotiation on more contentious issues is a useful tactic to promote more productive negotiations for several reasons. It provides an opportunity for the negotiators to become familiar with each other's style, and thus possibly prevent later problems due to misunderstandings (Graham & Walters, 1973). Of perhaps even greater importance, however, is that communication over simple issues can assist in establishing norms of cooperation and concern for each other's needs between the parties. It also provides a setting in which each party can experiment with the effects of granting concessions to the other and to strengthen norms of reciprocation. This reservoir of experience with a cooperative party may provide a supportive psychological setting when the parties later attack more difficult problems.

In general, we believe in Walton and McKersie's (1965) statement that:

> Integrative bargaining proceeds most vigorously when the parties see a high likelihood of success. The appropriate impression is created by a pattern of early success. Therefore the parties often prefer to take up those issues in which the integrative potential is greatest and easiest to discern. The success in the search process on these initial issues prepares the way for search on the tougher issues. (p. 151)

Rules of Accommodation

Some bargainers believe that, in the spirit of "all's fair in love and negotiations," any tactic can be justified if it strengthens one's own position. This orientation is perhaps supported by the clearly distributive character of certain situations, and a belief that displays of power are ultimately the most effective ways of gaining one's objectives. Regardless of whether this is an effective strategy in dealing with an avowed enemy, it is clearly inappropriate when bargaining with another with whom a long-term relationship is expected and the desire to find some process of accommodation exists.

Ikle (1964), for example, notes that in negotiations between friendly countries there are certain implicit rules of bargaining that are expected to be observed, and that failure to do so may result in termination of the negotiations. Among these expectations are that "unambiguous lies must be avoided, explicit promises have to be kept, invective is never to be used, explicit threats must not be issued, agreements in principle must not be blatantly violated when it comes to the execution of details, and mutual understandings must not be deliberately misconstrued later on" (p. 87). Additional "rules," which are not as strict as those above, but which can, if breached, erode the relationships between the two countries are that "the opponent's domestic difficulties should not be exploited in public, debts of gratitude should be honored (e.g., a concession acknowledged as such must be returned when the opportunity arises), motives should not be impugned, and the discourse ought to be reasonable in the sense that questions are answered, arguments are to the point, facts are not grossly distorted, repetition is minimized, and technical discussions are kept on a factual level" (p. 87).

"Friendly countries" may have severe conflicts of interest, but they understand the need to establish and maintain accommodative relationships because their self-interest clearly places primary importance on long-term relationships rather than short-term gains. That relationship between "friendly countries" and "accommodative interaction" is reversible. Not only do negotiators who value their relationship with the other party behave in certain ways, but behaving in those ways tends to confirm and intensify the feelings of mutual regard for each other's welfare and thereby increase their friendly relationships. In like manner, just as enemies might choose to ignore these accommodative interactions, violating them will communicate to the other that one does not anticipate friendly relationships between the parties. The use of invective, distortion, reneging on agreements, and similar behaviors at the academic bargaining table identifies the user as an unscrupulous adversary and invites reciprocal treatment. Behaviors can, therefore, be used as a signal to the other team. To the extent that one indulges in these behaviors, one signals a lack of interest in cooperative interaction, makes the other defensive, and provokes aggressive behavior. If parties wish to move toward constructive and creative relationships, they should immediately alter their communications and behaviors toward the other in the direction of accommodation.

Those who argue that they should not change their behavior until the other party becomes more reasonable fail to understand the power of cooperative bargaining styles to elicit reciprocal behavior from the other. As Ikle pointed out,

> Another reason for the observance of rules of accommodation, in addition to the idea that they may lead to friendlier relations on a bilateral basis, is the expectation that other nations will reciprocate the negotiating style. That is, the rules establish a mutually useful form of conduct, rather than serving as an expression of good will. Each government knows that it will always be engaged in negotiation, and it may expect that its own negotiation methods will be reflected in those of its opponents. Hence governments may adopt those methods which they would like to see adopted generally. (p. 90)

An additional reason for conducting academic bargaining under the rules of accommodation is that it is consistent with the norms and traditions of the academic enterprise. The violation of these norms in order to pursue some presumably greater end may mean that in the final analysis the institution that emerges from the bargaining interaction is not worth the saving.

Issue Control

It has been pointed out that conflict between groups is to some extent related to the size of the issues, with larger issues escalating conflict and making resolution more difficult. Laboratory evidence (Deutsch, 1973) supports the concept that conflict can be managed more easily with greater potential for constructive bargaining if issue size is limited. Fisher (1964) has suggested the means by which issue size can be controlled, and we can examine them to determine their implications for bargaining tactics. There are five dimensions which are related to the size of an issue:

1. the parties on each side of the issue
2. the immediate physical issue involved
3. the immediate issue of principle
4. the substantive precedent which settlement will establish
5. the procedural precedent which settlement will establish

For each of these dimensions, one or both parties have alternative definitions available to them. For example, a conflict may be defined by one party as a disagreement between Professor Smith and Dean Jones, and by another as a conflict between the faculty and the administration. If treated as a problem between two individuals, conflict size will be smaller than if it were considered as one between two large organizational units.

In the same way, the physical issue in a conflict can be considered to be Professor Greene's course schedule, or the entire academic calendar of the institution, or transformed from a technical scheduling matter to one concerned with major principles such as academic freedom. In each case, resolution is easier when the parties are limited, the physical issues kept small, and principle is not involved.

Questions of substantive and procedural precedent are somewhat more difficult to control in the bargaining environment. They are particularly critical, however, because constructive and creative bargaining is likely to result in the invention of new procedures or activities to meet the specific needs of the parties. The parties must find means by which the level of conflict related to their consideration can be reduced by limiting their precedential implications.

Procedural precedent may often be related to the question of scope of bargaining. Where one party wishes to restrict scope, a proposal by the other, regardless of its substantive merits, may be resisted because it appears to enlarge scope to an unacceptable level. The parties may fear that, having agreed to a specific proposal, they are thereby admitting the negotiability of all other matters of a similar nature. Substantive precedent may be established through the specific content of the proposal. Since such proposals may involve new and previously untried practices (particularly when the parties have been involved in problem-solving interaction), it is difficult to know with any degree of certainty what the consequences of adopting them may be. Since contract clauses are difficult to remove from subsequent contracts, parties may be reluctant to enter into an agreement that may tie their hands in the future.

The issue of precedent escalates conflict size in such situations. To avoid this, we propose a new category of collective bargaining provision called the Experimental Clause, which can reduce conflict and encourage creative approaches to bargaining by removing the precedential aspects of new approaches.

If, during the course of negotiations, the parties developed an interesting idea that they were unwilling to fully consider because of its precedential aspects, they could mutually decide to consider it as an Experimental Clause. In doing so, they would both agree to the following understandings:

1. It is adopted without prejudice to the question of scope or bargain-ability. Should the issue of scope arise at a later time, it would be dealt with under the procedures established by law, but neither party could use the previous existence of an Experimental Clause as grounds for their argument.

2. At the expiration of the contract, the two parties could either agree to include the same matter in one more successor contract, as it is or as modified as mutually agreeable in response to the experience of administering it. Alternatively, the parties could agree to retain it in the contract but remove it from experimental status. The last alter-native would be that either party could remove it from considera-tion in a successor contract by unilateral action for any or no reason. Should the other party wish to negotiate such a clause in future contracts, they could attempt to do so as they would any other matter, but they would be precluded from using any data or expe-rience gained during the period that the Experimental Clause was in force as the basis for their claim.

3. An item could only be considered an Experimental Clause for two contracts. At the end of that time, the parties would have gained enough experience to determine whether they wish to retain it in traditional contract form, or whether either party wishes to remove it.

4. In order to prevent contracts from becoming entirely "experi-mental" (itself perhaps a useful idea, which will be discussed as a strategy in a following chapter), it is suggested that there be no more than a small fixed number of Experimental Clauses in any contract. That number itself might be experimental, but two or three appears to be a reasonable initial limit.

The concept of the Experimental Clause is consistent both with traditional academic problem solving, and with academic bargaining. Colleges and universities often establish controversial or relatively unpredictable programs on an experimental basis, not only to mini-mize opposition to them, but also to collect information upon which a later and more binding decision can be based. Freed from the question of precedence, and its effects of requiring the bargainers to be unduly concerned with every possible negative consequence no matter how improbable, negotiators can focus their attention on the possible bene-fits. Should either unanticipated problems emerge, or the benefits to either party not be as great as imagined, the clause could be removed at the sole initiative of either, and its previous use would not be prejudi-cial to either party. The ability of the parties to extend an Experimental

Clause for one successor contract would permit them to obtain even more experience with issues that have long-term implications, or to see what the effects of a modification to an original agreement might be before making the decision to incorporate it in the future as a regular contract item.

Although there has been no report of the use of the Experimental Clause in higher education, similar concepts are not new and have precedents in industry. In 1963, for example, the United Steelworkers of America and the managers of the major steel corporations nego-tiated an amendment to their contract that included a number of provisions that had been recommended by a joint study committee. The provisions were considered as part of an "experimental agree-ment" subject to continuing review by a joint Human Relations Com-mittee. "The idea of an experimental agreement represents a major break from the tradition that, once something is done or agreed to in a contract, it can never be undone" (Healy, 1965, p. 221). The experi-mental use of new ideas for periods of about three months with contin-uing evaluation by the parties was also seen as a part of the cooperative relationship between the International Longshoremen's Workers Union and the Pacific Maritime Association, developed in response to joint needs to deal with automation on the waterfront (Healy, 1965).

The Tactics of Debate

The object of a debate is to modify the image that one party has of another, and thereby to promote agreement. Rapoport's (1974) anal-ysis of the components of a debate, which serve as the focus for this section, suggest activities that can be adopted by one party at the table in an effort to affect the other, or that can be used in part by one group in its pre-negotiation preparations.

Rapoport's argument assumes that the image of an adversary is stable because the threat or psychological aggression of debate makes the consideration of new images impossible. New images can only be considered, then, if the level of threat is reduced. The reduction or removal of threat in debate settings has three components, including (1) conveying to the opponent that he has been heard and understood, (2) delineating the region of validity of the opponent's stand, and (3) inducing the assumption of similarity.

Communicating Understanding.   The Blake and Mouton experi-ments, which have already been considered, illustrate the fact that in competitive situations such as academic bargaining groups do not

accurately hear or understand the position of the other. Rapoport also assumes that groups listen defensively and filter out information that might disrupt their image. To combat this, he suggests that every debate begin with the presentation of material to which the other team will carefully listen without becoming defensive. Since the other team will listen nondefensively to its own argument, each team should begin by presenting a summary of the opponent's argument as clearly and as eloquently as possible. "The purpose is to convey to the opponent the assurance that he has been understood, so as to reduce his anxiety on that account, and to induce him to listen" (p. 289). Each team would be required to persist in an attempt to present the other's position until the other team agreed that in fact the summary was an acceptable statement of their position.

Rogers (1952) has suggested this technique as the most effective means of promoting real communication and understanding between persons, particularly when they are involved in situations that generate strong emotions and the ability to achieve the frame of reference of the other person is therefore reduced. Believing that the tendency to judge and evaluate the statements of others without fully understanding them serves as a primary communications barrier, he suggests that individuals in an argument adopt as a rule that "Each person can speak up for himself only after he has first restated the ideas and feelings of the previous speaker accurately, and to that speaker's satisfaction" (p. 85). In translating this concept into the area of industrial relations, he asks:

> What would happen to a labor-management dispute if it was considered in such a way that labor, without necessarily agreeing, could accurately state management's point of view in a way that management could accept; and management, without approving labor's stand, could state labor's case in a way that labor agreed was accurate? It would mean that real communication was established, and one could practically guarantee that some reasonable solution was reached. (p. 85)

While Rogers' guarantee of a solution in bargaining situations is perhaps unduly optimistic, at least in part because it overlooks the fact that there may be real differences of interests between the parties, there are obvious advantages to adopting this process as a tactic to encourage more constructive bargaining. It assures that each party will have a full and accurate understanding of the other's position, a condition otherwise almost impossible to achieve in a conflict situation. It nimizes defensiveness, and so permits more effective communication in the debating activities that follow. And finally, as Rogers points out, it can be initiated by one party without waiting for the other to be ready, and since it is self-reinforcing its adoption by one is likely to reduce defensiveness in the other as well.

Experimental data collected in a simulated debate has indicated that role reversal (requiring each debater to take the role of the other and present the other's case) can be effective in some situations in significantly increasing the accuracy with which persons know the other's position (Johnson, 1967). Debaters in a role-reversal condition followed rules requiring them to accurately summarize their opponent's argument before they were allowed to present their own. The positions assigned to some negotiators were not necessarily in conflict, and those assigned to others were mutually incompatible. All subjects were told before the debate that their positions were mutually exclusive, and the situation was portrayed to them as win-lose. Although role-reversal led to greater understanding, the other party perceived the opponent as increasing understanding only when their positions were factually compatible. When they were factually incompatible, however, role playing pointed up more clearly the discrepancy between the positions and led to the perception that their positions were not understood by the other.

Where for any reason the parties do not wish to engage in role reversal as part of the intergroup bargaining process, it may still be used as an effective intragroup technique. In this setting, trying to present to one's *own* group the position of the other as fully and accurately as possible may assist in clarifying the actual position of the other, as well as possibly leading to more empathy with the other's position.

Maier (1970) has proposed that teams not only try to present the other group's position, but that they use their prenegotiation sessions for simulated bargaining at which, for example, half of the union team would take the role of the administration and the other half the roles of the union. This would permit the team to see the issues being bargained from both points of view. If the union team prepared itself in the same way, it could facilitate communications and make it easier for the teams to identify common interests when the real bargaining began.

Delineating Opponent's Region of Validity. After reducing defensiveness and reaching an understanding of the other's position through role reversal, Rapoport suggests that the parties should then present to each other their perception of the circumstances and conditions under which they think the other's position is justified. Since almost any statement can be shown to be true under some conditions, the parties at this point focus their attention upon defining for each other the region in which they believe the other's position to be valid. This posture, which is essentially a cooperative act since it focuses upon agreement rather than disagreement, minimizes threat by giving even further evidence that the parties understand each other's position. Although it focuses upon agreement, it also by implication begins to outline the areas of disagreement by identifying the boundaries that separate these areas. "The idea, as pointed out, is to steer the debate away from polarities and toward the examination of contexts. If both parties do this (if one starts, the other may follow — imitation is a surprisingly widespread principle of human conduct), progress may be made toward the resolution of the issue" (Rapoport, 1974, p. 302).

Inducing Assumption of Similarity. The first two phases of the debate indicate to the opponent an understanding of their image, and the conditions under which that image is agreed to be a valid one. The last, and most difficult, phase is to

> induce the opponent to assume that you are like him; that if he feels that he deserves to be believed and trusted, then you can also be believed and trusted; that if he feels that he has been relieved by the removal of threat, then it is to his advantage to relieve you, in order that threats (and the inevitable limitations of outlook that go with them) do not interfere with the co-operative potentialities of the situation (Rapoport, 1974, pp. 387-388).

Rapoport suggests that not only must each group begin to make the assumption that the other side manifests to at least some degree their own favorable characteristics (honesty, trustworthiness, concern for the long-term interests of the institution, commitment to academic value), but that they also manifest at least to some degree the unfavorable characteristics with which they are likely to depict the adversary. The parties thus see that at least to some extent their own positions may be self-serving, unfair, or unreasonable. If both sides begin to question their traditionally unquestioned righteousness, and admit that the position of the other side has some merit, the possibility of moving from intransigent positions toward agreement is increased. As Rapoport points out, asking ourselves to what extent we resemble our opponents is done on practical, not moral grounds. To convince others, we must be heard, and to be heard we must be listened to. Opponents will listen when parties make statements that suggest that they understand their own shortcomings; perhaps then they will begin to raise the same questions about themselves.

MANAGING POSTBARGAINING CONFLICT

Inexperienced parties engaged in collective bargaining often assume that the process concludes with the signing of a contract. In fact, negotiations consititute only half of the bargaining obligations of the parties; the other half includes those activities that are related to the day to day administration of the contract provisions. From an operational standpoint, the process of contract administration is critical because it is in the application of the contract to specific cases that the meaning of its provisions is clarified and defined. To the extent that interpretations of meaning develop from the implementation of the contract, and its substantive provisions are altered in certain respects from those envisioned by the parties at the table, contract administration is in some ways an extension of the negotiating relationship. From an intergroup perspective, the contacts between the parties in administering one contract constitute the prenegotiation experiences that will affect the successor contract. Contract administration, therefore, is a process with significant implications for the course of conflict between the parties. If done with an understanding of its importance in defining the future relationship of the parties, it can be a powerful means for supporting creative academic bargaining. In working together to give meaning to the contract, the parties can demonstrate their commitment to collaborative interactions, gain experience in reciprocating cooperative initiatives of the other side, and strengthen interpersonal ties and channels of communication that will support creative bargaining in future negotiations.

Educating Contract Administrators

The terms of the contract will impose certain obligations upon members of the faculty as well as officers of administration. It is obvious that every person on campus affected by the terms of the contract should immediately receive a copy of its provisions. Since most of these persons will not have participated in the bargaining sessions that preceded the agreement, however, they will not be aware of the meanings the negotiators may have attached to certain words or phrases, and might therefore in good faith carry out the letter of an unartfully worded provision only to find that they have acted contrary to the spirit of the agreement. In other cases, articles that appear to be unambiguous to its drafters may have different meanings to those who must implement them because of the different perspectives afforded by their roles. Particularly when the parties still view each other with suspicion, even honest misunderstandings may be attributed by the other party to a disposition to purposefully misinterpret the contract to gain advantage rather than as reflecting a problem related to the wording of the document itself.

Given these potential difficulties, an important tactic to support constructive bargaining is to hold meetings during which the provisions of the contract and their interpretations are discussed with faculty and administrators. The usefulness of such meetings would be increased if they were jointly conducted by union and administration representatives who had participated in the bargaining process. Although there may be reasons why special meetings should be conducted for occupants of specific roles, such as departmental chairpersons, it would be desirable if general meetings were held with both faculty and administrators present in the audience so that all persons could hear the questions and answers of the other group.

A major aspect of this contract briefing would be to implicitly or explicitly indicate to the campus community the philosophy that will influence its interpretation. A conservative orientation will place emphasis on the specific words and stipulations of the contract and attach a legalistic interpretation to its provisions. Grievances, for example, may be denied because they are filed a day after the deadline indicated in the contract, rather than being considered on their merits. Those who advocate this position argue that the contract is a legal document whose provisions must be exactly followed if the contract is to have any meaning. In general, accepting this interpretation of contract administration encourages greater attention to detail in negotiating future contracts, an increase in the size of the contract and the items covered, and a tendency toward adversarial processes at the table. Strict interpretations of the contract, particularly when they disadvantage one party in a manner not understood at the bargaining table, are usually seen as punishing tactics.

Parties wishing to promote constructive bargaining should attempt to avoid legalistic interpretations of the contract if at all possible. Where disagreements exist, they should become the subject of a meet and discuss session, and agreed upon interpretations should be published and circulated to all faculty and administration to permit consistency in application.

Meet and Discuss

During the course of negotiations, one party (usually the union) may demand a clause in the contract requiring the parties to meet and confer on a scheduled basis to discuss any problems being encountered in administering the agreement. Being a demand of one side, it is often rejected by the other, or alternatively, serious disagreements arise concerning the number of meetings to be held, the scope of discussions, the parties present, the legal status of any agreements reached during such meetings, and similar matters. As is the case with so many other issues concerning intergroup communications, meet and discuss meetings can lead to either constructive or destructive conflict, depending upon the existing relationships between the parties. In general, however, the potential of increased communications channels for improving the levels of cooperation between the parties outweighs its potential for increased competition, particularly if at least one of the parties understands the dynamics of the process and attempts to use it productively. The inclusion of such meetings in bargaining contracts is a tactic supporting contructive bargaining.

Studies of the operation of meet and discuss provisions actually operating in the field (Mortimer & Richardson, 1977) indicate the benefits and problems associated with them. In one institution with good union-administration relationships, the contract called for continuous consultation between the parties. The union believed these meetings, which were held with the president, were extremely important as a forum in which agreements were reached that made it less likely that the administration would make decisions that later would result in a grievance or other problem.

In stark contrast to this use of continual communication to alleviate potential causes of destructive conflict was the situation in another institution that also had a meet and discuss provision in the contract, but in which the union and administration relationships were considered adversarial. In this situation, the joint committee was "regarded as a forum within which the president of the college and the president of the Faculty Federation could exchange accusations. In addition, the president could use it to criticize the Federation and to communicate decisions he had already made" (Mortimer & Richardson, 1977, p. 64).

The fact that the same process can have quite different effects in differing situations demonstrates the difficulty of making simplistic generalizations such as "if only the parties would sit down together they would be able to resolve their differences." On the one hand, unless there are opportunities for communication between groups involved in conflict situations, there is no chance for the conflict to be resolved. On the other, as Sherif (1962) has pointed out, communications between competing groups can serve as the means for further accusations and recriminations, and the discussion becomes "bogged down in direct and indirect reference to the vicious circle of 'Who's to blame?' " Intergroup communication can be constructive, Sherif believes, when the groups share superordinate goals that are urgent and compelling for both groups. If the parties can come to see common institutional interests as overriding their group-related differences, then meet and discuss sessions should be exceptionally productive and useful.

Such sessions can serve several purposes. They can be a forum in which ambiguous items determined during bargaining can be discussed and clarified to the extent necessary in a less competitive environment. They also provide an opportunity for clarifying issues in such matters as grievances, in some cases thereby resolving them before they go through the formal adversarial grievance process. Finally, they permit the airing of problems that might otherwise become visible either indirectly through increased tensions or grievances, or would not be noted at all until the next contract negotiations. The value of meet and discuss provisions to prevent problems from festering and angering faculty has been noted (Dubeck, 1975; Kiep, 1976). The use of this process therefore serves as a mechanism for issue control, by providing a means by which individual issues can be treated as they arise and thereby increasing the chances of resolution, rather than having them accumulate and in doing so increase the level of conflict.

The "meet and discuss" concept, of course, does not have to be restricted to formal settings and definite agendas. When Swift and Company restructured its bargaining with the Amalgamated Meat Cutters and Butcher Workmen of North America to increase understanding and cooperation between the parties, an important aspect included a series of informal meetings at nearby resorts. "Brainstorming" sessions were held while the parties socialized together, and no record was made of comments made by either side. The meetings were used, as are meet and discuss sessions, to consider problems and how they might be approached by the parties, but an additional advantage was the opportunity it provided for principals to meet each other as people rather than merely as role incumbents (Healy, 1965).

Impasse

Impasse during the course of administering a contract usually occurs as a result of a grievance filed by a faculty member that is denied by the administration. Many, but not all, contracts provide in the grievance process for binding arbitration of grievances as a last step. Binding arbitration usually results in a win-lose confrontation between the parties, and as a quasilegal process its results are often based upon strict interpretations of contract language rather than an attempt to create solutions consistent with academic values and the common interests of the parties. Because such grievances often relate to the meaning of the terms of a contract, and an unresolved grievance therefore often represents differences in contract interpretation rather than merely a question of applying rules to specific cases, it is considered in this section as a form of contract impasse, rather than as just a contract dispute.

One tactic for more productively dealing with impasses of this nature is to jointly agree on a permanent neutral or a standing panel of neutrals who will provide assistance to the parties when issues of this nature develop. At minimum, this will assure that consideration of grievances will be made by someone familiar with the campus and the parties, rather than by an externally selected person who may have no understanding of the academic environment. It would be even more useful if, in addition, this person or panel were given an opportunity to observe the negotiations themselves, and therefore would be in a position to better understand the intentions of the parties when they drafted the language that later was disputed. Finally, if the neutral role was defined in terms of med-arb, rather than merely arbitration, the presence of an unresolved grievance could be used by the parties as an opportunity to work together to mutually clarify a problem area in the contract, rather than solely as a forum in which contending interpretations would be adjudicated. As in other recommendations in this book, a primary purpose of this tactic is to focus the attention of the parties upon the joint utility of considering the contract as a living document serving their mutual interests, rather than one which restrains their actions and leads to winning and losing.

This chapter has presented a number of tactics which can be adopted by the union or administrative academic bargainer who wishes to move away from destructive, adversarial, distributive bargaining orientations and toward a more accommodative and creative negotiating relationship. Although acceptance of these tactics by one or both parties are unlikely to directly result in sustained, dramatic changes in either the structures or outcomes of bargaining, they can be effective in limiting destructive aspects of bargaining, helping the parties to see and understand each other's positions more clearly, and preparing the institution for consideration of more powerful strategic changes that can promote a new orientation toward creative bargaining.

Tactical approaches to bargaining begin with an acceptance of both sides of the legitimate roles of the other; without this acceptance, the need for one or both parties to maintain a defensive posture will preclude the use of bargaining for constructive purposes. The parties must reject either unconditional cooperation or compromise as acceptable postures toward bargaining; they should instead adopt a position of flexible rigidity, in which they maintain high aspirations but are flexible in terms of the means adopted to meet those ends.

The constructive and creative bargainer should avoid any anti-union or anti-administration activity prior to a bargaining representational election, should put departmental chairpersons in the bargaining unit, avoid planning prebargaining strategy, and train negotiators in group processes and communications skills.

Bargaining positions taken should be fair. They should include neither demands at a level so high that they cannot be accepted even as a basis for beginning negotiation by the other side nor a large number of inconsequential or throwaway items. Negotiators should be trained in the communication of such fair demands, and should also consider the possibility of bringing items to the table as problems or felt needs, rather than as demands or solutions. Fair opening bids should be coupled with reciprocal concession rates, and parties could experiment with plans of unreciprocated concessions in an effort to induce trust in a reluctant cooperator. Negotiations should begin with simple issues that are easiest to resolve, the rules of accommodation should be scrupulously adhered to, and the size of the conflict should be managed by issue control. One creative means of controlling issue size would be consideration of the concept of the Experimental Clause, which would encourage creative bargaining initiatives by limiting their precedential impact. During the negotiating debate itself, parties should practice paraphrasing the position of the other party to assure understanding of the opponent's position, and should admit the weaknesses of their own position as well as the strengths of those of the opponent to induce assumptions of similarity between them.

Since contract administration is an extension of the negotiation process, and serves as the prenegotiation phase for the next contract, attention should be given to assuring that all institutional constituents are fully informed both of contract provisions and of the intent of the parties. Extensive opportunities for meet-and-discuss sessions should be considered as a means of continuing constructive communications between formal negotiation interactions, thus preventing problems of interpretation or administration from accumulating and increasing issue size. Consideration should be given to appointing a neutral or panel of neutrals familiar with the campus to perform arbitration or med-arb functions related to interpretations of the contract, and of having this person or panel observe negotiations so that the intentions of the parties are more clearly understood.

All of these suggestions assume that, while one or both parties have an interest in changing their bargaining relationship to make it more constructive and creative, they still continue to function under traditional bargaining processes. There is no reason why this need be so, except perhaps the lack of interesting alternatives that can allow bargaining parties to more fully consider new ways in which they can function together. Since these new alternatives would attempt to change the environment in which bargaining takes place, they are strategic in nature, rather than tactical. These strategic orientations to creative academic bargaining are the subjects of the following chapters.

7

The Strategies of Creative Academic Bargaining: Increasing Problem-Solving Potential

> *The adversary posture, with only occasional excursions into formal integrative bargaining, somehow seems to be collective bargaining's "natural" state. (Barbash, 1976, p. 306)*

> *Neither the occurrence nor the outcome of conflict is completely and rigidly determined by objective circumstances. This means that the fate of the participants in a situation of conflict is not inevitably determined by the external circumstances in which they find themselves. Whether conflict takes a productive or a destructive course is thus open to influence even under the most unfavorable objective conditions. Similarly, even under the most favorable objective circumstances, psychological factors can cause a conflict to take a destructive course. (Deutsch, 1973, p. 11)*

THE PREVIOUS CHAPTER considered a number of alternative behaviors and activities that could be adopted by one party in the bargaining relationship so that a collaborative and constructive orientation to bargaining becomes more probable. Each of these tactical suggestions assumed a traditional form of bargaining relationship that was structured so that demands and counteroffers were exchanged across a bargaining table between two parties, interacting through representatives, and working toward the achievement of an agreement before a stated deadline. Even when the effective use of tactics leads the parties into a more constructive relationship, however, the structural elements of traditional bargaining will be likely to inhibit development of the most effective processes for joint problem solving, which could lead to higher mutual payoffs for both.

In his analysis of the mediation of industrial disputes, Clark Kerr

(1954) identified the concept of "preventive tactical mediation" as one of three different approaches to the reduction of union-management conflict. He described this orientation as taking for its province

> more than the individual dispute but less than the total relevant environment. It deals with the relationship of the parties in general. It may be concerned with a long-range change in the attitudes of the parties toward each other or toward their mutual problems, with the nature of the leadership on one side or another, with the pressures to which the parties may be subject, with the timing of contract expiration dates, or with the alliances of the parties. It seeks to manipulate the parties and their relationship in advance in favor of nonviolent conflict. (p. 243)

It is in this orientation toward changing the relationship between the parties that we shall discover the strategies of creative academic bargaining.

Many of these strategies are central to the concept of "preventive mediation" as developed by the Federal Mediation and Conciliation Service. The activities of preventive mediation have been defined as including continuing liaison with labor and management officials, prenegotiation contract discussions, postnegotiation contract review, joint labor-management committees, labor-management conferences, special consultative and advisory services, and training activities (Stevens, 1967). All preventive mediation services are "voluntary, informal, participatory, and all seek to improve the labor-management relationship in a plant, an industry, an area, or community, or within a segment of Federal, state or local government" (Federal Mediation and Conciliation Service, 1970, p. 42).

The concept of changing the structures and patterns of interaction between the parties is in the long run essential for constructive relationships because traditional structures, time restrictions, and the dynamics of intergroup conflict prevent even bargainers of good will from developing the most creative and acceptable solutions to mutual problems. Some of the problems associated with the traditional bargaining approaches have been stated by Hildebrand (1961).

> Contract deadlines may deny opportunity to formulate complex proposals, let alone to devise mutually acceptable solutions. . . . Worse still, even if the issues can be defined, questions of work rules, incentives and job protection are often too subtle to be worked out adequately, by overburdened bargainers, for lack of both time and expertise. Finally, compromises in this difficult field are not easily made in the tense atmosphere of the bargaining table, because the institutional ties of the bargainers will deny them the freedom to explore such issues, even if they are blessed with considerable insight into each other's needs. (p. 138)

In the next three chapters, we shall suggest a number of ways in which the relationships between administrations and unions can be altered through structural and procedural changes in these traditional bargaining relationships. With few exceptions, most of these suggestions have been utilized in various industrial settings in the past. Some have been successful, others less so. It is ironic that some of the academic alternatives to the "traditional industrial model" may have been initially explored in industrial settings, perhaps even more so because the academic environment appears much more favorable to their successful implementation than the industrial settings in which they often achieved only limited success.

The characteristics of these strategic bargaining approaches follow:

1. A desire on the part of both parties to alter their traditional bargaining relationship
2. The use when necessary of third parties at various stages of the bargaining
3. The bilateral agreement of the parties to whatever changes are undertaken

The strategic approach contemplates the possibility of extremely significant changes, and it is in some cases related to a willingness of the parties to assume high risk. However, because they confront the basic causes of destructive bargaining, rather than merely addressing their symptoms, they have the potential for effecting long-term and significant change in the relationships between them.

Chapters 7 to 9 describe several major conceptual orientations to strategic change. This chapter discusses changes that can be made in the bargaining interaction to *increase the problem-solving potential* of negotiating teams. Chapter 8 considers the use of *third parties in the bargaining process* itself, with attention given to creative ways in which neutrals can be employed before, during, and after negotiations to promote constructive conflict management. Attention is also given to the role of third parties to *develop more productive intergroup relationships*. Finally, chapter 9 presents *new bargaining structures*, which are alternatives to those now inhibiting the full utilization of the potential of integrative bargaining.

EFFECTIVE PROBLEM-SOLVING APPROACHES

Parties who wish to move from distributive to integrative orientations in academic bargaining must adopt a problem-solving approach toward managing their conflict. Many critical elements related to effective problem solving are under the mutual control of the parties in academic bargaining, but usually remain unexamined either because the parties do not fully understand their importance, or because they incorrectly assume that they cannot be altered. For example, previous discussions of the sociopsychological consequences of competitive groups clearly indicate that problem solving is inhibited by the tendency to prematurely adopt a solution, present a united front to the opponent, and stifle internal dissent. How can the traditional processes of bargaining be altered to minimize these barriers to problem solving? Finding creative solutions to complex problems becomes less likely when the participants in a group are under strict time limits. Is it possible to develop forms of academic bargaining in which the pressures caused by deadlines are either reduced or eliminated? Specific proposals dealing with these, and other elements of effective problem solving, are the subject of this chapter.

Institutionalizing Dissent

Material presented in chapter 4 suggested that groups with deviant members, or groups with high internal conflict, were more likely than homogeneous groups to develop creative solutions to problems. There is also evidence that if negotiating groups are internally divided, they are more likely to reach agreement than if members of each group agree with one another.

This assertion is supported by the experimental work of Evan and MacDougall (1967). They formed two-person negotiating groups in which both members of a team agreed with each other's position and were opposed to the unanimous position of another team. This situation was considered to represent a state of "bilateral consensus." A second set of negotiating teams each consisted of two people who took different positions, one extreme and one moderate, creating a condition of bilateral dissensus. In the third condition, one team was composed of two members who agreed with each other, and the other included two persons who disagreed, a condition of unilateral dissensus. Members of teams with different positions (dissensus) were encouraged to articulate their differences during the negotiation with the other team.

The findings indicated that more terms of agreement were reached under the bilateral dissensus condition than the other two. That is, where bargaining teams each consisted of an extremist and a moderate, and both teams were encouraged to publicly display their internal dissensus during negotiations, they were more likely to reach agreement and to have more integrative results than if the teams adopted a single public posture and evidenced intrateam solidarity. The researchers suggest that the reason for this result is that the moderates on each team played a mediation role, and that the "average" position of the extremist and moderate on each team was much closer together than would be the position of teams composed of only extremists.

Much of the process of academic collective bargaining is predicated upon the concept of consensus. All members of the team are expected to support the positions taken at the table, team members who are not designated as spokespersons are expected not to speak at the bargaining table without permission from their chief negotiator, and if there is any need to discuss possible intrateam disagreement it is done in caucus where it cannot be perceived by the other team. In general, bargaining is governed by the principle of unanimity, and particularly as teams become involved in the escalation of competition and destructive conflict, dissensus among members is not tolerated. The effect of encouraging bargaining team consensus rather than dissensus is likely to be a lower level of agreement between the parties, a greater likelihood for impasse, and less probability that an integrative solution will be discovered.

Evan and MacDougall (1967) appreciate the problems in establishing dissensus on bargaining teams in actual negotiation settings.

> The bilateral dissensus strategy simulated in this experiment has an appearance of unreality. It is indeed difficult to find actual bargaining relationships in which bilateral dissensus is exhibited. It would almost appear as if the "institutionalization of dissent" in both trade unions and business organizations is a prerequisite for the emergence of a bilateral dissensus strategy. (p. 411)

To some extent, the creation of study groups, which are discussed in chapter 9, "institutionalize" dissent and make it possible for persons from both bargaining teams to explore similarities and differences away from the conformist pressures of the bargaining table. The establishment of some kind of process that might serve at least in part the same function at the table itself is somewhat more difficult to create. We would like to suggest, however, that one way to make dissensus during negotiations more likely would be for the union and the administration to participate in the selection of members of other teams.

This may appear as a radical proposal, but in fact it is consistent with traditional academic practice. In establishing presidential or dean's search committees, for example, the appointing administrator may ask the faculty governance body to submit a panel of potential members, including twice as many names as there are vacancies. This essentially creates a committee over which both the administration and faculty have veto control. A similar process is often found in the selection of an arbitrator; the state employment board submits a panel of names to each party, and they alternatively delete names from the list until only the one who is most acceptable, or at worst least unacceptable to both parties, remains.

Using this concept, the parties could agree that they would submit to each other before negotiations a list of potential members of their own bargaining team, and give the other side an opportunity to express preferences, to suggest additions, or perhaps in a setting in which experience and confidence in the process had developed, to actually select from the panel one or more team members. The union, for example, would have an opportunity to suggest or select as members of the administration team one or more administrators whom they believed were sympathetic to the union, and would thus be able to help their administrative colleagues more fully understand the faculty position. The administration would have the same privilege in influencing the membership of the union team. This "institutionalization of dissent" would increase dissensus on both teams, inhibit the development of unanimous and rigid positions on either side, promote integrative solutions, and act as a mediation device to assist in resolving difficult interorganizational issues.

The logic of this proposal is not that different from the "exchange-of-persons" strategy (Stern, Bagozzi, & Dholakia, 1977, pp. 370-371) as a means of reducing intraorganizational conflict. Through the bilateral, temporary exchange of persons in various offices in the same organization, it is possible for participants to gain greater understanding of the roles of others, and to therefore work more cooperatively with other groups when they return to their original assignment. The value of exchange of persons is well understood in those academic institutions in which faculty members regularly assume administrative roles for brief periods and then return to their faculty responsibilities.

Reducing the Effect of Deadlines

Negotiations leading to contract renewal are often referred to as "crisis bargaining" because they take place under a specific deadline imposed by the expiration date of the contract. The existence of a deadline provides a psychological motivation for the bargainers to achieve closure; this incentive is often increased by the implicit potential for action by one or the other party if the deadline is not met, or by an explicit threat.

Deadlines have a dual effect in distributive bargaining. On one hand, they have a dramatic power to move the parties toward agreement. On the other, they inhibit the bargainers from engaging in problem-solving activities that usually require more extended time periods to conduct properly. Industrial relations experts have commented on the problems related to crisis bargaining. Simkin (1967), for example, states that "First and foremost, the dominant issues present in some disputes simply do not lend themselves to crisis bargaining. [These are] issues not susceptible to quick solutions hammered out in those last frantic hours when the clock is running down" (p. 321). From the perspective of the behavioral science researcher, time pressures have equally undesirable effects. For example, time limits appear to reduce the aspirations of bargainers (Pruitt & Lewis, 1977). Since the maintenance of high aspiration levels is essential to the development of high-quality solutions in integrative bargaining, time limits may reduce the probability of achieving integrative agreements.

Negotiations leading to contract renewals often begin a stated period before the contract expiration, such as 60 days, and this time period may be written into the contract itself. One of the preventive mediation techniques pioneered by FMCS is to begin negotiations well in advance of the contract expiration, thus avoiding the crisis orientation that might otherwise exist (Federal Mediation and Conciliation Service, 1970). The purpose of these so-called "early bird" settlements is to reduce the destructive effects of a deadline showdown. Academic institutions wishing to promote integrative bargaining orientations might therefore begin contract renewal negotiations at least six months prior to contract expiration. If contract expiration dates and deadlines are maintained (a process for eliminating them completely is discussed next), it would be most useful to have them occur during times such as the end of the spring semester that permit bargaining to continue into the summer without the pressure of a new semester facing the negotiators. Contracts terminating immediately prior to the beginning of the fall semester may be an effective device for increasing bargaining power in a distributive bargaining relationship between competitors, but is dysfunctional in problem-solving orientations.

As is true with many other proposals in this chapter, minimizing the effects of deadlines through "early bird" bargaining can be a useful strategy for constructive bargaining *if* it is coupled in thoughtful ways with other approaches that together orient the parties toward collaboration rather than competition. Adopted as an isolated measure, extended negotiation periods may serve only to increase the time that the parties have to develop strong adversarial relationships, and expiration dates at the beginning of the summer rather than the end may be used as a stalling technique rather than as an extended period to assist problem-solving efforts.

Continuous Bargaining

In general, unless there is a clause permitting an item in the contract to be reopened by one of the parties, there is no requirement that parties engage in negotiations during the life of a contract. Under traditional union-management relationships, the parties are expected to abide by the agreements they have made, even if the circumstances that led to them have changed, or one of the parties finds the meaning of the agreement altered through an arbitrator's ruling. Parties are generally unwilling to discuss changes in mid-contract, and consider contract negotiation a cyclic event, which, once completed, mercifully does not need to be done again for one, two, or three years. One experienced academic negotiator has said (Howe, 1970) that the accomplishment of a contract should clearly terminate bargaining, and that bargaining should not be a continuing, year-long process.

This approach is consistent with the notion of distributive bargaining and win-lose negotiations in which the final agreement codifies the power relationship of the parties at the time it was completed, therefore making it always to the disadvantage of at least one of the parties to change. Although they are commonly accepted in all bargaining situations, there is no reason why bargaining must conform to specific schedules or deadlines, if the parties agree otherwise. Particularly for parties committed to the development of constructive and collaborative activities, it would appear more sensible to deal with problems as they emerge, rather than permit them to fester until the arbitrary date upon which contract renegotiations can begin (Walton & McKersie, 1965, p. 145). One way to permit problems to be considered as they emerge is to conceive of bargaining as a continuous, rather than as a cyclical process. The concept of continuous bargaining has precedents in both the academic and the industrial world.

One academic institution, which has developed a process of signing codicils to their contract, or agreeing on memorandums of understanding during its life, believes that this constant updating makes the contract more workable, and contributes to the collegial relationship that characterizes their bargaining. The contract in this setting is treated by the parties as a constitution rather than as a negotiated labor agreement, and is viewed by both sides as "a growing, changing document" (Walker, Feldman, & Stone, 1976).

Healy (1965) has reported on a number of industrial bargaining situations in which the parties permit bargaining of issues by committees and the addition of agreements reached into contracts even though the contract itself is not up for negotiation. In some cases the inclusion of the minutes of a joint committee that meets regularly is inserted into an unexpired agreement.

Continuous bargaining need not be an either-or proposition, but it can be implemented gradually if the parties desire. Colleges and universities wishing to consider the concept of continuous bargaining might begin by forming a joint study committee during the term of their present contract to study a clause regarded as troublesome by one of the parties. If agreement could be reached, the revised wording could be inserted into the contract. Initially, the parties might wish to limit the number of clauses for which this could be done, and identify the process itself as experimental and in existence for a limited period of time unless renewed by the parties.

If both parties found the process agreeable, and developed experience in using it, it is possible to conceive of an eventual situation in which, except for salary and fringe benefit provisions, "contracts" would have no termination dates. A policy once established through the continuous bargaining process would remain in force until either party wished to have it changed and initiated bargaining concerning it. Although such bargaining could occur in traditional fashion, it would probably be most constructive if it were to occur in study committees, and then ratified by the parties. Done in this manner, each provision could be dealt with as a specific problem and evaluated on its merits, rather than viewed as a potential trade-off for other items also under discussion. Parties would also be likely to feel freer to experiment with innovative approaches, knowing that if their agreement turned out to have unanticipated consequences, study and possible change could occur at any time.

Strengthening Cooperative Orientations

Experienced negotiating teams often spend a considerable period of time preparing for their participation at the bargaining table. Unfortunately, as has been already indicated, much of that time is spent in unilateral preparation of bargaining strategy, which has been shown in laboratory experiments to be likely to lead to impasses and inflexible positions. Taking positions prior to negotiations creates a win-lose confrontation and makes it increasingly difficult for the parties to understand the positions or arguments of the adversary. Representatives become committed to the positions of their group, and are unable to make concessions without being branded as traitorous or disloyal. When this happens, exploration of the problems underlying the issues on the table becomes exceptionally difficult, and "official" discussion at the table becomes formalized and rigid. Parties use the caucus, or bilateral agreement, to occasionally go "off-the-record" to conduct exploratory discussions, but even in such situations emphasis is likely to be placed upon questions of tactics and strategy rather than upon developing a clearer understanding of mutual problems (Douglas, 1962).

Prenegotiation Study of Issues.   A number of experiments concerning the effects of prenegotiation experiences in small groups (Druckman, 1967; Druckman, 1968; Bass, 1966) suggest the usefulness of having bargaining opponents meet prior to the start of negotiations to engage in mutual discussion of the issues. The prenegotiation instructions used by Druckman (1967), for example, said:

> The next 40 minutes will be spent in bilateral study. You are to use this time for learning as much as possible about company and union perspectives. Study the issues in order to gain understanding about both points of view as well as areas of greater or lesser agreement between proponents of either. *Do not formulate or plan any strategies for bargaining from either position. Do not take a position and argue its merits against someone who might profess to the opposite position.* Finally, do not form coalitions with other team members to bargain or debate from a position. (p. 282; emphasis added)

The results of experiments of this nature suggest that while *unilateral study of strategy* leads to hardening of positions and difficulty in reaching agreement, *bilateral study of the issues* prior to engaging in bargaining results in quicker agreement and more yielding on the part of the bargainers (Druckman, 1967). Creative academic bargainers should therefore not only avoid unilateral meetings for planning strategy but should encourage frequent bilateral meetings of the parties outside of the bargaining context to discuss problems and issues.

Prenegotiation Meetings.   A study of bargaining in the industrial sector has indicated the contribution that prenegotiation meetings have made to industrial peace in actual bargaining settings. After reviewing a number of union-management relationships, it was found that

> some kind of prenegotiation in advance of formal conferences on formal contract terms contributes to peaceful relations. Surprises of any kind are likely to upset negotiations. Each party has greater confidence if it has a thorough understanding of the issues to be raised by the other, as well as of the social, "political," or economic background of the various demands. (Golden & Parker, 1955, p. 44)

Both field studies of actual bargaining situations, and laboratory research in simulated settings, suggest that parties wishing to develop constructive academic bargaining processes should consider the establishment of regular meetings prior to formal negotiations at which they can discuss educational problems and other matters of mutual concern. Unlike the meet-and-discuss sessions recommended in the previous chapter, these prenegotiation meetings would not be used in order to discuss matters of contract administration. They would also differ from the study committees outlined in chapter 9 because they would not serve the function of making recommendations to the parties. Rather, they would serve as a medium for communication of information and attitudes that would assist the parties to engage in collaborative activities at the bargaining table. Such meetings could perform the following functions:

1. Serve as a forum in which the parties could freely discuss major issues in higher education in general, such as tenure, governance, finance, governmental involvement, or enrollment trends, without the need to take or defend positions. At the bargaining table, parties often erroneously assume that information considered to be "common knowledge" by one team—such as the recommendations of national commissions, or demographic trends — is also well known to the other. Prenegotiation meetings could provide mutual educational experiences that would increase the commonality of information available to the parties.

2. The meetings could provide a setting in which either party could present campus-based data and information to the other which it felt would be of general interest. The administration, for example, could provide an analysis of present and projected enrollments and budgets, which could then be discussed and analyzed outside the context of the bargaining table. As the parties become more sophisticated, they might use the meetings as an opportunity for data collection and feedback to the group. In discussing various techniques for influencing organizational change, Katz and Kahn (1975) indicate the usefulness of data feedback and group discussion.

> The presentation of survey findings to the various organizational families sometimes brought new problems to light. More often it gave an objective and factual basis to problems that had either been brushed aside or dealt with by some opinionated gesture." (p. 53)

The administration and union group might collaborate in a joint survey to collect information from the faculty and the administration prior to negotiations. The forms upon which the data would be collected could be designed, administered, and analyzed by a joint subgroup, with findings discussed in full session. This process might prevent the participants from making erroneous assumptions about certain situations and could make agreement in later negotiations more likely by increasing the amount of shared information.

3. Participation on prebargaining meetings for the expressed purpose of increasing communication with the other, and working together to more fully understand major problems, would be likely to lead to expectations of cooperative and collaborative behavior at the bargaining table and to reciprocal responses to collaborative initiatives.

4. Prebargaining meetings could be used as an opportunity to initiate conversations in areas that might be of concern to one of the parties in future negotiations. If parties could be encouraged to place such items on the meeting agenda prior to their introduction into actual bargaining, it could avoid surprising the other side and assist one side in being better able to understand the priorities of the other.

5. Prenegotiating meetings could increase accurate communications between the parties by encouraging full participation of all members, not just group representatives, and by eliminating the distortions created through competitive adversary bargaining. The establishment of cordial and collaborative interaction in prebargaining sessions could also serve to create more common attitudes, which, combined with an increase in shared information, could assist the decision-making process. The channels of communication and interpersonal interaction established during these meetings are likely to continue into the bargaining relationship as well.

6. These meetings could provide opportunities for experimenting with new forms of intergroup collaboration. For example, a joint subcommittee might be created to research a specific matter and report back to the total group, or as suggested earlier, might engage in a joint research effort. The meeting can also be used to experiment with new modes of interaction, such as role reversal, which might, if found to be useful, ultimately be employed at the bargaining table itself.

Conditions for Prenegotiating Meetings.   If prenegotiating meetings are to be useful in preparing the parties for collaborative negotiating activities, certain conditions must be met. First, such meetings should occur on a regular basis, perhaps once a month. Less frequent meetings might be considered as indicating lack of commitment to the joint effort and require the imposition of time limits because of the large number of agenda items that would be likely to accumulate.

Second, the meetings should have a mutually determined agenda distributed to the participants ahead of time, but should remain informal. Each participant should be free to express any and all views without any expectation of future commitment, and no records should be kept in which any comments can be attributed to any participant by name.

Such meetings should be extended (half or full day) and should take place off campus with meals and other informal opportunities for socializing. Holding such meetings off campus makes moot questions about proper on-campus locations (often administrative conference rooms are the only campus facilities that can provide an acceptable setting), indicates to both groups the importance of the meetings, and provides an atmosphere free of distractions and interruptions.

Finally, the parties should give consideration to the presence of third party neutrals. Particularly during the early stages of their relationship, a neutral can call the attention of the parties to inadvertent behaviors that might move the meetings away from a problem orientation and toward intergroup conflict. These behaviors are often subtle and can rapidly escalate without the knowledge or intent of the parties.

Just as destructive bargaining relationships are likely to be related to reduction of communication between the competing parties, so constructive bargaining and problem solving are reinforced by opportunities for increasing positive and nonthreatening contact between bargaining groups. The value of contact between groups before table negotiations begin has been summarized by Rubin and Brown (1975):

> Prior to bargaining—that is, prior to the development of a bargaining stance from which it may be awkward or costly to retreat—the availability of interpersonal experience . . . provides each party with the opportunity to discover, at relatively minimal expense, something more about what the other is like. Prenegotiation experience may help the parties to develop a more realistic, less stereotypic view of each other before positional lines are drawn and commitment processes have begun to operate at full strength. (p. 240)

Superordinate Goals: Productivity Bargaining

The concept of productivity has been anathema in higher education because of its industrial connotations, and because the unique nature of the academic enterprise makes it difficult if not impossible to quantify "outputs" except in the most superficial and trivial sense. Its image as a concept has also been damaged in colleges and universities because of the imposition of so-called productivity savings requirements (i.e., mandated budget cuts in public institutions without reductions in workload), and the linking of the concept of productivity with staff reductions and challenges to tenure.

The concept of productivity is not a new one to colleges and universities. Over two decades ago, a review of the course distributions and offerings of a number of colleges led to recommendations that, if implemented, would have reduced costs and permitted significant increases in faculty salaries (Ruml & Morrison, 1959). Unfortunately, these recommendations were offered to trustees with the admonishment that they should take back from the faculty the authority which they had delegated in the past to control the curriculum. As would be expected, the proposal was not well received in faculty circles.

Yet there obviously is room to increase productivity in some institutions, in terms both of effectiveness and efficiency. Since the faculty and administration together have the technical expertise to evaluate institutional changes that could increase productivity, both groups must be involved in any such activities if they are to be effective. Productivity changes can be made if the processes used are consistent with the norms of the organization (Birnbaum, 1978).

Because productivity changes, to be effective, require joint decision making, the issue is one that might appopriately be considered in collective bargaining, and increased productivity might assume the position of a superordinate goal that could provoke collaborative activities between the parties.

There are incentives for both groups to participate, since their mutual service orientation should make concepts of increasing efficiency and effectiveness in the public interest supportable. Administrators would have an additional incentive, because increased productivity would reflect favorably upon their professional skills and provide increased credibility with trustees or legislative finance committees. For the faculty, however, productivity has too often been related to increased workload or other impositions and is often accurately seen as diminishing the effectiveness of the institution. If collective bargaining is to be used to develop joint processes for reviewing issues related to effectiveness and efficiency, a means must be found to provide positive incentives for faculty participation.

The concept of productivity bargaining is not new in industry. The Scanlon Plan (Lesieur & Puckett, 1969), for example, has been adopted by a number of companies as a means through which management and labor could jointly study productivity matters and share the benefits of actions taken to improve it. In most settings, the process works through a series of productivity committees located in departments, consisting of representatives of management and the union. Productivity improvement suggestions are forwarded to an organization-wide screening committee. After thorough discussion of each suggestion, those found to be useful are accepted and implemented. Accompanying the process of selecting ideas for implementation is the creation of formulas by which the savings generated are distributed between management and labor. In general, most such distributions allocated 25% of the savings to the company and 75% to the workers in the form of bonuses over and above their salaries. Although evaluative research on the effectiveness of the Scanlon Plan in the many organizations in which it is in use is sparse, it appears as if the plan works very well in some companies, and not well in others (Tannenbaum, 1974). No data appear to be available that would suggest the specific organizational characteristics that would be likely to make effective use of the plan. A similar effort relating productivity and wage bargaining in the public sector has been reported by McKersie (1976).

Although we do not know of any academic contract dealing with productivity in this manner, there are situations that are not that dissimilar. At Hofstra University (Memo, 1977), for example, the administration and union negotiated a contract provision that related enrollment to additional salary compensation. In addition to bargained salary increases, the contract called for faculty to receive half of any additional tuition and fee income above that budgeted for the year, with the other half remaining in the university budget.

Savings related to productivity changes would not necessarily have to be reflected in salary but could be distributed in the form of free time, additional budget allocations to library or other academic resources, support of teaching assistants, or any other proposal acceptable to the parties. In all cases, there would have to be guarantees that all resources generated through such a program would be available to the participants over and above that which they would have otherwise received, so that it is not used merely as a device to increase workloads. This is obviously an easier challenge for a private institution to meet than a public one, but the unexplored potential for problem-solving orientations related to productivity bargaining appears to justify at least their experimental use in a number of settings. A caution is in order, however. From the perspective of intergroup relations and problem solving, productivity may serve as a superordinate goal which can elicit collaborative behavior. However, if emphasis is placed on utilitarian rewards, it may contribute to the de-emphasis of normative values that we have identified as the most critical danger of bargaining, and may even anger those participants who feel that monetary rewards are inappropriate recognition for increased commitment to institutional goals.

Increasing Alternatives

When competitive groups independently develop their own solutions to a problem, each group is likely to believe that its product is superior to the other, to become committed to that solution, to selectively filter information pertaining to the quality of the solution, and to fail to recognize the characteristics of the proposals of the other side. In bargaining, through a similar process, each party becomes committed to the demands or counteroffers it presents, and the examination of alternatives becomes extremely limited. Since a major principle of problem solving is the creation of a large number of alternative solutions from which the best can be selected, a situation that essentially makes available to the parties only two solutions has low potential for integrative approaches.

One possible means of increasing problem-mindedness would be for the parties to prepare their demands or counteroffers in terms of a range of alternatives, rather than as a single response. The concept of the "range of alternatives" has been proposed by Blake and Mouton (1962) as "conducive to obtaining better end products than both groups representing only their most preferred position to the other, failing to consider alternatives, or keeping them hidden" (p. 116). Translating this suggestion into bargaining processes, the parties could agree that demands or counteroffers would consist of at least two quite different items dealing with the same problem, either one of which meets the minimum requirements of the party presenting it. The parties could decide to do this for a single issue in a contract on an experimental basis, or for some or all of the contract provisions.

Requiring that the parties submit ranges of proposals to each other has a number of advantages. Since there is a tendency for groups to stop problem-solving activities once an acceptable solution is discovered, the requirement that a range of alternatives be presented requires that the search for creative solutions continue. In addition, the need for both parties to find at least four possible ways to resolve a problem (two from the party making the demand, and two from the party responding) serves to reinforce the concept that alternatives *are* available if problem-solving techniques are utilized to find them. This may assist the parties in using the bargaining table to find other choices together that neither was able to discover separately. Finally, requiring a party to present two or more alternatives may diminish a commitment to either of them, and thus make it easier for the parties to hear the positions of the other and work collaboratively.

Although the conceptual orientation is quite different, in some ways the process resembles the dual last-best-offer package approach to binding arbitration. In both cases, the preparation of numbers of alternatives increases the possibility that the solutions of the two groups will have overlapping provisions, which may facilitate final joint agreement on a single solution.

Reducing Nonrationality

In focusing attention upon intergroup and interpersonal processes related to bargaining, there is a tendency to overlook the cognitive aspects of conflict. While it is true that competitive orientations reduce the ability of individuals and groups to fully hear and completely understand the position of the other side, it is also true that even in the absence of such intergroup processes the accurate communication of a position may be extremely difficult. Particularly as issues become more complex and ambiguous, limited human rationality increases the probability that each side does not really understand the position of the other and therefore is inhibited from reaching agreement with the other. This problem can be referred to as "cognitive conflict," and it can exist and create difficulties in problem solving within, as well as between, groups. To the extent that cognitive limitations frustrate the ability of the parties to agree, cognitive aids may be useful in clarifying their positions to each other and assisting in the bargaining process.

Collecting and Presenting Data.   Probably the simplest form of cognitive aid is the collection and presentation of data related to specific topics under negotiation. Parties often come to the table with specific demands related to problems for which data can easily be made available, but which often is not. In the absence of data, it is difficult for the other party to clearly understand the demand, and to appropriately respond to it. For example, demands for revisions in the grievance process may be based upon the belief of one side or the other that the current process "isn't working," but the demanded changes are often unsupported by data and in fact may be unrelated to the actual cause of the problem. The presentation of data relating to the number of grievances filed, the stages that they reached in the process, the time taken for each grievance, its disposition, faculty or administrative attitudes toward the existing process, and similar matters would enable the parties to better understand the factors prompting one party to ask for revision, and permit analysis of the effect of the proposed change on resolving the underlying cause of the problem. Obviously, both intergroup and cognitive processes would be facilitated if the groups made this data collection and analysis process a joint, intergroup activity.

Using Interactive Computer Programs.   A more sophisticated cognitive aid has been suggested (Brehmer & Hammond, 1977) that uses interactive computer programs to permit the positions of each, and the degree of their disagreement on a specific issue, to be visually displayed and compared on a computer terminal. Particularly when conflict between the parties is caused by their inability to correctly predict the response of the other to a proposed initiative, the computer provides a means of obtaining clearer information, assuming the parties are willing to provide accurate communications to each other.

Using Neutrals.   Although experimentation with the use of computer programs as a cognitive aid may be an approach with which individual institutions may wish to experiment, it is possible that the use of a neutral by the parties during bargaining can perform some of the same functions. The neutral can serve cognitive functions by interacting individually with each party concerning a specific issue, and then where conflict appears to be related to cognitive issues, calling the parties together to present a report that clearly defines their positions to each other, presenting their similarities and differences, and suggesting steps that could be taken by each side to move toward agreement in ways consistent with their bargaining positions. This process, which might be considered as fact-finding, but with recommendations during the bargaining interaction rather than following impasse, might be more effective than a more statistical and abstract comparison offered by the computer. Not only would the neutral have a greater ability to interrogate each party concerning positions, preferences, and values, but the suggestions made by a neutral seen as an expert would be more difficult to dismiss as superficial or arbitrary than those prepared through prepackaged programs.

There are three basic strategic approaches to creative academic bargaining. First, if creative bargaining should be based on problem solving rather than competition, the negotiating process should be altered to increase its problem-solving potential. Second, if two parties are having difficulty in bilaterally establishing constructive relationships, then neutral third parties can assist them. And third, if the structure of bargaining itself tends to lead toward destructive rather than constructive conflict, it can be changed by agreement of the parties.

The first basic strategy consists in determining the specific aspects of the traditional bargaining relationship that inhibit problem solving and then having the bargainers agree to change them. Many critical elements related to effective problem solving are under the mutual control of the parties in academic bargaining, but they often remain unexamined because they are incorrectly assumed to be unalterable. For example, since uniformity of opinion inhibits the development of creative solutions by problem-solving groups, bargainers could make group processes more effective by institutionalizing dissent through permitting each team to influence the selection of the members of the other team. Problem-solving ability is also reduced by the presence of deadlines that do not allow thorough consideration of alternatives. Parties could minimize this problem through "early bird" bargaining, or by considering the adoption of continuous bargaining that would create contracts without termination dates and enable either party to raise any issue for bargaining at any time it was felt to be a problem.

Bargaining teams often engage in unilateral prenegotiation planning of strategy, a process which has been found to make agreement more difficult. Prenegotiation meetings can support creative bargaining approaches if they are used instead for bilateral study of the issues, or for joint consideration of current educational problems that may at some point have an effect upon the institution.

Problem solving can be increased, and competitiveness decreased, if the parties establish superordinate goals requiring the efforts of both to achieve. One such goal could be that of productivity, with both the administration and the faculty sharing in the benefits of increased efficiency and effectiveness. Since problem solving is inhibited by the tendency of groups to move too quickly toward acceptance of solutions, bargaining could be more productive if bargainers submitted a number of alternative proposals to each other for each item, instead of only one.

Finally, although destructive conflict is often caused by problems in communication related to intergroup competition, it is also true that it can be related to cognitive conflict caused by the complexity of proposals. This problem of nonrationality can be significantly reduced through the use of cognitive aids such as the collection and presentation of data, the use of interactive computer programs, or the use of neutrals.

Each of these strategies is under the control of the two bargaining parties and can be implemented in the bargaining process if they wish to do so.

8

The Strategies of Creative Academic Bargaining: Third Party Interventions

THIRD PARTY NEUTRALS have always played a role in labor-management relations, and this role appears to be assuming even greater importance with the advent of bargaining in the public sector. Traditionally, the use of third parties has been limited to the impasse procedures of mediation and, more recently, fact-finding and arbitration. With the concept of "preventive mediation" has come experimentation in new forms of neutral involvement.

This chapter presents a number of strategic approaches to creative bargaining that rely upon third party involvement. These have been somewhat artificially divided into two groups: those that may occur prior to bargaining, such as intergroup workshops, imaging, confrontation meetings, and total organization development activities and those that may take place during or after the bargaining process itself, such as neutral advisement, process consultation, and innovative impasse procedures. Obviously, the principles used in all of these processes can be utilized to design interventions that may take place at any time. Indeed, a primary purpose of this chapter is to suggest that, contrary to traditional bargaining practice, neutrals can be useful in various ways not only before, but during or after the actual bargaining interaction as well. While this is probably true in any bargaining situation, these possibilities may be of particular value to the academic bargainer.

Chapter 5 presented the functions of the mediator as described by Kerr. Before beginning a review of other third party processes, it would be useful to consider in more general terms the role of the third party in intergroup conflict in any social setting. It will then be possible to relate these functions to the specific strategies that will be outlined in the next two sections. The seven functions of neutrals discussed here were developed by Deutsch (1973), to which reference may be made for more extended descriptions and examples. In considering the following material, the reader might find it useful to stop after each item and consider how the function might be effectively performed either before, during, or after bargaining has taken place; what kinds of structures one could imagine that would permit a third party neutral to most effectively perform these activities; and what kinds of skills and understandings neutrals should have so that their activities would be seen as legitimate and useful by administrative and union leadership.

Deutsch's (1973) listing of the seven functions of the third party follow:

1. *Helping the conflicting parties identify and confront the issues in the conflict*

Problems in communication and cognitive functioning related to the conflict situation often prevent the parties from being able to completely and accurately identify the precise nature of the conflict. Until the parties understand the real nature of the conflict, they will be unable to confront it and deal with it in a constructive manner.

Occasionally, the parties, already deeply embroiled in conflict, may be unwilling to explore some very important, but also very volatile issue for fear that it will escalate the relationship out of control. Deutsch suggests that "the mere presence of a supportive, skilled, neutral, discrete third party may sufficiently relieve the anxieties of the conflicting parties about the possibilities of an uncontrolled, catastrophic blowup so that they would be able to deal with issues that they may otherwise think would be too hot to handle" (p. 382). Often, parties cannot focus on the real issues because there are differences in the motivations, power, or legitimacy of the two parties that are leading to suppression or conflict evasion. The neutral can increase the motivation of the less-motivated party, change the perception each has of the other's power, or work with one side to modify their picture of the other as illegitimate, and thus make the balance between them more equal and their attention to the real problems between them more probable. The neutral can also work individually with each party to get past the rhetoric that develops during sustained conflict, and after developing an understanding of the real issues between them, help them to perceive issues with greater clarity.

2. *Helping provide favorable circumstances and conditions for confronting the issues*

Not only what the parties do, but when, where, and how they do it may be significant in the development of more constructive relationships. By controlling some of the interaction between the parties, the neutral can ensure that the level of tension is high enough to promote problem solving, but not so high that the parties become defensive and are incapable of constructive interaction. The neutral can remove the parties from their traditional locations, eliminating distractions and creating a new setting on neutral turf. The neutral can also control the information exchange between the parties, preventing parties from exchanging threats or other communications that might inhibit their progress, and making it possible for parties to make concessions through the neutral without appearing to be weak or losing face.

3. *Helping remove the blocks and distortions in the communications process so that mutual understanding may develop*

Conflict distorts communication and makes it difficult for individuals or groups to clearly hear what the other side is saying and feeling. The neutral can assist by providing communications training to the parties so that they are better able to communicate

4. *Helping establish such norms for rational interaction as mutual respect, open communications, the use of persuasion rather than coercion, and the desirability of reaching a mutually satisfying agreement*

The need to follow the rules of accommodation if the parties to a dispute are to be able to move toward constructive management of conflict has already been discussed. The neutral can be a powerful force in the acceptance of rules by both parties and in assuring that basic elements of fairness are employed by both even in the midst of great conflict. This may be one of the most important functions that a neutral can play in working with higher education institutions because the participants often either do not realize what the rules are, or have stereotypical or erroneous impressions about how the "bargaining game" is to be played. Deutsch's description of some tactics likely to be utilized by inexperienced disputants will be familiar to anyone who has participated in or observed spiralling conflict at the academic bargaining table:

> hitting the other side's sensitive spots; generalizing rather than being specific, so that issues in conflict become broad and diffuse rather than limited and clearly focussed; defining issues in absolutist terms that leave no room for give and take or in moralistic terms that imply that if the other side yields, he is confessing guilt; issuing ultimatums and threats that imply that the other has no alternative but to yield; and bluffing indiscriminately so that it is impossible to know when one should be taken seriously (p. 384).

As has already been seen, each of these deviations from rational norms and a problem-solving orientation is likely to intensify destructive conflict. A sensitive neutral can instruct the parties in more appropriate verbal behavior and help them to see the effects of their rhetoric on the response of the other so that they can begin to learn to monitor and control their own communications processes.

5. *Helping determine what kinds of solutions are possible and making sugges-tions about possible solutions*

A third party can assess the aspirations and expectations on each side and determine alternative possibilities for settlement that can be pre-sented to them. Occasionally, this may require the third party to assist the disputants in redefining the problem so that solutions become accessible that were not previously considered; in other situations, the neutral may assist a party in changing the level of expectation so that solutions once considered not acceptable may now be reassessed.

6. *Helping make a workable agreement acceptable to the parties in conflict*

Parties may refuse to adopt a productive solution because they believe that it would appear as a retreat or loss of face. The third party may get one or both of the disputants to perceive the solution in such a way that accepting it does not violate their principles, or the third party may bring pressure to bear on one or the other by threatening to leave the situation, or publicize the disagreement.

7. *Helping to make the negotiators and the agreement that is arrived at seem prestigeful and attractive to interested audiences, especially the groups repre-sented by the negotiators*

We have already mentioned the problems of the negotiator who must bargain with constituencies to accept the results of the negotia-tions, even if they are not fully consistent with the original goals of the parties. The bargainer is able to accept agreements that contain less than had originally been hoped for because of having had the experi-ence of unsuccessfully attempting to get more; the constituency has not been in that situation and is often less willing to lower their aspirations even when they had been set at an unrealistically high level. The neutral third party can assist in the "selling" of the agreement by endorsing it and proclaiming its merits. There are many ways in which this can be done, such as publicly praising the negotiators for their bargaining skill or focusing attention on those elements of the agree-ment that were consistent with the objectives of the bargainers. Particu-larly in an academic setting, there might be value in identifying innova-tive new approaches taken in the agreement, and emphasizing those aspects of the agreement that support commonly accepted academic virtues such as academic freedom, teaching effectiveness, or increased participation in decision making.

In addition to performing specific functions, third parties can some-times be effective merely by their presence, as Walton (1969) has noted.

The simplest and most passive third-party intervention is to be present and available in the confrontation. Depending, of course, on his particular personal and role attributes, the mere presence of a third party in the situation can perform a synchronization function. In addition, his presence can influence the group norms governing openness, can reassure the participants who see him as a source of nonevaluative acceptance and emotional support if needed, and can decrease the perceived risks of failure because he is presumed to possess skills that can facilitate dialogue. (p. 148)

With this orientation to the uses of neutrals, we now turn our attention in this section to specific ways in which third parties can be used in academic bargaining to increase its integrative potential.

INCREASING INTEGRATIVE POTENTIAL

Noncrisis Neutral Advisement

Bargainers in industrial settings are generally reluctant to involve third party neutrals in negotiations until impasse has been reached, because of their belief that the "best" bargains are those reached by the parties without external "interference." To some extent, this reaction may be related to the needs of professional bargainers to clarify their roles and exercise control over the bargaining process (Jones, 1975). Adherence to this philosophy has often caused mediators to "lament that they are too seldom called into a case early enough, before all the elasticity has been stretched out of the disputed items" (Douglas, 1962, p. 55). One might expect, therefore, that while the use of third party neutrals in crisis (i.e., impasse situations) may assist the parties to resolve their current dispute, it usually comes too late in their interaction to have a major impact upon building constructive relationships and creative bargaining.

Public Sector Bargaining.   One attempt to provide noncrisis third party assistance has been reported by Loewenberg (1975). Although the results were equivocal, this pilot project conducted in Pennsylvania is of interest because it was concerned with public sector bargaining, the area in which most higher education negotiations is concentrated.

The rationale for the project was that public sector bargaining in general was immature and its participants inexperienced, and that "ignorance and inexperience breed mistaken expectations, misunderstanding, and unrealistic strategies" (Loewenberg, 1975, p. 2). In order to compensate for this inexperience, six sets of parties involved in bargaining agreed to work with six experienced labor neutrals in their prebargaining and bargaining activity. The six groups included two school districts and their education associations, three city or county units and their uniformed personnel associations, and a city and its nonuniformed personnel union. It was believed that participation of the neutrals in their activities would facilitate the bargaining process by increasing knowledge about the collective bargaining relationship and the processes and substantive issues of bargaining; developing respect for the process and its participants; opening two-way communications between the parties; providing a mechanism for problem solving; and developing the capacity of the parties to resolve their own problems in the future. Rather than participating only when the parties reached impasse, the neutral advisers were to have early and continuous involvement with the parties, both before and during bargaining.

The actual activities of the six advisers differed considerably in each setting, making firm categorization of their behaviors, and their consequent effects on the relationships between the parties difficult. However, they encompassed the following (pp. 25-29), although probably no adviser engaged in each of these activities in any one setting.

1. *Assisting the parties in procedural aspects of negotiations* (advising on the meaning of contract language, mediating claims of bad-faith bargaining, assisting the sides to understand the positions and feelings of the other, guiding bargaining sessions, outlining the technical requirements of a fact-finding presentation)
2. *Providing factual information to the parties* (collecting data for the parties, indicating how other parties had handled similar situations)
3. *Assisting the parties in analyzing positions* (analyzing their own stand, assessing new information, considering other side's contentions)
4. *Offering informed judgments* (serving as a sounding board for either party, indicating how a specific situation might be viewed by a neutral at impasse)
5. *Acting as liaison to state mediators* (providing background information, or serving as a co-mediator)
6. *Assisting in contract administration* (assisting the parties to establish grievance machinery, serving as a part of the grievance process)
7. *Helping to study and resolve problems* (helping to clarify issues, investigating alternatives, assisting the parties in determining a resolution)
8. *Directing parties to formal training sessions* (identifying conferences, organizations, and workshops that would be of use to the parties)
9. *Changing attitudes and feelings*

The findings of the project were that in three of the pilot settings, relationships between the parties had become more sophisticated, trustful, and professional; the relationship in one setting had improved somewhat; and in the remaining two settings no change was seen. Unfortunately, no data were presented that would identify the criteria or process through which these assessments were made. In some ways, the project itself was a self-fulfilling prophecy. "If one or both parties opposed bargaining or basically had little use for the demonstration project, the impact of the project was doomed to be minimal. If parties were willing to accept bargaining and were seeking assistance, then the possibility existed for effective intervention by neutral advisers. In the cases in the project where such willingness existed, the project generally succeeded in meeting its goals" (Loewenberg, 1975, p. 50).

Other factors may have interfered with the effectiveness of the program. The neutral advisers, for example, were originally limited to 12 days of consultation with their clients, an extraordinarily short time to learn of their situation, develop trusting relationships, and provide assistance. This was extended in actual practice so that an average of 17 days was spent by each adviser with his clients. There was significant confusion by the clients of the exact purpose of the project and the function of the advisers, which may have had an adverse impact on their effectiveness. Although the advisers themselves were experienced labor neutrals, they were primarily trained in arbitration rather than in methods of assisting the parties in prenegotiation or negotiation activity. Their orientation to their new roles was limited, and there were no protocols or training sessions that would have developed some mutual sense among them of what activities or behaviors might be effective in their settings. The demonstration project, therefore, was more of an ad hoc field venture than either an experiment or an example of action research. Yet while it is difficult to draw firm conclusions concerning its possible effectiveness, it seems that the idea is potentially sound and could be useful in academic bargaining.

Academic Bargaining.   Certainly, the problems of immature and inexperienced bargaining relationships are present in many college and university bargaining settings. It may be possible to utilize the model of the Loewenberg project, with some modifications, as the basis of a design for implementing and assessing the effectiveness of non-crisis neutral advisement in academic bargaining.

If successful, this may be the first step in a more comprehensive orientation to the possible use of neutral advisers. Their use is consistent with academic norms, and, in some respects, is similar to using advisers in other academic settings such as departmental visitation committees, accrediting visits, and preaccrediting advisement. Since the availability of qualified neutrals is likely to remain a major issue, and the parties are likely to find neutrals useful only when they are acceptable, it may be desirable at some time to establish a national program for training and certifying such neutrals and providing workshops for their potential clients. Such a program, directed by a panel of persons appointed by leading national unions and administrative groups, could legitimize the use of neutral advisers, assure proper training, examine potential neutrals on their understanding of union-management relationships, bargaining law, the academic environment, and consulting skills, and evaluate and disseminate to potential user institutions information about their performance.

The availability of such a "Board of Academic Neutrals" could serve as a resource for both unions and administrations in institutions convinced of the desirability of constructive and creative bargaining and anxious to solicit reputable and skilled neutrals who could assist them in their efforts. This concept is consist with Keaton's (1972) suggestion that "To be truly effective, mediation in the public sector should not only be an impasse resolution device. It should be available at all times. This is particularly true when the parties are inexperienced" (p. 105). In the academic environment, all bargaining institutions should have such resources available.

Impasse

An earlier chapter discussed the traditional impasse resolution processes of collective negotiations and indicated problems associated with their use in academic bargaining. Although institutions adopting the tactical and strategic suggestions in this book related to creative bargaining may be less likely to have need for impasse procedure, even collaborative bargainers working together in good faith will occasionally find themselves in situations in which resolution of their differences becomes extremely difficult. This section considers a number of alternatives to the traditional use of mediators, fact-finders, and arbitrators, many of whom are often selected by a state or federal agency. Each of these alternatives involves the use of one or more neutrals, although several suggest the use of persons who are members of the academic community but not direct parties to the dispute, as opposed to professional labor relations neutrals. In all impasse processes, however, the neutral participants *must* have a high level of understanding and sensitivity to the unique properties of the academic organization and the nature of academic work.

Problems associated with the use of neutrals not familiar with the characteristics of colleges and universities are already being seen. A recent review of grievance arbitration cases in higher education, for example, indicated that in many cases arbitrators were applying industrial standards in making decisions, and were either unaware of, or insensitive to, the unique nature of university structure and governance (Finkin, 1976).

Although this review was concerned with grievance arbitrators, the same problems may well arise as institutions make increasing use of neutrals to provide other forms of service. We have already noted the tendency of groups whose solution in a competitive situation was not selected as best by a judge to have negative feelings about the judge's competence and fairness. This dynamic is likely to reduce the interests of the parties in implementing the final decision. This problem can be increased in magnitude when the neutral is seen even before the award as not being expert in college and university operations, and perhaps it can be reduced if the parties acknowledge such expertise before the initiation of the impasse process.

In some ways it is difficult to separate the impasse situation from the other phases of bargaining. Clearly, an impasse exists when the parties are unable to agree and do not believe that further interaction will be fruitful. However, many activities occurring before or during negotiations have as one of their major purposes the prevention of impasse and are therefore related to the problem.

Impasse procedures are divided into three categories: the use of neutrals to provide preimpasse assistance; the use of neutrals to provide impasse assistance; and the use of neutrals to make impasse awards.

Using Neutrals for Preimpasse Assistance.   One procedure for preimpasse assistance and impasse prevention is to build the involvement of neutrals into the process and structure of bargaining itself. This was one of the outcomes of the Long-Range Committee formed by Kaiser Steel Corporation and the United Steelworkers of America in the 1960s. The group was a study committee charged with the responsibility for recommending a long-range plan for the "equitable sharing of the company's progress between the stockholders, the employees, and the public." Its membership included three persons selected by the company, three selected by the union, and three public members all of whom were experienced labor neutrals. Various rationales have been given for the inclusion of public members, incuding their role in representing the public interest, and their ability to function as knowledgeable neutrals in providing technical assistance or mediation re-sources to the parties. It was also suggested that—

> Because the parties, in the past, had been so heavily engaged in conflict, there were always the seeds of distrust that accompany such a relationship. Therefore, many observers believe that both parties felt "safer" with the presence of respected third parties in their midst. The argument goes that, if one party doubts the objectivity of the other party, the presence of a neutral would insure that the first party gets a reasonable and objective hearing. (Healy, 1965, p. 250)

Using this model, if academic bargainers believed that they were about to engage in negotiations over particularly difficult issues, they might jointly select a neutral who would participate with them during the entire bargaining process. Alternatively, and perhaps of even greater utility, the parties might agree to remove such an item from the bargaining table and remand it to a tripartite study committee whose membership included one or more neutrals of their selection.

Using Neutrals for Impasse Assistance. Turning now to the use of neutrals in impasse situations, the establishment of an Academic Dispute Settlement Commission, with permanent mediation boards, has been suggested (Hobbs, 1971) as one means of providing specialized neutral assistance to bargainers at impasse. This proposal, of course, does not necessarily suggest a function any different from that encountered in traditional dispute resolution, but it does provide that, because of the special qualifications of its members, such boards would be better able to meet the needs of academic institutions.

A somewhat different model is suggested by Clark's (1977) description of the negotiation of a settlement of a suit at a state university after a judge had made a finding of discrimination. In this case, attorneys representing faculty and administration met together with an administrative representative who was knowledgeable about the institution and familiar with negotiations but who had not been involved in any way in the decision-making chain related to the discriminatory acts. In this case, therefore, an internal neutral served to assist the two parties to reach agreement. A university is probably one of the few institutions in our society in which there are individuals who, while by definition are members of either the faculty or administration and therefore parties to the bargaining dispute, might be acceptable as neutrals by both parties. Use of this model would suggest that such persons could be used to work with the parties in case of impasse. Again, it would be preferable if this were to occur in small-group, off-line settings in which participants could interact informally and deal with a single issue as a problem.

In this same situation, certain kinds of decisions were to be made regarding issues such as back pay. Rather than submit them to arbitration, the parties jointly named a four-person faculty committee. They were provided with all the administrative assistance required and utilized the services of an outside, expert neutral as well. Even though the members of the team were all from one "side" of the dispute, they were mutually acceptable to both parties and they decided that all decisions would be made by unanimous vote. Their success in this assignment was related to the fact that "even though their initial nominations came from one of the sides, they never thought of themselves as representatives of the plaintiffs or the administration. Instead, they regarded themselves as faculty representatives charged with resolving a faculty problem" (Clark, 1977, p. 238). This exercise suggests the possibility of forming neutral committees of faculty and administrators on a campus to which the bargaining parties could remand for study and recommendation one or more issues that did not appear to be soluble at the bargaining table.

Using Neutrals for Impasse Awards. Where impasse cannot be avoided either through preimpasse intervention, or the involvement of a neutral after the declaration of impasse, and where one of the parties is not willing to defer a solution, a final award must be made. Several processes are available using specialized neutrals.

Establishing Tripartite Arbitration Panels. One process is the establishment of a tripartite arbitration panel, including a union representative, an administration representative, and a neutral. This structure would "presume that the arbitrator would be educated to the nuances of the case not only in its presentation but by debate within the committee as well" (Finkin, 1976, p. 433). As an alternative, this possibility could be combined with the tripartite impasse assistance group mentioned above, with the neutral, this time drawn from outside the campus, engaging in med-arb. During the mediation phase of the process, the neutral would serve as a member of a problem-solving group attempting to mediate the differences in the approaches of the parties and suggesting alternative solutions that may not have occurred to them. If the parties later declared that they were at impasse, the work of the neutral would continue, but this time as an arbitrator with the authority to make a binding final award if continued attempts at mediation were not successful. In order to assure that even at this stage the award is one which best meets the needs of the parties, they might follow Fuller's

(1971) suggestion that the arbitrator submit the award in draft form to the representatives of the parties for comments and suggestions. After receiving them, and encouraging the parties to reach voluntary settlement, the arbitrator would prepare and publish the final award.

Hobbs' (1971) concept of an ad hoc academic arbitration board established by an Academic Dispute Settlement Commission offers another approach. Indicating that the parties themselves could decide whether the awards of such a board would be advisory or binding, Hobbs suggests that their essential features would be that (1) board members would be knowledgeable in academic and legal matters, (2) arbitration would take place only after mediation had failed to lead to resolution, and (3) all decisions would be reviewable in the courts. This is similar to Finkin's (1976) suggestion for the establishment of standing panels of arbitrators experienced in academic affairs. Such panels might be nominated by faculty and administrative groups, might serve geographical areas, and could serve as a resource not only for unionized institutions but for others as well who would prefer arbitration to more time-consuming or costly alternative processes.

Establishing Regional Standing Panels.   Rather than establish panels that would perform traditional arbitration functions by visiting the site of the dispute and holding hearings, an additional alternative is establishing a regional standing panel that would meet on a regular basis and decide cases brought to it in written form. If such a panel consisted of a small number of persons selected by union and administrative groups, it could follow the model set by the Council on Industrial Relations, which was established jointly by the National Electrical Contractors Association and the International Brotherhood of Electrical Workers. This council was established to adjudicate contract and grievance disputed in the electrical industry upon the submission of either party or a joint submission.

The council was headed by two co-chairpersons, one from management and one from the union, and included ten additional members, five each from management and the union, and two nonvoting officers chosen on a rotating basis from management and the union.

The parties to a dispute submitted written briefs and could make personal appearances at the quarterly meetings of the council. Representatives of the national union and contractors association would meet with local union and management persons to attempt to mediate disputes prior to consideration by the council.

An extraordinary aspect of the council was the method by which they reached decisions. After hearing a case, the council went into executive session. All decisions rendered by the council required unanimity among all members and awards were announced with no reasons given for the decisions.

In presenting an outline of the council's operations as it functioned in 1965, Healy (1965) noted that the council had succeeded where similar industry-wide panels had failed because of the binding, rather than advisory, nature of their awards. In addition, although decisions regarding 122 management chapters and 540 union locals were made centrally by a national council, it did not require the use of "neutrals" as we generally understand the term, and thus kept the decision-making process between the parties. The process apparently worked because of the superordinate commitment that the participants had to "the good of the industry" and the legitimation provided by a unanimous vote of people who were thoroughly familiar with the industry. Experience at Rutgers indicating that the actions of a seven-person joint faculty-administration grievance appeals committee have usually been by unanimous vote suggests that this concept could be applied to higher education as well (Begin, 1978, p. 297).

Establishing Special Agencies.   A primary purpose of these suggestions is to find a means by which impasse in academic bargaining can be creatively responded to by neutrals who have an understanding of the educational enterprise. Unless some appropriate mechanism is found, disputes that cannot be resolved directly by the parties concerned will eventually (in the public sector) come under the jurisdiction of existing public employment labor relations boards. Helsby (1977) notes that no state has established a special agency to meet the needs of higher education institutions.

> Because of the unique nature of the higher education collective bargaining equation, public sector board and commission personnel feel particularly unqualified and ill-equipped to handle the jurisdictional problems related thereto. Almost without exception, boards and commissions which have jurisdiction over higher education concur that a cadre of specially trained mediators, factfinders, arbitrators, hearing officers and other neutral board and commission personnel are needed to properly deal with disputes in higher education (p. 20).

The selection and preparation of such persons can proceed in two different ways: experienced neutrals can be identified and given additional background and training in the area of higher education, or experienced academics can be selected and trained to perform the functions of neutrals. The latter appears to be the preferable course for several reasons.

First, the nonacademic with an industrial background will have difficulty being accepted by the parties and may not fully understand the structures, norms, and even the vocabulary of higher education (Pisarski & Landon, 1976). Second, the fact that all arbitrators bring to each situation certain values that will influence their findings (Bankston, 1975) suggests that arbitrators with values developed in the academic milieu will be less likely to reach decisions that inadvertently subvert academic values than those whose training and experience has been in other sectors.

Finally, an experienced neutral is likely to have been trained primarily as an arbitrator rather than as a mediator and to be oriented toward adjudicating differences rather than assisting in intergroup development. In addition, it is likely that persons experienced as third parties in labor relations will have developed a traditional orientation toward union-management relations that might make it difficult for them to feel comfortable with participating in the kinds of activities related to creative academic bargaining.

Process Consultation

An earlier section described the potential use of neutral advisers to work with bargainers before and during formal negotiations. Many of the activities of these persons, such as assisting the parties in collecting and analyzing data, or advising on the meaning of proposed contract language, presumed a substantive knowledge of both collective bargaining and the academic environment. For this reason, they could be considered to be expert consultants, in many ways performing the same functions as do the expert consultants used by higher educational institutions in other settings.

A less common use of neutrals in organizational settings can be described as "process consultation." The expertise of the process consultant is not in the substantive areas in which the parties are negotiating, but rather in the processes through which they interact with each other. The process consultant sits as an observer in intergroup meetings and intervenes at various points in their interaction to comment upon the structure of the agenda, problems in communications, the behaviors of the participants, and similar matters concerning group process. The consultant may also propose intergroup exercises to give the participants practice in working with new problem-solving techniques, or provide coaching to groups or group members in communications skills, such as paraphrasing or impression-checking. In some ways, the activities of the process consultant may parallel those of the traditional mediator. However, mediators are usually persons trained in industrial and labor relations, or the law, who develop insight into the functioning of groups in conflict through experience. They are able to facilitate agreement on issues in dispute by gradually developing packages that both parties can agree to and controlling communications between them to facilitate their adoption. The mediators' primary concern is with reaching an agreement; presumably, once agreement is reached, the relationship between the parties will improve and the conflict between them reduced.

Process consultants, on the other hand, are trained in the applied behavioral sciences. Working on the principle that group processes can be analyzed and improved in any setting, they focus attention on such issues as the way groups structure their activities, communicate with each other, deal with conflict, go about problem-solving and decision-making activities, distribute influence, react to leadership, and similar matters. The process consultant's primary concern is with assisting groups to more fully understand their similarities and to increase the adequacy with which they communicate with one another; presumably, this will increase their ability to solve problems and decrease conflict.

The most critical difference between the mediator and the process consultant is that the mediator attempts to have the parties reach agreement by controlling communications; the process consultant attempts to improve the problem-solving capabilities of the groups by increasing the adequacy of their communications. While the mediator may focus attention on constructing a solution that both parties will accept, the process consultant emphasizes the need for the organization to learn how to diagnose its own problems and fully participate in the creation of solutions (Schein, 1969).

Descriptions of the use of process consultation (Schein, 1969; Walton, 1969; Schmuck et al., 1977) in industrial and educational settings note its utility in "confrontation" situations, that is, those in which two individuals or groups decide to directly face their differences rather than ignore them or smooth them over. Although there appear to be no published reports of the use of process consultation in an actual negotiation setting, the institutionalized confrontation of collective bargaining would appear to offer a natural setting for it.

Categories of Interventions.   Process consultants engage in two different, but related activities in working with groups. The first involves data collection, which may be done through observation of the groups, through interviews with group members, or through questionnaires or similar instruments. Through these data techniques, the consultant begins to understand the processes through which the group usually transacts its business. Rather than prescribe a specific solution to the problems facing the groups, as an expert consultant might do, the process consultant uses these data to select interventions that are likely to facilitate the continued problem solving of the group itself. A number of these interventions have been classified by Schein (1969) into four categories that broadly define the specific behaviors in which process consultants might engage.

Affecting the Agenda.   The first category of interventions is concerned with assisting the group in setting its agenda. During the course of the meeting, the consultant might ask group members how they reacted to an activity or interaction between members that had just taken place, thus temporarily changing the agenda of the group from the substantive issue under discussion to a consideration of their own operation. The consultant could propose that the group allocate a portion of its agenda at each meeting for process analysis at which group members can reflect upon the dynamics of the meeting in which they have just participated. This not only assists the group members to improve their skills for more effective future meetings, but also sensitizes members to process issues and reduces their reliance upon the consultant for this assistance. The consultant can also raise with the group questions about their satisfaction with the way in which the substantive agenda of the group is determined and suggest alternative processes by which an agenda might be constructed. Finally, the consultant can affect the agenda by providing conceptual or theoretical material at critical times that permits a group to gain more insight into its own process. Information concerning the communications and cognitive distortions created when groups compete, for example, might assist them in recognizing the early stages of an incipient escalating win-lose situation, and enable them to deal with it before it became too destructive to control.

Providing Feedback to Group.   The second category of interventions are those that provide feedback to the group, or to group members, about the effects of their own behavior. The feedback may be provided directly by the consultant, or the consultant may intervene in an ongoing meeting to ask people to react to an event that has just taken place. Feedback also takes place when the consultant presents to the group summaries of information collected that give the group more insight into its own procedures, or the way in which the operations of the group are perceived by others.

Counseling Group Members.   Interventions can also take the form of coaching or counselling group members, subgroups (such as individual bargaining teams), or the entire group composed of the negotiators of both sides. The consultant can propose exercises that give groups experience in decision making by consensus, for example, or can provide training in communications skills if the parties do not seem to be able to listen to what the other is saying.

Suggesting New Structures. Finally, the consultant can intervene in group structure by suggesting the use of study committees or other subgroups at appropriate times, by reminding the group of the advantages of altering group membership to deal with certain issues or offer specific expertise, or by suggesting alternative models of assigning work or establishing lines of authority than might otherwise occur to group members. This latter possibility might be particularly important in view of the commonly accepted and ritualized structures of collective bargaining that for the most part are accepted as "given" by the parties, and usually not challenged regardless of their effectiveness in promoting or inhibiting constructive bargaining.

The interventions of a process consultant are designed to perform certain functions in intergroup conflict. Through their use, the consultant can help to maintain the motivation of both groups toward constructive bargaining, assist in balancing the power of both groups, pace the negotiations process so that decisions are not made prematurely before differences and similarities are fully explored, assist the parties in more completely understanding the position of the other group and the perceptions that other group has of their own position, and maintain a productive level of tension in the relationship (Walton, 1969).

Monitoring Interaction Process. The process consultant cannot only be useful in working with each of the parties separately during their participation in bargaining, but he or she can also monitor and influence behavior at the bargaining table itself. The consultant can referee the interaction process, terminating discussions that are repetitious or counterproductive, or assuring that the parties have equal time in expressing their positions; initiate agenda items that tend to bring the real differences between the parties into clearer focus; paraphrase and restate the issues and the views being expressed by both bargaining groups to make communications between them more reliable; offer observations and feedback to the parties on their interaction; work with the parties to diagnose the latent sources of conflict between them that might be resulting in the substantive issues under discussion; or prescribe different discussion methods that might be more productive at different phases in the bargaining process (Walton, 1969).

Probably of equal importance, the mere presence of the consultant as a third party during the course of group interaction has several positive consequences. The process consultant can provide emotional support to the parties, and a role model that encourages the open expression of disagreements and recognition of the constructive possibilities for managing conflict (Schmuck et al., 1977). At the same time, the presence of a consultant presumed by the parties to be an expert in intergroup processes may lead the groups to believe that there is less possibility that the interaction will have destructive consequences. As Walton (1969) expressed it, because of the presence of a process consultant, a party "perceives less risk that the confrontation would bog down, become repetitive, and result in more frustration and perhaps bitterness. The third party may have slightly increased the potential payoff from these confrontations in the sense that participants believed that he could assist them in learning something of general value about their behavior in such situations" (p. 108).

Bargaining Evaluation

We have already discussed the use of third party neutrals in working with the parties prior to and during bargaining. An interesting use of neutrals *subsequent* to bargaining has been proposed by Walworth and Angell (1977). They suggest that after the completion of bargaining, the parties complete a self-evaluation, including management's evaluation of their own and the union's performance, and the union's evaluation of the same topics. A questionnaire might be developed to collect data from a representative sample of campus faculty and administrators as part of the self-evaluation process. As is now the case with regional accrediting reports, the self-evaluation could then be sent to an external visiting team of three persons, including a national union representative, a management consultant, and a neutral chairperson. They could review the report, visit the campus and conduct interviews, and prepare their own report for dissemination on campus evaluating the state of union-administration relationships, and making recommendations for improvement. The concept of using neutrals to evaluate and strengthen the bargaining relationship offers significant possibilities for developing creative bargaining approaches. Rather than having the visiting committee formed on traditional labor-management lines, it could also be composed with more functional purposes in mind. A neutral with a rich understanding of the academic environment, and two team members whose areas of expertise were in academic bargaining and intergroup conflict resolution, respectively, might provide a more useful balance of evaluation resources for the bargaining campus interested in creative bargaining.

IMPROVING INTERGROUP RELATIONS

As indicated in the previous section, there are a number of ways in which third parties can support the development of constructive academic bargaining by participating in prenegotiation, negotiation, and postnegotiation processes, or through their involvement in creative impasse activities. For the most part, these interventions contemplate that, except for the presence of the neutral, the structure of bargaining would continue in its normal form.

The interventions presented in this section are different. Rather than working with the parties in the bargaining context, they use neutrals to create new and artificial structures—such as workshops—within which the parties can examine the basic nature of their relationship. Through the processes of learning how each perceives the other's behavior, clarifying goals and objectives, and focusing on common problems, faculty and administrative groups may increase their joint problem-solving ability, and thereby influence the course of future negotiations.

Each of the programs presented in this section has been developed in settings outside of higher education, and there are no reports of their use in academic bargaining situations. However, the principles upon which they are based appear applicable to colleges and universities, and the descriptions here may encourage their experimental use by unionized institutions.

Workshops

A decade ago, Patten (1970) noted that collective bargaining was an institutionalized form of conflict resolution and suggested that consideration be given to using principles of behavioral science and laboratory training to assist the parties in finding ways of strengthening their relationships and developing consensus on major issues. The use of such processes, he argued, would develop the social and problem-solving skills of the participants, rather than supporting their drift into impasse, which requires the use of third party decision making. Giving specific emphasis to the use of training groups (T groups) in order to foster the development of open, authentic, and trusting relationships between the parties, Patten suggested that such training could be used either as a prelude to, or accompanying the process of, contract negotiations.

Ten years later, there is little evidence of the use of these techniques in labor-management relations, and no reports in the higher education literature to suggest that they have been employed in academic bargaining. However, there have been a number of reports of workshops utilizing behavioral science techniques, some including T group methodology, focused upon the reduction of intergroup conflict in international relations (Levi & Benjamin, 1977; Doob & Foltz, 1973; Kelman & Cohen, 1976; Kelman, 1972; Cohen, Kelman, Miller, & Smith, 1977). Although the results of these workshops have been ambiguous, their assumptions and processes appear to be consistent with academic norms and the problems of academic bargaining, and they may be considered as a means of altering traditional bargaining relationships.

Two different orientations to such workshops have been described. Although both depend upon behavioral science insights into processes through which conflicting groups can engage in more productive problem solving, they differ in their focus upon interpersonal communication and group process in one model and seeking alternative solutions to a specific problem related to intergroup conflict in the other. Both approaches will be briefly described.

Group Process Model.   The group process model is represented by a workshop experience involving a team of American behavioral scientists working with a group of Catholic and Protestant citizens of Belfast, Northern Ireland (Doob & Foltz, 1973). The project was conducted during a nine-day, live-in workshop held at a neutral site. The participants were all leaders or important figures in formal or informal groups in Belfast, an area of particularly bitter conflict between religious groups.

The purpose of the workshop was "to bring together persons of influence in two of the strife-torn neighborhoods in order to have them establish some degree of mutual trust and then to develop plans for establishing or improving relations between them" (Doob & Foltz, 1973, p. 492). The behavioral scientists who conducted the workshop hoped that the experience would help the participants increase their understanding of the other side, discover realms of common interest, and make initial attempts to engage in small projects cooperatively that might serve as models in their broader communities of a new form of interaction between the groups.

The first five days of the workshop were based upon Tavistock approaches to group development, in which small groups met in the presence of an authority figure (a consultant), who refused to participate in the activities of the group except for occasional interventions to interpret a specific bit of group behavior. This forced the groups to study their own behavior and to confront their usual relationships to authority.

During the last four days, the workshop was based on orientations associated with the National Training Laboratory. These included the creation of small groups which worked on the planning of activities to be implemented when they returned home. An understanding of group process was developed through participation in role playing, simulation, and similar exercises. The membership of each of the problem-solving groups formed during this stage was self-selected as were the problems they chose to consider.

During the workshop, the emphasis was on group processes and on an understanding of the ways in which they had dealt with conflict in the past. The problems they selected to work on, while important, were in reality vehicles for the development of more effective intergroup relationships. Commenting on the relationship between the workshop and the real world situation, the behavioral scientists wrote:

> some of the participants nakedly expressed the conviction that they were experiencing [at the workshop] the very kinds of hating and loving emotions evoked by the conflict in Northern Ireland. In the workshop, however, they could appreciate fragments of their own irrationality and, with the appreciation, seek to more rationally appraise their past behavior and even anticipate their future behavior back at Belfast. Self-knowledge concerning authority, therefore, could be the initial step toward discovering ways through which the communities of Belfast might conceivably live together (p. 502).

Although it was not possible to fully evaluate the effectiveness of this workshop approach, several outcomes were fairly certain. The two religious groups learned that, contrary to their expectations, the other side was not monolithic. "[F]rustrations, doubt, and weakness, it soon became abundantly clear, were shared by both sides. And that simple realization was a powerful source of eventual understanding and co-operation" (p. 504).

The structure of the workshop, the process interventions of the behavioral scientists functioning as neutrals, and the inclusion of participants of all political persuasions including extremists were all critical to making the workshop more than just a place where "people of good will" could get together to discuss their problems. As we have indicated previously, in order to manage conflict it is not enough merely to provide a setting in which communication can take place; in some cases the communications channels will not be used, and in others they will be used to exacerbate the existing conflict. The workshop offers the possibility of a setting in which union and administrative representatives can examine the relationships between the two groups and to some extent free themselves of the stereotypes that develop during intergroup conflict. Increasing the ability of the participants to communicate effectively and engage in joint planning may have significant carry-over effects when they next meet at the bargaining table.

Problem-Solving Workshops.   Unlike the preceding example, problem-solving workshops focus their attention upon content, rather than process for its own sake. As would be expected, therefore, the format is somewhat different, and the intent to have the workshop make an impact upon policy and decision makers is more explicit. The pilot operation of such a workshop to confront issues related to Israeli-Palestinian conflict is described by Cohen, Kelman, Miller, and Smith (1977). This description of the approach relies upon a model specified in Kelman and Cohen (1976).

The goal of the ten-day to two-week workshop is to develop an atmosphere in which creative problem solving between contending groups becomes possible, and eventually has an impact upon the policy-making processes of the principal parties represented by the members of the workshop. Workshop members are not official representatives of their countries, or groups, however, since that might commit participants to an "official" point of view and inhibit a problem-solving orientation. The groups from which they are drawn are informed of their participation, and the workshop members are selected so as to include in each group at least some persons who have access to the policy leadership of their respective sides. The members of each workshop group are selected so as to represent two specific areas of expertise; the examples provided by Kelman and Cohen included five economists and five educators on each ten-person team. They would participate in the workshop with eight to ten staff members, who might have expertise in group process, conflict theory, mediation, or the specific substantive areas to be discussed.

At the beginning of the workshop, the neutrals meet separately with each national group to obtain their views of the conflict between them and their analyses of conditions for its resolution. Following these sessions, the groups are reorganized along professional lines, and the bilateral groups meet under the auspices of the neutrals to discuss "problems within their domain that have to be confronted regardless of the particular political organization of the geographical region they share."

> The educators might focus on educational issues endemic to the region — such as the educational implications of religious, linguistic and cultural diversity,. . . Depending upon the degree of movement in the discussion,

participants are encouraged to explore ways in which they may be able to contribute to conflict resolution—through their professional specialties—and to develop proposals acceptable to both sides (p. 82).

During these meetings, which last for about a week, the consultants work with the groups to assist in the development of trust, encourage the adoption of an analytic stance, keep the group process moving in constructive directions, and call to the attention of the group facets of their interaction that might be related to their conflict. In addition to the group meetings, evening sessions are held at which theoretical concepts concerning conflict resolution may be presented and analyzed by all participants.

After spending a week studying these functional problems, the parties convene again in their national groups and present to them the proposals developed in the bilateral sessions. This serves as a reality check for the proposals, by assessing their acceptability by others who did not have a role in preparing them. Following these sessions, participants return to their expert groups to report reactions and to discuss plans for implementation and follow-up.

Various aspects of the workshop format serve specific functions. The workshop setting itself frees the parties to some extent from the norms that typify the conflict relationship, such as rigid adherence to group positions, legalistic arguments, and denial of the legitimacy of the other side's claims. The theoretical and conceptual inputs allow the parties to "gain some degree of distance from their own conflict and approach it indirectly, by way of general propositions or other cases" (p. 86). Both content and process observations by the consultants during the process assist in the preservation of a problem-solving orientation.

Kelman and Cohen argue that the most useful participants in workshops of this kind are not policy makers themselves, who may feel constrained by their roles to fully participate, nor persons so far removed from the policy process that their new insights can have no impact on high-level decision making. Rather, they should be individuals at an intermediate distance from official leadership, who are influential with specific constituencies, whose views represent those of some segment of opinion, and who have at least potential access to the political leadership.

Transferred to an academic setting, problem-solving workshops of this kind need not include union and administrative leadership, but might instead focus on senior faculty and middle-level administrators. It would not be difficult to find groups of such persons who shared common professional backgrounds and/or a common substantive interest in a particular aspect of institutional functioning. With the know-

ledge of the union and administration, but without their endorsement
and free to discuss substantive matters without committing either
party, participants in such a workshop could propose solutions to
problems that would come to the attention of union and administrative
leadership. The development of these new lines of communication and
interaction, as well as the assessment of possible solutions that are
considered valid by a group of influential persons whose perceptions
are important to their respective groups, could serve as a means of
reducing extreme positions and fostering increased collaboration between the groups themselves. A variant of the Kelman-Cohen approach, which is task oriented but takes place over only two days, has
been described by Levi and Benjamin (1977), again involving Arab and
Israeli participants.

Both the process and the problem-solving approaches share many
common characteristics, although their focus may be different. The
process orientation places primary emphasis on producing interpersonal change in partcipants, and in focusing their attention upon the
processes by which individuals relate to each other so that cooperative
activities in the future become more probable. The problem-solving
approach uses process as a means to an end, rather than as an end in
itself, and places emphasis upon intergroup change.

Although the potential use of a problem-solving approach might
appear to be more acceptable from a college and university perspective, either orientation offers an unusual opportunity for the bargaining college or university to experiment with new techniques for dealing
constructively with conflict.

Imaging

Destructive conflict caused by intergroup competition leads to misunderstandings of the other's positions and distortions in their communications systems that perpetuate and intensify the conflict. Parties
may develop "images of the enemy," which are resistant to change and
make it difficult for them to engage in collaborative activities.

"Imaging" is an intergroup process, guided by behavioral scientists
functioning as third party neutrals, which assists the parties in more
accurately assessing the goals and perceptions of the other and in
achieving a better understanding of the effects their own activities are
having on the behavior of the group. The process is based on the
theory that the images each group has of the other can be altered
through controlled confrontation, and that changes in perceptions and
communications will enable the parties to increase levels of trust,

identify more clearly the real issues between them, and move toward a more constructive bargaining relationship with greater emphasis on problem solving. A similar process, called an "intergroup," has been described by Burke (1974).

The original description of the process, called the union-management intergroup laboratory (Blake, Shepard, & Mouton, 1964; Blake, Mouton, & Sloma, 1965), which shall be summarized here, is of particular interest because it deals with union-management conflict in a naturalistic rather than an artificial setting. Their description of this two-day process refers to real people involved in a real bargaining relationship, and the content and tone of their interaction, as well as the high levels of conflict between the parties, will be instantly recognized by anyone who has been involved in difficult academic negotiations. Blake, Shepard, and Mouton (1964, pp. 155-195) present a complete description of the process, together with summaries of inter-party conversations at crucial stages, which should be of interest to all academic bargainers.

The union-management intergroup laboratory required 18½ hours of activity divided into eight phases (Blake, Shepard, & Mouton, 1964, p. 160). The activity in each phase, and the time period involved, is shown below to assist the reader in understanding the brief summary of each activity that follows.

Sequence and Phases of the Intergroup Laboratory

Phase	Activity	Time (hours)
1	Orientation	½
2	Intragroup development of own image and its image of the other	5
3	Exchange of images across groups	1
4	Clarification of images	2
5	Intragroup diagnosis of present relationship	4
6	Exchange of diagnoses across groups	3
7	Consolidation of key issues and sources of friction	2
8	Planning next steps	1
		18½

Phase 1. *Orientation of participants to the laboratory.* The orientation serves to remind the groups that they are not participating in a bargain-

ing session or engaged in a win-lose confrontation with the other. Rather, the purpose is to identify and attempt to plan for the elimination of problems in the relationships between the groups.

Phase 2. *Intergroup development of images.* During the first major activity, each group meets separately to complete two assignments: the preparation of a description of their own image of their behavior in their relationship with the other group and their image of the behavior of the other group. These descriptions are entered by each group on newsprint pads for the information of both groups in the next stage and for the use of the other group in phase 5.

Phase 3. *Exchange of images.* Meeting in joint session, the two groups post their written images of each other and themselves, and then describe for the other (ideally without interruption) the meaning of each of their descriptions.

Phase 4. *Clarification of images.* After having heard the images each group has presented of themselves and the other, the groups are then given an opportunity to ask questions that will clarify their meanings. This is not a session for argument or debate, although it may be difficult to prevent it completely, but rather a chance for resolving ambiguities.

Phase 5. *Intragroup diagnosis of the present relationship.* Having seen and had an opportunity to clarify the image that each group has of the other, and having noted the significant discrepancy existing between the behaviors and attitudes that each group ascribes to itself, and those attributed to it by the other, the groups return to their own meeting rooms to answer the following questions: "One, what is it we do (the union or management) that has contributed to the image the other group has of us? Secondly, what is it in our own beliefs and actions that leads us to the conclusion we have reached about ourselves?" This phase of the process is the crucial one, for it is in this process of self-diagnosis that the parties should be able to begin examining their own behavior as seen by the other so that insight can be gained into the causes of their present relationship.

Phase 6. *Exchange of diagnosis.* After having prepared their self-diagnosis of the difficulties in their relationship, the parties then reconvene together to discuss them. Although debate at many stages may be heated, the previous interaction and communication between the parties should make it possible for them both to more adequately communicate their feelings and attributions toward each other and to hear what the other party is actually saying. Similarities as well as differences between their positions become clearer, and the interaction becomes less oriented toward attack and defense and more focused upon matters of clarification.

Phase 7. *Consolidation of key issues.* In this phase, the parties jointly, with the assistance of the neutrals, identify the major critical issues in their relationship that must be improved.

Phase 8. *Planning next steps.* Before concluding the workshop, the parties discuss what next steps should be taken to begin working on the problems that they mutually identified in the previous phase.

Although a union-management intergroup laboratory process has probably not been used in a unionized college or university, the imaging process that is at its core has been used in developmental activities in school systems (Schmuck et al., 1977). While it obviously cannot by itself reverse a long history of destructive conflict between the parties, it can serve as a first step in a continuing program designed to move them toward more constructive conflict processes. Imaging may be particularly useful in some settings because, unlike some other processes, it is designed to function even in situations in which conflict between the parties is relatively intense.

The consequences of intergroup workshops have been summed up well as follows:

> The Intergroup Laboratory permits those groups in conflict to come together and work through the tensions and frictions that have built up during extended hostility. Confrontation at this level permits participants to get beneath the issues separating them and to gain knowledge of the misunderstandings and associated tensions. Once areas of friction have been identified and tensions reduced, the two groups can effectively solve their operational problems. (Blake, Shephard & Mouton, 1964, p. 194)

Confrontation Meeting

The confrontation meeting format, developed by Beckhard (1969), offers another model in which a neutral can work with groups in conflict. Although originally designed primarily as a process for establishing organizational goals, with slight modifications it might serve several functions in the academic bargaining process.

The confrontation meeting takes place over approximately six hours and can be divided into two periods on consecutive days. As modified to deal with bargaining, it would involve a relatively large number of persons. For the purposes of this example, we can imagine a group consisting of 20 administrative members (including all the members of the bargaining team) and 20 union members, including their negotiators. Alternatively, the group might be tripartite, composed of equal numbers of administrators, union leaders, and faculty senate officers and members.

During the first half of the meeting, the total group would be divided into subgroups of five or six people; for illustration using the tripartite model, each group would consist of two administrators, two union leaders, and two senate members, none of whom were otherwise directly related in the organization. Each group would be given an hour to make a list of items in response to the following assignment:

> Thinking of yourself as a person with needs and goals in this organization, and also thinking of the total organization, what are the behaviors, procedures, ways of work, attitudes, etc., that should be different so that life would be better around here?

The total group then would reassemble, and their lists posted. Categories of problems would be developed, and the first portion of the meeting ended.

The second half of the meeting would begin with consideration by the entire group of the appropriate forum in which the problems identified on the previous day should be considered. In the example, it might be assumed that some of them would be assigned by the group to the faculty senate, others to the union, some to the administration, and others to particular agencies already existing on the campus, such as a university budget committee or an institutional curriculum committee.

The total group would then divide into functional groups, so that individual meetings would be held by the senior administration, the faculty senate leadership, the leadership of the union and administrative bargaining teams, and senior officials of the appropriate institutional committees. Each group would be asked to go through the list of problems that had been identified as being within their jurisdiction, and to identify those upon which they would commit themselves to work. The subgroups would then reconvene into a single group, and each would report to the full committee the priority items upon which it was going to work. A follow-up meeting would be set at which each group was to report to the entire membership on the progress it had made in dealing with the specific problems to which it had made a commitment.

The confrontation meeting may be an interesting process for pre-bargaining activity. It operates best in situations of high organizational stress (Beckhard, 1969), which will often typify the institution involved in academic bargaining, particularly during its early years. It can serve as a means by which the allocation of issues to the faculty senate or the union can be mutually addressed in an institution wishing to create or preserve a dual governance system, and it can help to establish the academic bargaining agenda. In addition, because it requires administrators and other faculty groups to make commitments regarding certain issues, it can remove certain matters from the bargaining table. In bargaining situations, items may be included in the demands of one party, not because they necessarily wish to assert jurisdiction, but because they believe that the matter is important and they have no assurance that it will receive appropriate attention outside the bargaining framework. The confrontation meeting permits them to participate in the assignment of such issues to other arenas and to hear periodic reports on the progress being made.

Relationship by Objectives

Relationship by Objectives (RBO) is an innovative program developed by the Federal Mediation and Conciliation Service (FMCS) combining several aspects of workshops, imaging, and confrontation meetings and is used in situations of intense labor management conflict. Since it has been employed as a preventive mediation device only since 1975, there are no data concerning its effectiveness. Anecdotal reports, however, suggest that it has changed the bargaining environment, reduced grievances, and increased communications between labor and management where it has been tried (Weimer, 1977; "U.S. Mediators Try a New Role," 1975). The structure and process of the program has been described by Popular (1977).

The program involves from 20 to 40 union and management participants, including both leaders and middle level persons from both groups. Two different RBO formats have been used: one is based upon an intensive three- to four-day meeting in a retreat setting; the other, called a Six Pak, is based on six separate meetings that may occur over a three- or four-week period. During the program participants meet in three different formats: small labor-management committees, separate labor and management groups, and meetings of the entire group. Each meeting is attended by an FMCS mediator who functions as a third party neutral.

Joint Committees.   The program begins with small joint committees watching a movie dramatizing poor labor-management relations in an industrial setting, and then asked to analyze the problems depicted in the film and recommend solutions. This unusual process provides an opportunity for labor and management to begin working together as teams, and to gain insights into their own problems by observing and analyzing a nonthreatening situation which is in many ways similar to their own.

Separate Labor and Management Groups.   Labor and management are then split into separate groups and asked to begin work on their own problems by asking themselves what they, and the other party, should be doing to improve their relationships. When the two groups meet together, mediators draw up four lists for review by the participants. The lists include what the union believes it should do and what the company should do and what the company believes the goals of the union and itself should be. The groups then consolidate these four lists into one list of mutual objectives. The smaller joint labor-management committees are then assigned one of these objectives and asked to develop action steps, which are subsequently reviewed by the union and management groups meeting separately.

Meetings of Entire Group.   The entire group then meets to negotiate out differences that remain. The final step in the RBO process includes automatic 90-day follow-ups by FMCS mediators who keep track of the progress of the parties and the status of their mutually agreed upon goals.

Because RBO is a federal program only available to parties organized under NLRA, it is not now accessible to public colleges and universities. As a no-nonsense, practically oriented, and tested program solidly based upon behavioral science concepts, it would appear to offer a most productive approach to creative bargaining in unionized institutions. Development of such a program by a state employment relations board, a university industrial relations or organization psychology department, or a national academic organization would offer an important resource to unionized institutions presently faced with disruptive bargaining conflict.

Organization Development

Organization development (OD) is an orientation toward planned change in organizations relying heavily upon behavioral science insights into interpersonal and intergroup relations. Although there are extensive reports of its use in elementary and secondary school settings (Schmuck et al., 1977), little has been reported about its use or effects in college or university settings. One of the few projects in the literature utilizing OD approaches to the building of campus change agent teams (Sikes, Schlesinger, & Seashore, 1973, 1974) dealt only with small subunits of colleges and universities, and the projects themselves had little if any impact on the operation of the organizations in which they were developed.

While there are many problems associated with the potential use of organization development approaches, some of which shall be mentioned later in greater detail, its general orientation and values are consistent enough with the stated norms of higher educational institutions to justify exploration of its use in the development of creative bargaining relationships.

Probably the most widely cited definition of organization development is that given by Beckhard (1969):

> Organization development is an effort (1) planned, (2) organization-wide, and (3) managed from the top to (4) increase organizational effectiveness and health through (5) planned interventions in the organization's "processes," using behavioral science knowledge. (p. 9)

Examining the various elements of this definition indicate some of the possible uses of OD in the unionized institution as well as some of its shortcomings.

Planned Effort.   Optimally, OD is a planned effort. This implies that it is not merely a one-time activity casually implemented because a single person or group thought that participation in a specific activity might be "interesting." The requirement for planning implies that there be an organizational commitment for change, an analysis of present levels of organizational functioning and effectiveness by qualified experts, the preparation of long-range plans of approach by the expert and organizational representatives working collaboratively, and the commitment of resources (time and personal involvement, as well as financial) to carry through the program. This planned, comprehensive approach to organizational functioning is one of the great strengths of OD but also poses one of the greatest problems for its use in the unionized institution. OD activities are concerned with such fundamental facets of institutional operation that a successful effort may take between two and five years to result in substantial change (Boyer & Crockett, 1973). Changes that occur in both administrative and union leadership over this period of time, coupled with the increasing turbulence of an environment that seems to place new and unforseen pressures on an institution on almost a yearly basis make it difficult to assume the continuity of operation within which an OD effort might be most effective.

Organization-Wide.   The organization-wide orientation of OD means that emphasis is placed upon changing the total communications, decision making, and other related systems of the organization, and not just on attempting to alter the way in which individual subunits function. Since one of the objectives of OD is the development of organization-wide consensus, this total organizational approach is more likely to be an effective strategy. Collective bargaining, too, has an actual or potential impact on these same organizational systems, so that the total organizational coverage and many of the areas of concern are similar in bargaining and in OD. Unfortunately, both OD and collective bargaining make general assumptions about reasonable regularity in the structure and processes of the organization, including the existence of a clear authority system. In many ways, colleges and universities are characterized more by political decision processes than by the bureaucratic structures typical of the business and industrial organizations in which OD was developed. At least partly for that reason, Bennis (1973), an OD expert as well as an experienced academic administrator, has indicated that OD has not been successful in universities. It has, he notes, been useful in organizations that are self-contained, large, and rich, with easily identifiable and measurable products. Higher educational institutions, in general, do not conform to these characteristics.

Managing OD from the Top.   Managing OD from the top is considered to be a requisite for successful implementation. Without the involvement and commitment of top management, any changes resulting from the OD effort may easily be vitiated and the system returned to its initial state. This top-down, management-oriented philosophy is an effective means of ensuring a supportive climate for organizational changes that occur. At the same time, it identifies OD as primarily a management process, which retains management control of organizational processes albeit with perhaps more understanding of the needs of "employees" (Barbash, 1976). Indeed, case studies of organization development activities appear to contain almost no references to the presence of unions, and the OD literature is almost barren of examples of OD activities that focus attention on union-management relationships (Kochan & Dyer, 1976). The reports by Blake and Mouton (1968) of union-management intergroup activities developed within a comprehensive OD program for industry and by Nadler (1978) concerning joint labor management change workshops focusing upon quality of work and organizational improvement issues represent two of the rare examples of OD in unionized settings. At least in part, the failure of OD to speak to the needs of unionized organizations has been due to its development in hierarchical organizations and the consequent inability to comprehend the political and adversarial relationships that characterize most union-management interactions. In addition, OD tends to see all conflict as yielding to problem-solving approaches and is often unable to come to terms with the essential elements of distributive bargaining that are functional when the parties are faced with objective conditions of scarce resources (Strauss, 1976).

Ironically, however, although OD was developed in the industrial sector and then found to be difficult to apply in unionized settings, the existence of unionization in academic institutions might prove to increase the utility of OD approaches in an organization framework that previously has been resistant to them. This may be partially so because the college and university are unique in their involvement of "employees" in performing functions which, in almost all other settings, would be the prerogatives of management. Perhaps of even greater importance, the implementation of bargaining on a campus increases the hierarchical properties of the organization, thus making it more similar to more traditional OD environments, while at the same time it legitimates the structures and processes that make possible the confrontation necessary to successful OD efforts. It has been suggested (Weisbord, 1978) that OD may not function effectively in universities because of their multiple and unclear goals and the relatively low level of collaborative activity required between its participants. For these reasons, it may be appropriate to consider the development of OD activities in unionized institutions that are single purposed and relatively highly structured, rather than in more complex universities with amorphous authority systems and unclear goals.

Increasing Organizational Effectiveness and Health.   Because OD programs attempt to increase organizational effectiveness and health, they focus upon major changes in structure, managerial strategies, and organizational norms. Some of the characteristic goals of OD programs (Beckhard, 1969) include:
- increasing collaboration and diminishing competition among organizational subunits
- opening up the communications system to increase the adequacy of information up, down, and laterally in the organization
- increasing the organization's ability to plan and to cope effectively with changes in its environment
- changing decision-making patterns so that decisions are made on the basis of expertise and the availablity of information, rather than on position in the organizational hierarchy
- diversifying the structural forms of the organization so that some processes and decisions are handled by the stable and ongoing structure, while others, as appropriate, are performed in temporary systems or other structures more suitable to it

Each of these OD orientations is compatible with the expressed values of higher educational institutions, and they are in many ways consistent with the objectives articulated by academic unions.

Intervening into the System's Process.

In working with organizations in a program of planned change, the OD consultant plans a number of activities, or interventions into the system, based upon behavioral science knowledge. Some activities previously described in this chapter, such as the participation of process consultants, imaging, and the confrontation meeting, are examples of the interventions that might be part of an OD program. They do not, however, constitute an OD program themselves, since they have been identified as discrete activities rather than as part of a continuing, planned program.

In general, OD interventions fall into one of four categories: training designs based upon sequential plans to change the knowledge, behavior, and norms of individuals in the system, and altering the organizational structure to support these changes; data feedback designs that collect information from the system, disseminate it to system members, identify the discrepancies between what is actually happening, and assist the organization to solve problems related to these discrepancies; confrontation designs, which provide a structure for uncovering conflict between groups and working on strategies for managing these conflicts so that they lead to increased problem-solving adequacy in the system; and process observation and feedback designs, in which neutrals observe the ongoing functioning of a group and sensitize it to its own processes and their consequences (Schmuck et al., 1977).

Through various combinations of design elements, OD interventions can be focused upon team development, intergroup relationships within the system, the development of planning and goal-setting processes for individuals, teams, and the system, and improving the knowledge, skills and abilities of organizational members at all levels (Beckhard, 1969). A successful OD program may include interventions selected from among each of the designs, based upon the diagnoses made at the initiation of the effort, changes in the system as the program progresses, and the increasing sophistication of the participants over time.

Of all the strategic approaches to creative academic bargaining, the development of OD programs is in many ways both the most comprehensive and the most problematic. The political nature of the governance processes in many academic institutions probably reinforces an orientation toward compromise rather than problem solving. The initiation of bargaining, as Blake and Mouton (1964) have pointed out, may exacerbate that tendency by trading off faculty security and academic management items without solving the real problems of either. At the same time, bargaining may lead to destructive conflict and the attempt by one side or the other to impose its own desired solutions through coercion or the application of whatever sanctions might be available to it.

Given our present level of understanding of union-administrative relationships in higher education, and the question of whether adversarial relationships and OD concepts are compatible (Milstein, 1977), an OD model that can meet the needs of the unionized institution has not yet been developed. Perhaps the description of some of the purposes and activities of OD given in some of the present references in the field will encourage a creative institutional administration and union to experiment with the use of behavioral science interventions to deal with specific problems, or to try and create a new OD approach that appears to meet the needs of the unionized institution.

For the present, it can be said that OD offers a promising but still unclear process through which the problems of the unionized institution might be fruitfully explored.

The second basic strategy leading to more constructive bargaining is the use of third party neutrals. Behavioral scientists have identified a number of constructive functions third parties can perform in intergroup conflict situations. Unfortunately, the traditions of bargaining support the idea that the best bargains are those developed by the two parties alone. The use of third parties in the process is thus often seen as a reflection of an immature bargaining situation, inexperienced bargainers, or an admission of weakness by the side proposing it. This view acknowledges the legitimacy of third parties only at impasse. However, once impasse has been reached, the positions of both sides are usually more firmly held, their adversarial relationships intensified, and they have often exhausted most of the flexibility in the bargaining relationship. Under these conditions, the ability of the third party to encourage creative bargaining initiatives is severely limited.

Rather than considering the use of neutrals solely as an alternative at impasse, creative academic bargaining can make use of third parties at various stages, such as prior to the commencement of bargaining, while bargaining is continuing, and even after bargaining has been concluded. Neutrals can help the parties more fully realize the integrative potential in their relationship by providing noncrisis neutral advisement both before and during bargaining itself. They can also assist the parties by serving as members of joint study committees or through the establishment of impasse procedures involving standing panels of experienced and knowledgeable persons at either the campus or regional levels. Neutrals serving in these capacities can either be professionals who fully understand the academic environment, or academics who are seen by both sides as being able to objectively balance faculty and administration concerns.

Process consultants could also be used in the bargaining relationship and could contribute to creative bargaining by helping to set the agenda, providing feedback, counselling group members, or suggesting new structures. Finally, third parties can help both sides to evaluate bargaining after the process has been concluded, thus permitting both sides to gain a better understanding of their relationship and greater insight into the effects of bargaining on campus functioning.

In addition to helping the parties exploit the integrative potential of bargaining, neutrals can assist the parties to improve their intergroup relations. This is usually done prior to the commencement of bargaining and can include the use of group process or problem-solving workshops, or participating in imaging exercises or confrontation meetings. The RBO program offered to business and industry by FMCS might be a useful and appropriate process for academic bargaining as well.

Although organizational development approaches have not been applied or tested in academic bargaining, the principles upon which OD are based appear consistent with many aspects of organizational functioning in higher education. OD is both the most comprehensive and the most problematic strategic approach to academic bargaining, and creative uses of it should be explored by unionized colleges and universities.

9

The Strategies of Creative Academic Bargaining: Structural Approaches

THE DIFFERENCES BETWEEN the behaviors required of integrative and distributive bargaining pose a significant dilemma for the academic negotiator concerned with the establishment of cooperative union-administration relationships. The tactics of distributive bargaining, it will be remembered, are effective in assuring competing parties that they will maximize their payoff in a zero-sum game. Since the resources over which they are bargaining are limited, any concessions won by one party come at the expense of the other. The most common bargaining subject for which distributive tactics are appropriate, and for which problem-solving orientations are most likely to be ineffective, is salary; except under unusual circumstances, the parties are unable to increase the total sum available to them and, therefore, must bargain over how it is to be distributed.

In contrast, there are many areas of bargaining in which the parties, through the use of problem-solving approaches, can increase the payoffs to each through cooperation. This approach, called integrative bargaining, is of little value in negotiating salaries, but it can be useful in dealing with other financially oriented matters such as fringe benefits and is of greatest value in dealing with bargaining issues related to the distribution of influence, job security, and other items unconstrained by finite resources.

Although collegial norms would suggest the desirability of using the tactics of integrative bargaining in an academic setting, the need to utilize distributive techniques in dealing with salaries makes it difficult for even the negotiator with collaborative intentions to adopt a consistent bargaining orientation, and the interactions developed during the distributive phase of bargaining are likely to interfere with attempts to engage in problem solving on other items. This basic dilemma of the academic bargainer is of more than theoretical interest, because the specific behaviors required by the two bargaining orientations are not only quite different, but in fact are incompatible. The distributive bargainer attempts to limit information given to the other side, so that the bargaining process itself is conducted in an information-impoverished environment. Communication between the bargaining teams is stylized and restrained, and only the chief negotiators are permitted to talk during the bargaining sessions without explicit permission. The parties issue demands to each other and attempt to misrepresent their preferences so that the other cannot understand their priorities or the major problems in back of each demand. Unwanted demands are often placed on the table solely for use in later trading, and time limits are imposed to facilitate the final concession-granting that leads to agreement. Because of the threats of the environment, risk taking is inhibited, and both parties assume defensive postures in their relations to each other. Parties attempt to become committed to firm positions as soon as possible.

In contrast, integrative bargaining requires full and open communication between all participants (the input of those with minority positions is particularly helpful) and the full sharing of all available information. Leadership in integrative groups is more concerned with facilitating the communications process between members than with serving as the group's representative in negotiation. Parties do not issue demands to each other, but rather attempt to describe in as complete detail as possible the problems they are facing. A premium is placed on clearly communicating preferences so that the parties can jointly search for solutions that meet the needs of the other as well as themselves. Only real problems are discussed, and an attempt is made to provide a supportive environment in which new ideas can be explored and risks can be taken. Time limits are either not used or are very flexible to encourage careful consideration of numerous alternatives, and parties remain exploratory and tentative throughout the process.

It has been pointed out that—

Generally speaking, the tactics appropriate for pure distributive bargaining conflict with those appropriate for pure integrative bargaining. At virtually every turn the negotiator finds himself in a dilemma: Should he conceal information in order to make his tactical commitment more credible, or should he reveal information in order to pursue integrative bargaining; should he bring militant constituents into the session to affirm feeling, or should he use small subcommittees in which new ideas can be quietly explored? (Walton & McKersie, 1965, p. 182)

A bargainer attempting to switch back and forth between strategies depending on whether a specific agenda item is generally integrative or distributive in nature would have to constantly change behavioral patterns, as would the opponent who would have to share the same perceptions and the same behavioral range for the same items. More-over, this kind of mixed-motive bargaining, which attempts to move between two contrary forms of behavior, poses other bargaining prob-lems. For example, the free exploration of alternatives during a prob-lem-solving process might reveal information about preferences that the other party could use to its advantage when the next distributive item appeared on the agenda.

One solution to this dilemma, suggested by Walton and McKersie (1966), is to separate the two kinds of decision processes as much as possible. The bases for separation or differentiation they suggest are by agenda, by people, by ground rule, by time, and by space. Several of these proposals have already been discussed, although not identified in quite this way. For example, the establishment of ground rules that permit the parties to go "off the record," or hold side-bar conferences, is a means by which alternatives can be explored without commitment, thus permitting integrative techniques to be used as a supplemental process to distributive bargaining.

SEPARATION BY TIME AND BY PEOPLE

Separation by time can be accomplished in several ways. One possi-bility suggested by Walton and McKersie (1966) would be for institu-tions to utilize the flexible deadline approach developed by General Motors and the United Automobile Workers. In this situation, bargain-ing deadlines were not established in advance. Rather, the parties could engage in bargaining without the threat of strike as long as both believed that progress was being made. This freedom from deadlines should have the effect of facilitating a problem-solving orientation and the exploration of issues. At either party's discretion, however, notice could be given that bargaining was commencing, and traditional dis-tributive approaches were then appropriate. Through this means the expectation was that in the first, nonbargaining phase, the parties could explore issues and discover ways in which the total payoffs could be increased. In the second phase, they would then bargain over how the additional resources developed in the first phase would be al-located.

The joint fact-finding committees mentioned earlier separate the bargaining issues by people. The use of experts from both sides to meet jointly, either to develop mutually agreed-upon facts, or to develop the largest possible number of alternatives, can occur in a problem-solving environment and then be reported back to the negotiators at the table for use in distributive bargaining.

The two major means of separating distributive from integrative decision process, which have not yet been mentioned and which are the subjects of this section, are separation by agenda through the concept of dual governance and spatial separation through the use of joint study committees. Also included are brief comments on the possible use of separation devices based on indices, and the idea of tier bargaining.

SEPARATION BY AGENDA

Dual Governance

Probably the most perplexing issue in academic bargaining is that of scope: Upon what matters should the union be permitted to bargain? In the private sector, the phrase "terms and conditions of employment" is reasonably well delimited, and management is assumed to retain all rights to run the enterprise subject only to restrictions placed upon it by the terms of the contract and the union's right to grieve over contract interpretation. With the expansion of unionization into the public sector, and the inclusion of white collar and professional employees into bargaining units, there has been a tendency for the scope of bargaining to expand and for unions to become more interested in influencing management decision making on matters of basic policy.

Role of Faculty Senate.   The role of faculty members in their institutions is significantly different even from that of most other professional workers in public or private employment. The extensive nature of these differences, which are assumed to be familiar to the reader, have been concisely summarized as follows (Carnegie Council, 1977):

> Faculty members are distinguished from other employees, among other ways, in their self-determination over matters of teaching and research; in their sharing of responsibility for department management; in their supervision of other persons, from teaching assistants to secretarial personnel; in their need, because of the special nature of their duties, for special protection for their academic freedom; in their participation in the selection and advancement of their colleagues; in their evaluation of the performances of students and those persons who report to them; in their participation within a national or regional rather than a local labor market; and in their actual or potential coverage by specialized tenure regulations.

> Faculty members are, in fact, partly employees, partly managers, and partly professional colleagues. (p. 9)

The involvement of faculty, not only in activities that reflect their roles as employees, but also in processes that in other settings are clearly the prerogatives of management, has caused ambivalence in the academic community on the organizational and structural means by which these various interests should be expressed. The question of scope is structurally related to the existence at many unionized campuses of senates or other faculty representative bodies which, to varying degrees depending upon the history and traditions of individual institutions, have been responsible for fulfilling the faculty's role in governance. Where senates do not exist, the union may in fact provide the only meaningful opportunity for faculty to participate in governance activities of the institution. Where they do, however, there are three possible relationships that can develop between senates and unions (Garbarino, 1975). One (almost always the union) can co-opt the other, so that the leadership of both groups is identical; they can compete with each other over their respective jurisdictions; or they can cooperate by establishing separate and essentially nonoverlapping spheres of influence. When this latter condition exists, the institution can be said to have a dual system of governance.

Relationship between Unions and Senates.   Early analysts saw the relationships between unions and senates as essentially unstable because of overlapping membership and constituencies, unclear jurisdictions, and the authority ceded to unions, but not senates, in the law (Garbarino, 1975). Even where cooperative relationships initially existed, it was felt that the tendency for union contracts and areas of jurisdiction to expand, and the political nature of unions requiring them to constantly seek "more," would gradually move traditional governance issues into the bargaining arena. The end result of such an expansion could eventually be the extinction of the senate as an organizational structure.

Garbarino's finding that the threatened replacement of senates by unions was either premature or exaggerated has been supported by results of surveys of college presidents and union leaders (Baldridge et al., 1978). Both groups report that senates and unions have tended to function in discrete areas, with senates remaining active in academic matters and unions in economic ones. This pattern is consistent with recommendations of the Carnegie Council (1977) that academic bargaining be limited in scope to issues having a substantial monetary dimension, and that issues related to academic governance be dealt with through traditional forms of faculty participation in decision making.

Although functional and effective dual governing systems may be increasingly challenged in the future as the functions of traditional senates diminish while the scope of bargaining gradually expands (Begin, 1978, p. 259), at least at the present time they appear to be working well in a number of institutions. This approach is of great significance to creative bargaining because it offers a means by which the dilemma of integrative and distributive bargaining can be ameliorated through the separation of agendas. The union, responsible for the economic well-being of the faculty, can engage in distributive bargaining and its associated tactics in negotiating salaries, fringe benefits, and those aspects of employment conditions that would be common to employee bargaining in the private sector. The senate, or other representative body, could at the same time engage in the processes of integrative bargaining over governance issues with little or no direct impact on the economic well-being of the faculty. Thus, those items with integrative potential can be dealt with in a problem-solving setting and in the absence of the dynamics that characterize destructive conflict. In turn, those responsible for distributive bargaining issues can utilize the most effective tactics without fear that doing so will endanger the ability of faculty and administration to work cooperatively in academic and related matters. To be most effective, separation of these issues by agenda should also include separation by people, so that those on both sides who participate in union-administration negotiations are not the same people who participate in the more traditional governance processes.

For some bargaining issues, the line between economic and academic aspects may be difficult to draw, and coordination of senate and union activities made difficult. Begin and Weinberg (1976) mention several approaches to this problem. A special committee of the senate was formed at St. John's University (and suggested but never implemented at Rutgers University) with the responsibility of coordinating senate-union relationships. A slightly different approach was suggested by an AFT union at one of the New Jersey state colleges but rejected by the administration. Their plan called for a joint union-administration committee to decide if specific issues should be handled through the governance or the bargaining mechanisms. Institutions wishing to establish or support an existing dual governance approach might wish to consider these possible processes for maintaining the separation of distributive and integrative items. An alternative might be to form a campus committee, consisting of faculty who are not in either the union or the senate leadership, to study and recommend to the union, senate, and administration what they consider the appropriate forum for any issue to be. Such a committee might not only consider new items, but also at the request of any of the three groups review previous decisions to evaluate their effective placement after some experience in operation.

Means of Establishing Dual Governance.

There are essentially three means through which the structure of dual governance can be established: legislation, judicial or administrative interpretation, and practice. Neither the National Labor Relations Act, which is the controlling legislation for academic bargaining in private institutions of higher education, nor most of the states having legislation affecting bargaining of public employees (Carnegie Council, 1977), have provisions that recognize the unique characteristics and needs of colleges and universities. Angell (n.d.) has commented upon the significant problems current legislative provisions pose for the bargaining institution, particularly in their failure to recognize the existence of traditional governance structures and modes of faculty participation in governance.

Of the several attempts to establish specific legislative authorization limiting bargaining scope in order to foster the establishment of dual governance, perhaps the most clearly described took place in Wisconsin (Lavine & Lemon, 1975). After bills were introduced in the Wisconsin legislature by two rival faculty unions, the University of Wisconsin System Board of Regents prepared their own legislation that would have permitted limited bargaining on salaries, fringe benefits, and nongovernance working conditions by the faculties of the system. Their bill would have *prohibited* bargaining over any matter of shared governance, including such items as personnel policies, merit salary policies, academic matters, faculty governance structures, and similar issues. In proposing a bill of extremely limited scope, the board's stated purpose was to protect the existing governance structures already provided for in legislation, while establishing a dual governance structure through enabling bargaining over economic matters. The regents bill was not supported by either of the two contending unions, and none of the three bills proposed were enacted.

The abortive Wisconsin attempt is of unusual interest because it would have mandated a system of dual governance through the unusual expedient of *prohibiting* bargaining over governance activities. Other states legislatively providing for a narrowed scope of bargaining have done so through the inclusion of management rights provisions in the enabling legislation. These do not forbid management to bargain on any issue, but make bargaining on certain topics permissive. This allows management to determine, subject to consideration by the state public employment relations agency upon appeal by the union, that a certain matter introduced by the union need not be bargained unless management is willing to do so. Such determinations by the courts, the National Labor Relations Board, and state employment boards are the second means by which the limits of dual governance can be established.

Decisions of these agencies have increasingly recognized the unusual nature of academic governance and have separated the "management" role of faculty from those rights that they enjoy as "employees." One of the earliest and most widely cited of such opinions was delivered by New York's Public Employment Relations Board in ruling that a board of trustees did not have to negotiate with the union over the placement of students on faculty personnel committees unless it wished to do so:

> The right of the faculty to negotiate over terms and conditions of employment does not enlarge or contract the traditional prerogatives of collegiality; neither does it subsume them. These prerogatives may continue to be exercised through the traditional channels of academic committees and faculty senates and may be altered in the same manner as was available prior to the enactment of the [state public employment law]. We note with approval the observation that "faculty must continue to manage, even if that is an anamoly. They will, in a sense, be on both sides of the bargaining table." We would qualify this observation, however; faculty may be on both sides of the table, but not their union. (Board of Higher Education of the City of New York, 1974)

Recent decisions determining that governance issues are permissive subjects of bargaining with faculty unions (i.e., that boards may decide whether or not they wish to bargain about them) have also been made under the National Labor Relations Act. Although applying only to private institutions, they are likely to be followed by state agencies when similar matters are raised by unions in public institutions (Semas, 1977). Probably the most unusual legal interpretation limiting the scope of bargaining is that made recently by the Supreme Court of New Jersey (Ridgefield Park, 1978), which legally removes all "permissive" subjects of bargaining from the negotiation table until and unless the legislature changes the present law. In New Jersey, there are now only two categories of issues for bargaining: those that are "mandatory," and those that are "prohibited."

Through decisions such as these, judicial and quasijudicial administrative agencies establish the legal bases for systems of dual governance, and explicitly or implicitly support the creation and continuation of structures to implement them. Either legislation, or judicial or administrative interpretations, can remove governance issues as mandated items for negotiation, and in doing so remove them from the distributive bargaining agenda. As Begin (1973) has pointed out, this separation of integrative and distributive items has the potential to improve the cooperative relationships between the bargainers. Whether or not this occurs, however, is to a great extent a function of the degree to which the parties see such restrictions as legitimate and therefore acceptable. Where they do not, the union is likely to use the bargaining situation as the forum for testing and attempting to expand the limits of bargainability. Since it is extremely difficult to set practical and stable limits on what is bargained if either party wishes to expand them, regardless of its other virtues or weaknesses the separation of integrative and distributive items merely through law or interpretation is not by itself likely to lead to creative bargaining. It may in fact result in a relationship that is so frustrating to one side that its efforts will be focused on overturning or otherwise circumventing the established limits, with little or no attention given to ways in which the parties can operate creatively within them.

This suggests that if dual governance is to be an effective means of fostering creative bargaining, it must develop voluntarily as a matter of practice between the parties; it cannot merely be imposed. Regardless of the legal provisions under which they function, constructive bargaining is most likely to occur in situations in which the administration and union recognize the importance of separating integrative and distributive items in order to serve the long-range purposes of the institution and consequently the interests of the parties. This separation offers a means through which problem-solving approaches can be applied to professional matters, free of arbitrary time pressures and we-they orientations, and not subject to the tendency to trade-off or compromise rather than continue the search for mutually acceptable solutions.

Unions will be most amenable to this voluntary limitation on scope if their institution has an ongoing and relatively effective means of faculty participation in governance, and less agreeable where such mechanisms are relatively ineffective or impotent. In the latter situation, it may be useful for the parties to avoid bargaining over substantive governance issues, and instead to bargain over the roles of governance bodies such as the faculty senate. The provisions of the governance structure can then be incorporated into the agreement (Walters, 1973), a process referred to as "collegiality by contract."

Kemerer and Baldridge (1977) argue for political reasons that it is preferable to bargain with unions over the establishment of new governance mechanisms than it is to permit union leadership to directly participate in academic decision making. We support this view, although on the somewhat different grounds that distributive bargaining tactics that union leaders must employ on economic matters to best serve the needs of the membership are inappropriate to the problem-solving orientations that should characterize academic governance matters.

SPATIAL SEPARATION

Study Committees

A study committee is a group established by the two bargaining parties, charged with the responsibility for investigating one or more specific problems and making recommendations back to the bargaining teams (Carr & VanEyck, 1973). Committees may consist of members of the bargaining teams themselves, or of management and union representatives who are not on the bargaining team. Occasionally, it may be tripartite in nature, with neutrals acceptable to the parties named as full members. In all cases, the study committee meets away from the bargaining table itself and is expected to engage in a process considerably different from traditional bargaining. The use of joint study committees has been found to be a contributing factor to peaceful negotiations in the industrial sector. Their major impact, however, may not be so much in the substantive areas in which they deal as in their effect on the general tone of the relationship between the parties and the establishment of additional systems of intergroup communications, which make it easier for the parties to understand each other when discussing key bargaining issues (Golden & Parker, 1955). The formation of joint labor-management committees is now an accepted aspect of the technical assistance programs of the Federal Mediation and Conciliation Service and is recognized as an effective means of improving the relations between the parties (FMCS, 1978, p. 7). As negotiations in industrial settings increasingly include issues in addition to those traditionally concerned with economic security, such as quality of work and productivity, the need for nonadversarial processes have become recognized by labor and management alike. One study of union activists found that while about 80% of them believed that traditional adversarial processes were most effective and desirable in dealing with wages and similar matters, over half favored the establishment of joint programs outside the framework of collective bargaining to deal with other, noneconomic issues (Kochan & Dyer, 1976, p. 66). The federal government makes extensive use of joint committees in its negotiated contracts, and study of a small sample of federal organizations indicates that their use has been beneficial in all cases and has become a major problem-solving device in several (Martin, 1977). Some of the unique aspects of academic governance and academic bargaining suggest that joint study committees may play important substantive and procedural roles in the unionized university.

The use of study committees in industrial bargaining began during the 1950s and 1960s as negotiators realized that they were dealing with increasingly complex issues at the table, and that both the time pressures and the distributive tactics traditionally associated with bargaining were not appropriate for resolving them. The more complex the issue, the more likely it is that all the available information about it is not known by either side, that positions of the parties will become fixed and stereotyped, and that the disagreement will become ideological in nature. Under severe time limits, which inhibit problem-solving behavior, the parties are likely either to impasse, to sweep the issue under the rug, or to force a solution based on relative power that may culminate in a lose-lose situation. Hildebrand (1961) has pointed out the problems:

> Contract deadlines may deny opportunity to formulate complex proposals, let alone to devise mutually acceptable solutions. . .compromises in this difficult field are not easily made in the tense atmosphere of the bargaining table, because the institutional ties of the bargainers will deny them the freedom to explore such issues (p. 138)

Study committees can be used with three objectives in mind: to gain time, as a means of introducing experts to provide assistance on difficult problems, and as a device for constructively shaping the course of negotiations and the future relationships between the parties (Hildebrand, 1961). All three purposes are legitimate in various settings, but the greatest potential of study committees is in moving the parties toward more constructive and creative bargaining. To the extent that parties suggest the use of study committees with the sole or principal intent of delaying a decision in order to gain a partisan advantage in the process, the effectiveness of study committees as a problem-solving structure will be vitiated.

Although it has been reported that the use of study committees is common in academic bargaining (Carr & VanEyck, 1973), there is little in the literature commenting upon its effectiveness. Carr and VanEyck note the existence of such a practice at Central Michigan University, and call it a promising means for studying problems that may lead to changes in subsequent contracts or interim agreements between the parties. In Pennsylvania, the formation of statewide joint study committees in lieu of detailed governance provisions in the second State

Colleges and University contract has been seen as reflecting an intention of both sides to view bargaining as a cooperative, problem-solving process (Johnson & Gershenfeld, 1976).

Descriptions of three early uses of study committees in the industrial sector will suggest the potential range of activities of such groups in higher educational institutions. The first two examples involve major industrial unions in steel and meat-packing; they indicate the use of study groups to deal with specific problems while negotiations in a traditional collective bargaining format are proceeding on other items. In the third example, a union and management bargaining team, interested in developing more cooperative relationships, and working with a behavioral scientist, developed a procedure in which *all* major items were considered by study groups whose members composed the bargaining team itself.

The Armour Automation Committee. During the late 1950s, the consolidation of many meat processing plants and the increasing use of automation in the industry had resulted in losses of jobs and crises related to employee displacement and job security. Negotiations between Armour and Company, one of the nation's largest meat-packers, and its two major unions, were unable to cope with this extremely complex and difficult issue. Their solution, as described by Healy (1965), was to establish in the 1959 contract a study committee called the Armour Automation Committee. The committee was composed of nine persons, including four selected by management, two selected by each of the two major unions, and a neutral chairperson mutually selected by the parties. The stated purpose of the committee was to be

> studying the problems resulting from the modernization program and making recommendations for their solution including training employees to perform new and changed jobs and promoting employment opportunities within the company for those affected. (Healy, 1965, p. 142)

The findings of the committee were to be recommendations only, not binding on either side but forwarded to the company and the unions for their further consideration. The committee report was to be made at least six months before the expiration of the existing two-year contract. With the concurrence of the parties, the neutral chairperson appointed an executive director of the committee (also an experienced labor neutral). Although it did not fully resolve the problem for which it was created, a number of recommendations submitted by the study committee were incorporated into the successor contract.

While the Automation Committee was a constructive approach to bargaining in a very difficult and tension-filled setting, it failed to accomplish the major objectives which its creators had envisioned. The reasons for this failure are of interest to parties considering using the study committee approach. At least in part, problems in working together were related to high levels of distrust between the parties. The major problems were probably inherent in the design of the committee, however. The committee met on only a monthly basis and placed far too much reliance on the use of neutral consultants. The parties themselves did not work together in collecting data and were not directly involved in generating new ideas, but rather spent their time responding to the creative initiatives of others. There was not a clear sense of purpose for the group, partly because the infrequency of meetings inhibited the development of strong interpersonal bonds between them, but also because the principals were unsure at the time of setting up the committee exactly what its goals were.

The Human Relations Committee in Basic Steel.   In 1959, a 116-day strike by the United Steelworkers of America against the major steel companies was ended under a Taft-Hartley 80-day injunction. Two months later, the parties settled under strong federal pressure, thus ending an extremely costly strike for the parties and the national economy. This increase of the federal government's interventions into the industry led the parties to establish as a superordinate goal the creation of a means to protect collective bargaining in the steel industry. The 1960 agreement established two study committees, one of which quickly disappeared, and the other, called the Human Relations Research Committee (later the Human Relations Committee or HRC), which was to have a significant impact upon the relationships between the parties and their ability to bargain constructively.

The HRC was charged with planning and overseeing studies and recommending solutions to problems in such areas as wage and benefit adjustment guidelines, job classification systems, seniority, and medical care. The number of committee members was not specified, but the contract stipulated that it was to be jointly chaired by one union and one management representative (Healy, 1965).

HRC immediately set out to perform its functions through the establishment of subcommittees, each dealing with one area of its charge. Altogether, 35 company representatives and 31 union representatives were involved in the work of these subcommittees. Although HRC members were also members of the negotiating teams, it was agreed that the subcommittees would operate with a problem-solving rather than a bargaining orientation. To assist in this process, HRC established ground rules, including the right of any member to be completely released from any statement made at HRC without retribution, a ban on the exchange of written documents, and a decision that none of the study material generated would be used by either side in a grievance process.

As the work of the subcommittees progressed, meetings that had been held sporadically increased in frequency until some were meeting on a daily basis. The subcommittees were jointly collecting and analyzing information that previously had not been available either to the union or the company and preparing joint recommendations for use by the negotiators in the successor contract.

Twenty-six days after the initiation of negotiations, and three months before the expiration of the contract, the parties reached agreement on a new contract with a number of important and innovative provisions. Participants in the process stated that the cordiality that typified the bargaining was directly related to the work of the HRC and to the associations between negotiators that participation on the HRC had fostered.

The success of HRC demonstrated that critical problems were susceptible to solutions created away from the bargaining table.

> The parties learned first-hand in the heat of a 116 day strike that certain problems cannot be solved effectively by sheer economic power in an atmosphere characterized by suspicion and antagonism. They found that they lacked the factual data to really attack a problem objectively, and that they did not have enough time during the negotiating period to find the necessary facts. Further, they found that, because of the urgency and complexity of the problems confronting them, the parties could not afford to wait two or three years until the next negotiation before undertaking a solution. (Healy, 1965, p. 227)

Other factors contributing to the effectiveness of this study committee were the creative use of subcommittees whose members were technically competent to contribute to the solution of problems and whose work involved a large number of senior people on both the management and union side; the ability of the parties in the committee situation to objectively examine data and forego rigid and preconceived positions generated at the bargaining table; the increased flexibility of the parties, represented by their willingness to accept such new concepts as experimental agreements; and the establishment of lines of communication related to the close working relationships that developed on the subcommittees. During the process, neither side sacrificed any of its bargaining power or integrity; the final agreements were adopted because each side believed that they were in its own best interests.

The Hilltop Company.   The third example of the use of study committees was a real setting, identified with the fictitious name of The

Hilltop Company by Blake and Mouton (1962), in which management and union interests in developing a cooperative relationship led to the use of behavioral science consultants to facilitate the structuring and operating of the bargaining relationship.

Bargaining was done by a 16-man unit, including 8 union and 8 management participants. After identifying problem areas, four-man teams, including two union and two management representatives, were appointed to investigate and establish the factual situation related to each problem area. Each four-man subcommittee reported its findings of fact (with no recommendations) back to the entire group. This process of bilateral fact-finding resulted in quite different data than had been assumed by each party before the investigation had been carried out, and the members of the large group believed that the subcommittee reports had produced a higher quality of understanding than would have been otherwise possible.

The entire group was then divided into two subgroups of eight persons, each including four union and four management members. Each group was asked to develop its own best solutions for each of the problem areas, based upon the facts that had been mutually agreed to, and working independently from the other.

> Rather than a management proposal being presented and countered with an alternative proposal (the typical approach that leads too commonly to win-lose competition), each eight-man group explored the widest possible spectrum of alternative solutions in a tentative way prior to placing evaluations of utility on any of them. ... In the final stage, the two eight-man subgroups reunited into the total parent bargaining group of sixteen to compare the quality of the solutions by one group with the solutions that had been produced by the other. Since the octets were crossgroup in composition rather than being octets of management or the union they were able to evaluate solutions more objectively and, when necessary, to further modify the most highly agreed on suggested solutions as the basis for formalized agreements. (Blake and Mouton, 1962, p. 135)

The approach described in this situation was effective not only because the parties were both committed to cooperative relations, but also because the structure of the negotiations fostered creative problem solving and inhibited the establishment of distributive bargaining relationships based upon intergroup conflict.

Effectiveness of the Approach.   The effectiveness of study groups as a strategy for creative bargaining probably depends upon a number of variables, such as the desire of the parties to develop new relationships, their bargaining history, the size and complexity of the organization, and the skills of the chief negotiators or other bargaining principals. In general, it appears to hold considerable promise for higher education, since the bilateral committee is ubiquitous in colleges and universities, and the transfer of this organizational form to bargaining should not be difficult to accomplish once the concept is understood by the participants.

Many of the devices that have earlier been identified as required for a problem-solving, integrative approach are included in this strategy. The process operates so that the participants are problem oriented rather than solution oriented, it jointly collects facts which are shared by all the group members, it forms cross-cutting groups that reduce destructive conflict and at the same time increases dissensus for effective problem solving, and it functions outside the distributive bargaining process and therefore is not affected by the stereotypes, group loyalties, and reluctance to agree to proposals suggested by the "other side." The process permits participants to suggest alternatives in a tentative way, without commitment, and increases involvement so that all team members, not just the chief negotiators, fully participate.

Several additional factors may contribute to the effectiveness of joint study groups. It has been suggested that, because bargainers typically become highly committed to the position of their reference groups, they may not be the best or most flexible negotiators in problem-solving situations (Rubin & Brown, 1975, p. 53). Study committees permit the differentiation of role assignments, so that "nonmilitant" persons from both sides can participate in those activities that require nondistributive orientations. In addition, study committees provide for the sequencing of bargaining interactions, so that one group can first engage in problem-solving activities to seek creative solutions, and a different group can later bargain over how the benefits made possible by the new solution are to be distributed between the groups (Pruitt & Lewis, 1977). Finally, as Hildebrand (1961) has noted, the nonbinding nature of study committee recommendations, while appearing to be a weakness, is one of its greatest strengths. It can be a way of preparing opinion for what would be unacceptable proposals if advanced by either of the parties or a neutral, and the voluntary and tentative nature of the process makes it possible to consider matters that might otherwise be unthinkable.

Since it does not operate under strict time deadlines, it can deal with problems in depth, collect data as needed, and give problems the attention they deserve. The approach focuses participants' attention on the superordinate goal of solving the problem, rather than beating the other team, and the relationships created by the interaction of union and administrative representatives are likely to endure and be reflected in the administration of the contract and the general relationship between the parties.

Caesar Naples, an experienced and effective academic negotiator, has cautioned against the use of study committees on the grounds that

> such committees provide no opportunity for trading off one item for another and allow extreme concentration of effort, energy, and attention on one issue. They tend to raise expectations and make compromise more difficult. Generally, they should be used only in issues where resolution is truly possible and reasonably forseeable and which may require extensive consultation. (1976, p. 26)

In situations in which the parties view bargaining from a distributive rather than a problem-solving perspective, the use of joint study committees in an effort to defer action on a difficult issue will probably lead to greater difficulty in the future. Study committees should not be considered as a tactic for "cooling off" controversial matters, but as a strategy for maximizing their integrative potential. To be effective, both parties must believe in the collaborative interests of the other.

The use of study committees, particularly those that involve large numbers of organizational members who may not be part of the bargaining team, serves an important additional purpose. Bargaining involves not only the establishment of agreement between two negotiating teams but also requires acceptance by the faculty or administrative groups they represent. Intraorganizational bargaining takes place as each side attempts to reconcile the varying interests of its members in order to determine, for example, what issues the team shall present at the table, and what the bargaining strategy is to be. A more critical intraorganizational bargaining situation arises during bargaining itself. The negotiators, having revised their expectations of the negotiating outcome through interaction with the other side, must communicate these new perceptions to the leadership of the union or administrative organization and influence them to also change their perceptions and expectations. This is often difficult to do, and many negotiators find dealing with the unrealistic expectations of their own principals and constituencies to be more difficult than reaching an agreement with the putative adversaries. Experienced negotiators have developed a wide range of tactics to assist in this intraorganizational bargaining process (Walton & McKersie, 1965) and often will assist in the intraorganizational bargaining attempts of the other.

It might be expected that intraorganizational bargaining would be particularly difficult in higher education because of lack of experience by the parties, frequently unrealistic expectations, lack of leadership continuity (particularly on the part of the union), and difficulty in determining exactly what the real concerns of the faculty union are. The tendency of faculty unions to submit laundry lists of demands may, in good part, not be related to any intention to deceive the administration concerning their preferences, but rather it may reflect an understandable inability to "control" the faculty and thus permit the preparation of more focused demands. This same problem of diffused authority might make it comparatively difficult for a bargaining representative to get colleagues to understand why a settlement just offered, while not meeting all of their expectations, is reasonable and should be approved.

One way of dealing with this situation is to increase the number of persons who are actively involved in the negotiating process, so that they begin to understand its nuances, as well as develop a commitment to its outcomes. The use of study committees performs this function and serves to educate the membership and make communication between the bargaining team and the faculty clearer and more credible.

The effective use of a mechanism similar to a study committee in a unionized institution has been noted by Mortimer and Richardson (1977) in a report presenting a number of institutional case studies. At the institution with the most cooperative administration-union relationships (so good that it is "very difficult to distinguish where administration leaves off and the faculty leadership begins," an institutional planning commission was formed with a high degree of union participation, coordinated by the union vice-president who was released half-time from teaching for this purpose.

> A process of the sort developed by [this college] may offer great potential to institutions organized under collective bargaining because it provides a mechanism through which faculty and administration can contemplate change in a nonthreatening and non-adversarial set of circumstances and then commit themselves to necessary changes in advance of the implementation process. (Mortimer & Richardson, 1977, p. 180)

OTHER SEPARATION DEVICES

The Use of Indices

While the use of study committees can separate integrative and distributive items on the bargaining agenda, adoption by the parties of the principle of "indexing" salaries and fringe benefits can remove the need to engage in any distributive strategies or tactics from the table completely. This would permit the parties to establish a bargaining relationship based solely on problem-solving strategies and tactics.

The simplest form of indexing would be based upon an accepted standard such as the consumer price index. Agreement by the parties on a one-time basis that in the future faculty salaries would on average rise by an amount equal to the change in the consumer price index the previous year would negate the need to negotiate a salary package each year. If salaries were believed to be unfairly low so that merely changing them on a yearly basis to reflect economic changes would perpetuate an inequity, the parties could negotiate a formula through which, in addition to cost of living increases, the average salary would rise to a specified level over an agreed-upon time period. Having engaged in this distributive bargaining process once, the parties need not do it again.

Rather than using an arbitrary index, such as the cost of living, the parties might agree to a form of "pattern bargaining" on salaries and fringe benefits. Pattern bargaining occurs when negotiators tend to agree to terms that are similar or identical to those established earlier by other bargainers (Simkin, 1971). Parties could reach prior agreement that they will settle salaries and benefits on the basis of agreements reached elsewhere. Public institutions for example might use the average settlement earned by all other state employees, or identify one or more specific employee groups in public service and agree to be bound by the mean of their increases. Alternatively, institutions might decide to base their agreement upon the compensation increases granted in five or ten institutions that the parties judged comparable to their own, on the basis of size, program, geographic location, existing compensation levels, or similar factors.

The use of indices or patterns even outside one's own industry has precedent. The Tennessee Valley Authority (TVA) and its Trades and Labor Council, for example, are reported to have unusually harmonious working relationships. Although other factors in that situation, such as the existence of joint labor-management committees, may contribute to this relationship, the main reason is believed to be that "TVA follows the prevailing wage rates established in the area, and other industries do the hard bargaining" (Tannenbaum, 1974, p. 96).

Tier Bargaining

Thus far bargaining has been treated as a process taking place in a defined social and organizational setting between two groups that are interdependent in both their bargaining and nonbargaining activities, and which have continuing contact with each other. The suggested strategies and tactics assume the possibility that more constructive cooperation can take place between these groups, because, even though they may have somewhat different interests, they share common attitudes and organizational concerns. The locus of these recommendations has been the campus.

For many public institutions, however, bargaining is not done at the campus level, but it is centralized within state systems and takes the form of merely another bureaucratic and external political control upon the individual campus. The distance between the negotiators and their constituencies, the lack of knowledge of problems existing at specific institutions, the need to deal with all institutions identically and in the most general way, and the increased political involvement in system-level negotiations all operate to reduce the possibility that effective problem solving can take place, that the parties that have to implement the decisions will have played a part in creating them and will support them, and that integrative possibilities will be fully understood or explored. As it is traditionally organized, therefore, system-wide bargaining would appear to discourage creative bargaining initiatives.

Centralizing bargaining does have one advantage, however; it removes from the campus the destructive consequences of distributive bargaining. It thus offers the opportunity to separate distributive and integrative bargaining by agenda, time, people, and space, with the integrative bargaining done at one level, or tier, and items with integrative potential done at another. Forms of two-tier bargaining have been suggested by Cheng (1976) and by Garbarino (1975):

> Some of the recommendations for developing a new model of collective bargaining in higher education in the United States rather than transferring the American industrial model to the college and universities call for something like the German two-tier system. Particularly in the multicampus university systems which dominate faculty unionism, it might be possible to have one union organization that represents employee interests at the system level on general economic and policy matters, with implementation at the campus level in the hands of a work-council senate. (Garbarino, 1975, p. 140)

Two-tiered bargaining has been tried in Massachusetts, with economic issues bargained at the state level between system administration and a joint union committee, while other issues are negotiated on the individual campuses between campus faculty and administration. Garbarino (1977) has suggested that this pattern is well established in the private industrial sector, and that it could be of significant value in academic bargaining as well.

The concept of tier bargaining has been endorsed by the Carnegie Council (1977). They suggest that if the governor's office is involved in bargaining, unions on nonsystem campuses should bargain directly with the governor on monetary issues and with their boards on other matters. They also suggest the development of three-tier bargaining in multicampus systems, presumably with financial matters bargained with the governor, policy issues with the board, and local nonfinancial matters on individual campuses. This latter alternative holds considerable promise. However, it is likely that in most situations the "local" matters allocated to each campus may be so trivial in nature that the development of creative bargaining at this level will be inhibited. The following alternative orientation to three-tier bargaining may be a useful model that would continue the separation of distributive and integrative bargaining, permit basic policy to be established at the system level, and permit real integrative bargaining on important matters to occur on each campus as well.

First, bargaining on salary and fringe benefits would be established between the system-wide union and the governor's office. In many systems, the union engages in bargaining over salaries with the system board. Often the board is sympathetic to the union demands, but it is unable to respond positively to them either because of political constraints or because of its inability to make binding financial commitments. It seems pointless to have trustee boards bargain over matters that they do not control, particularly since these fiscal items are the most distributive in nature and cannot assist in the development of constructive bargaining relationships.

Strictly limiting bargaining at the top tier to salaries and fringe benefits may increase difficulty in reaching agreement, since there will not be available other, noneconomic issues that can be traded off in reaching a settlement. Bargaining under such conditions could also assume the position of a "take-it-or-leave-it" offer from the state with no viable recourse by the union. Therefore, such a tier system should be accompanied by the right to strike over economic matters, so that the bargaining process can be facilitated by the equalization of power between the parties. The right to strike has been considered as necessary for the maintenance of industrial peace in unionized organizations (Golden & Parker, 1955, p. 37). This right may also be essential for academic peace and can be defended as long as it is independent of other governance activities and faculty-administration relationships. Using tier bargaining to direct this distributive aspect of bargaining outside the university community, including the problems associated with the aftermath of a strike, should minimize the impact of distributive bargaining upon the development of constructive bargaining relationships at the other two tiers.

Second, bargaining on noneconomic policy matters should take place between the union and the system (with the campuses fully represented on the system bargaining team) and result in a master contract that does not mandate policies and procedures to be followed by the campuses, but rather prescribes broad policy directives within which bargaining can take place at the campus level. These broad directives would specify guidelines under which each campus would develop its own procedures and would also specify the faculty agency, whether senate or union, which would be responsible for jointly working with the administration in their development. Specific clauses in such a master contract might typically begin with a phrase such as the following:

The president and union of each campus shall develop a promotions process that meets the following standards . . .

The standards might include, for example, such matters as the process by which a faculty promotions committee would be selected, notification requirements, the process by which the president would notify the faculty of reasons for not accepting committee recommendations, the need to publish the promotions calendar and procedures, and similar matters. The standards could prescribe specific policy matters considered to be of importance to the parties, but be flexible enough so that each campus could develop its own, and optimally quite different, internal processes within them.

Third, bargaining would take place on each campus within the guidelines established at the state level. Unlike present suggestions that local items, such as parking, be decided at the campus level, this process would permit the major contract items to be bargained there, subject only to the constraints developed in the master contract. This approach would assure both system administration and the statewide union that reasonable system-wide standards and processes were being maintained, while encouraging each campus to develop policies consistent with its own needs.

The concept of tier bargaining is not only responsive to the need to separate distributive and integrative negotiating agendas and to permit creative problem-solving to occur at the campus level, but it can also serve to stabilize bargaining relationships by minimizing the negative effects of multilateral bargaining. Multilateral bargaining (Begin, 1979) occurs when third party interest groups participate in the negotiations process, and it is commonly seen when a union goes directly to a public official or agency to obtain something through an "end-run" that cannot be obtained at the bargaining table. It is caused primarily by lack of sufficient employer authority at the bargaining table, a common situation in public institutions in which trustees are unable to make binding financial commitments. The use of "end-runs" weakens bilateral relationships, reduces trust between the parties, and opens the possibility of third party involvement in increasingly greater numbers of bargaining areas. The institutionalization of multilateral bargaining through the assignment of specific bargaining areas to specific tiers with appropriate bargaining authority can control its expansion and protect institutions from its more undesirable consequences.

The third major strategy of creative bargaining is to change the bargaining structure so that the development of collaborative bargaining relationships in some areas is not inhibited by the need to use competitive approaches in others. Since the behaviors, tactics, and strategies of distributive bargaining are completely different from, and inconsistent with, those of integrative bargaining, the two can be separated by time, people, agenda, ground rule, or space. Dual governance is a common separation device, used to place items with integrative potential on a faculty senate agenda and those primarily distributive in nature on the agenda of the union. A common form of spatial separation is the use of study committees, which tends to make the participants more problem oriented, increases intragroup dissensus, allows persons outside the bargaining team to participate in the process, and assists in intraorganizational bargaining.

Other means of separating distributive and integrative items in bargaining include the use of indices based on changes in wages and prices, or some other criterion, to determine distributive matters such as salaries without the need for the parties to interact with each other. Tier bargaining permits negotiations over different issues to take place at different times. Tier bargaining might be particularly useful in large multicampus systems because it could reduce political involvement in governance and related academic issues, remove trustees and other members of the academic governance community from the need to engage in competitive interaction with the faculty, and permit bargaining to become a constructive and creative force on each individual campus.

Epilogue: The Future of Creative Academic Bargaining

There are a number of ways in which the parties to academic bargaining can significantly alter their relationship to promote constructive and creative outcomes of conflict. Through increasing the problem-solving potential of their bargaining, utilizing third party interventions to change the bargaining process or to support intergroup development, or altering the bargaining structure, it is possible to redefine the nature of academic bargaining. The movement from competitive orientations toward collaborative, cooperative ones not only may increase the payoffs for both union and management, but also can integrate bargaining into a constructive relationship fully accepted and supported by faculty and administration alike.

The behaviors and activities presented in the last chapters are much different from those that are commonly supposed to represent appropriate orientations toward bargaining. For the most part they are untried in institutions of higher education. Their implementation on a campus will require the taking of risks on the part of both sides. It should be remembered, however, that the adoption of collective bargaining during these early years is a risk in itself; its eventual outcomes are far from certain, and its effect upon the future course of higher education and the relationships of faculties to their institutions and their profession can at this time only be the subject of speculation. Yet experience with the bargaining relationship in other settings suggests that, at least in some situations, insititutions that fail to understand the powerful dynamics for spiralling conflict inherent in bargaining and do not take steps to control it may find the unusual bonds existing between faculty and administration disrupted, or conceivably destroyed. If this happens, the institution that remains may still be called a college or university, but it will have lost the norms and values that

245

constitute its essence and make it a distinctive agency of society. The risks may be great; the costs of not acting may be higher.

As is true with so many apparently radical proposals, the ultimate purpose of these recommendations is not to support significant change, but in fact to maintain the stability of traditional relationships and attitudes. This book as a whole is at least conservative; perhaps even reactionary. Consider, for example, what the governance processes of a unionized institution might look like a decade from now if creative bargaining approaches were adopted. Institutional policies of various kinds would be jointly developed by union and administrative representatives and incorporated into a contract. Through regular meetings held to discuss campus operations and emerging problems, and joint efforts to collect data concerning the attitudes of staff members and institutional effectiveness, the state of the campus would be constantly assessed. Contracts would have no expiration date, and any matter in them could be opened for renegotiation at any time either party believed that a problem existed. In most cases, a joint subcommittee would be established to consider the problem and recommend solutions to the union and administration. Salary negotiations would be conducted by a special union committee directly with representatives of the agency having appropriation authority and completely unrelated to other union bargaining activities.

Negotiations would be conducted by members of the union and administration who had received special training and developed skills in bargaining and group process. Lawyers and industrial relations specialists would not participate in the process. Although early in their relationship the parties would have profited from working intensively on their intergroup relations with a skilled behavioral scientist, their use of neutrals at this more mature stage in academic bargaining would be more limited. Experts would sometimes be asked to provide recommendations on particularly complex substantive issues, and process consultants would monitor some of their meetings on an irregular basis to provide feedback to the parties on the effectiveness of their communications and decision-making processes.

Conflicts would still exist on the campus, and occasionally they would flare and appear unmanageable for brief periods. But the understanding by the parties of the dynamics of win-lose confrontation, as well as the overlapping roles played by many participants on both teams and the clear and effective communications systems that had been developed would make it possible to channel conflict into constructive orientations.

Considered in this way, academic bargaining could be a most traditional form of shared authority; changing the name of "union" in the above description to "faculty senate" indicates that bargaining can, if properly managed, lead to levels of constructive interaction between faculty and administration typically seen only in few campuses. Indeed, because of its ability to change campus processes and structures, and its presumption of legal equality at the bargaining table, it may well be that academic bargaining is the *only* way that institutions characterized by administrative primacy or administrative dominance in decision making can move toward a governance system of shared authority.

This possibility is captured in the prescient comment of Carr and VanEyck (1973):

> There is something to be said for "bargaining by amateurs" in higher education, that is, for direct participation in the bargaining sessions by administrators and faculties. This practice might well prove, in time and with experience, to be simply a new manifestation of the shared authority principle of university governance. (p. 163)

This change will not happen by itself, however. Without intervention into ongoing systems, the forces in the environment, as well as in the structure of competitive groups, will prevent it from occurring. This book should help those concerned about starting this change.

References

AAHE Task Force on Faculty Representation and Academic Negotiations *Faculty participation in academic governance.* Washington, D.C.: American Association for Higher Education, 1967.

Adler, D. I.. *Governance and collective bargaining in four-year institutions 1970-77.* Washington, D.C.: ACBIS Monograph #3, 1977.

Alderfer, C. P. Group and intergroup relations. In J. R. Hackman & J. L. Suttle (Eds.), *Improving life at work.* Santa Monica, Calif.: Goodyear Publishing, 1977.

American Association of University Professors. Statement on government of colleges and universities. *AAUP Bulletin,* 1966, *54,* 155–159.

———. Statement on collective bargaining. *AAUP Bulletin,* 1973, *59,* 167–168.

Anderson, H. J. *New techniques in labor dispute resolution.* Washington, D.C.: Bureau of National Affairs, 1976.

Angell, G. W. Legislatures, collective bargaining and the public university. Washington, D.C.: ACBIS Monograph #4 (undated).

———. Two year college experience. In E. D. Duryea, R. Fish, & Associates (Eds.), *Faculty unions and collective bargaining.* San Francisco: Jossey-Bass, 1973, 87–107.

———, & Kelley, E. P., Jr. *Faculty bargaining under trustee policy* (ACBIS Monograph #7). ACBIS Project on Educational Employment Relations, 1979.

———, & Associates. *Handbook of faculty bargaining.* San Francisco: Jossey-Bass, 1977a.

Baldridge, J. V. *Power and conflict in the university.* New York: John Wiley, 1971.

———, Curtis, D. V., Ecker, G., & Riley, G. L. *Policy making and effective leadership.* San Francisco: Jossey-Bass, 1978.

Balke, W. M., Hammond, K. R., & Meyer, G. D. An alternative approach to labor-management relations. *Administrative Science Quarterly,* September 1973, *18,* 311–327.

Bankston, E. W. Value differences between attorney and economist labor arbitrators. *IRRA 29th Annual Proceedings,* 1975, 151–160.

Barbash, J. Collective bargaining as an institution — a long view. *IRRA 29th Annual Proceedings,* 1976, 303–310.

Barbash, J. The American ideology of industrial relations. *Proceedings of the Spring Meeting,* Industrial Relations Research Association, 1979, 453–457.

Bartos, O. J. Simple model of negotiation. *Journal of Conflict Resolution,* December 1977, *21,* 565–579.

Bass, B. M. Effects on the subsequent performance of negotiators of studying issues or planning strategies alone or in groups. *Psychological Monographs*, No. 614, 1966.

Beckhard, R. *Organizational development: strategies and models.* Reading, Mass.: Addison-Wesley, 1969.

Begin, J. P. *Faculty bargaining: a conceptual discussion.* Washington, D.C.: U.S. Department of Health, Education and Welfare, 1973.

————. Faculty governance and collective bargaining: An early appraisal. Washington, D.C.: ACBIS, Special Report #5 (undated).

————. Grievance mechanisms and faculty collegiality: the Rutgers case. *Industrial and Labor Relations Review*, 1978, *31*, 295–309.

————. Multilateral bargaining in the public sector: causes, effects, and accommodations. In J. W. Sutherland (Ed.), *Management handbook for public administrators.* New York: Van Nostrand Reinhold, 1979.

————. Statutory definitions of the scope of negotiations: the implications for traditional faculty governance. *Journal of Higher Education*, 1978, *49*, 247–260.

————, Settle, T. C., & Alexander, P. *Academics on strike.* New Brunswick, N.J.: Institute of Management and Labor Relations, Rutgers University, 1975.

————, & Berke-Weiss, L. *Community college collective bargaining in New Jersey.* New Brunswick, N.J.: Rutgers Univerity, September 1977.

————. Patterns of faculty collective bargaining in community colleges. *Rutgers-Camden Law Journal*, 1978, *9*, 699–714.

Begin, J. P. & Weinberg, W. M. Dispute resolution in higher education. In H. J. Anderson, *New techniques in labor dispute resolution.* Washington, D.C.: Bureau of National Affairs, 1976, 81–106.

Bennis, W. An O.D. expert in the cat bird's seat. *The Journal of Higher Education*, May 1973, *44*, 389–398.

Birnbaum, R. Productivity and the academic calendar. *Public Productivity Review*, 1978, *2*, 32–37.

Blake, R. R., & Mouton, J. S. Competition, communication, and conformity. In I. A. Berg & B. M. Bass (Eds.), *Conformity and deviation.* New York: Harper, 1961b, 199–229.

————. Comprehension of own and outgroup positions under intergroup competition. *Journal of Conflict Resolution*, 1961a, *5*, 304–310.

————. *Corporate excellence through grid organization development.* Houston: Gulf Publishing, 1968.

————. The intergroup dynamics of win-lose conflict and problem-solving collaboration in union-management relations. In M. Sherif (Ed.), *Intergroup relations and leadership.* New York: John Wiley, 1962, 94–140.

————. Loyalty of representatives to ingroup positions during intergroup competition. *Sociometry*, 1961c, *24*, 177–183

————. Reactions to intergroup competition under win-lose conditions. *Management Science*, 1961d, *7*, 420–435.

————, & Sloma, R. L. The union-management intergroup laboratory: strategy for resolving intergroup conflict. *Journal of Applied Behavioral Science*, 1965, *1*, 25–27.

Blake, R. R., Shepard, H. A., & Mouton, J. S. *Managing intergroup conflict in industry.* Houston: Gulf Publishing, 1964.

Board of Higher Education of the City of New York. 7 P.E.R.B. 3042 (1974).

Bonham, M. G. Simulating international disarmanent negotiations. *Journal of Conflict Resolution,* 1971, *15,* 299–315.

Boulding, K. Opening remarks. In E. Boulding (Ed.), *Conflict management in organizations.* Ann Arbor: Foundation for Research on Human Behavior, 1965.

Bowen, J. J. A college contract: before and after. *Phi Delta Kappan.* April 1977, *58,* 616–619.

Bowers, M. H. The dilemma of impasse procedures in the public safety services. *The Arbitration Journal,* September 1973, *28,* 167–174.

Boyd, W. B. Collective bargaining in academe: causes and consequences. *Liberal Education,* 1971, *57,* 306–318.

Boyer, R. K., & Crockett, C. Organizational development in higher education: introduction. *The Journal of Higher Education,* 1973, *44,* 339–351.

Brehmer, B., & Hammond, K. R. Cognitive factors in interpersonal conflict. In D. Druckman (Ed.), *Negotiations: social-psychological perspectives.* Beverly Hills, Calif.: Sage Publications, 1977.

Brown, B. N. Face-saving and fare-restoration in negotiation. In D. Druckman (Ed.), *Negotiations: social-psychological perspectives.* Beverly Hills, Calif.: Sage Publications, 1977.

Burke, W. W. Managing conflict between groups. In J. D. Adams (Ed.), *Theory and method in organization development: an evolutionary process.* Arlington, Va.: NTL Institute for Applied Behavioral Science, 1974.

Byrnes, J. F. Mediator-generated pressure tactics. *Journal of Collective Negotiations,* 1978, *7,* 103–109.

————. Representing the faculty in a unionized college: the tasks and roles of a chief negotiator. *Journal of Collective Negotiations,* 1977, *6,* 19–27.

Campbell, R. Collective bargaining: some reflections of a president. *Community and Junior College Journal,* December/January 1974, *44,* 25–28.

Caples, W. G., & Graney R. A. The technique of labor-management negotiations. In E. W. Bakke, C. Kerr, & C. W. Anrod (Eds.), *Unions, management, and the public* (3rd Ed.). New York: Harcourt, Brace & World, 1967, 308–312.

Carnegie Commission on Higher Education. *Governance of higher education: sex priority problems.* New York: McGraw-Hill, 1973.

Carnegie Council on Policy Studies. *Faculty bargaining in public higher education.* San Francisco: Jossey-Bass, 1977.

Carnegie Foundation for the Advancement of Teaching. *More than survival: prospects for higher education in a period of uncertainty.* San Francisco: Jossey-Bass, 1975.

Carr, R. K., & VanEyck, D. K. *Collective bargaining comes to the campus.* Washington, D.C.: American Council on Education, 1973.

Cheng, C. W. *Altering collective bargaining: citizen participation in educational decision making.* New York: Praeger, 1976.

Clark, B. R. Belief and loyalty in college organization. *Journal of Higher Education*, June 1971, 499–515.

Clark, D. L. Discrimination suits: a unique settlement. *Educational Record*, Summer 1977, *58*, 233–249.

Cohen, M. D., & March, J. G. *Leadership and ambiguity: the American college president.* New York: McGraw-Hill, 1974.

Cohen, S. P., Kelman, H. C., Miller, F. D., & Smith, B. L. Evolving intergroup techniques for conflict resolution: an Israeli-Palestinian pilot workshop. *Journal of Social Issues*, 1977, *33*, 165–189.

Corson, J. J. *The governance of colleges and universities* (2nd Ed.) New York: McGraw-Hill, 1975.

Coser, L. *The functions of social conflict.* New York: The Free Press, 1964.

Cross, J. G. Negotiation as a learning process. *Journal of Conflict Resolution*, December 1977, *21*, 581–606.

Deutsch, M. Conflicts: productive and destructive. *Journal of Social Issues*, January 1969, *25*, 7–41.

―――. *The resolution of conflict: constructive and destructive processes.* New Haven, Conn.: Yale University Press, 1973.

―――, Canavan, D., & Rubin, J. The effects of size of conflict and sex of experimenter upon interpersonal bargaining. *Journal of Experimental Social Psychology*, 1971, *7*, 258–267.

Doherty, R. E. On factfinding: a one-eyed man lost among the eagles. *Public Personnel Management*, September-October 1976, 363–367.

Doob, L. W., & Foltz, W. J. The Belfast workshop: an application of group techniques to a destructive conflict. *Journal of Conflict Resolution*, 1973, *17*, 489–512.

Douglas, A. *Industrial peacemaking.* New York: Columbia University Press, 1962.

―――. The peaceful settlement of industrial and intergroup disputes. *Journal of Conflict Resolution*, 1957, *1*, 69–81.

Druckman, D. Dogmatism, prenegotiation experience, and simulated group representation as determinants of dyadic behavior in a bargaining situation. *Journal of Personality and Social Psychology*, 1967, *6*, 279–290.

―――. The influence of the situation in interparty conflict. *Journal of Conflict Resolution*, 1971, *15*, 523–555.

―――. (Ed.). *Negotiations: social-psychological perspectives.* Beverly Hills, Calif.: Sage Publications, 1977.

―――. Prenegotiation experience and dyadic conflict resolution in a bargaining situation. *Journal of Experimental Social Psychology*, 1968, *4*, 367–383.

―――, & Mahoney, R. Processes and consequences of international negotiations. *Journal of Social Issues*, 1977, *33*, 60–87.

―――, & Zechmeister, K. Conflict of interest and value dissensus. *Human Relations*, 1970, *23*, 431–438.

―――. Conflict of interest and value dissensus: propositions in the sociology of conflict. *Human Relations*, 1973, *26*, 449–466.

―――, & Solomon, D. Determinents of bargaining behavior in a bilateral monopoly situation: Opponents concession rate and relative defensibility. *Behavioral Science*, 1972, *17*, 514–531.

Dubeck, L. W. Collective bargaining: A view from the faculty. Washington, D.C.: Academic Collective Bargaining Information Service, Orientation Paper #7 (October 1975).

Duryea, E. D., & Fisk, R. S. *Collective bargaining, the state university and the state government in New York.* Buffalo, N.Y.: State University of New York, 1975.

———, & Associates. *Faculty unions and collective bargaining.* San Francisco: Jossey-Bass, 1973.

Eisinger, R. A., & Levine M. J. The role of psychology in labor relations. *Personnel Journal,* September 1968, *47,* 643–649.

Esser, J. K., & Komorita, S. S. Reciprocity and concession making in bargaining. *Journal of Personality and Social Psychology,* 1975, *31,* 864–872.

Etzioni, A. *A comparative analysis of complex organizations.* New York: The Free Press of Glencoe, 1961.

———. *Modern organizations.* Englewood Cliffs, N.J.: Prentice-Hall, 1964.

Evan, W. M., & MacDougall, J. A. Interorganizational conflict: a labor-management bargaining experiment. *Journal of Conflict Resolution,* 1967, *11,* 398–413.

Federal Mediation and Conciliation Service. *Twenty-third annual report—fiscal year 1970.* Washington, D.C.: Author, 1970.

———. *Thirty-first annual report—fiscal year 1978.* Washington, D.C.: Author, 1978.

Feller, D. E., & Finkin, M. W. Legislative issues in faculty collective bargaining. In Carnegie Council on Policy Studies in Higher Education, *Faculty bargaining in public higher education.* San Francisco: Jossey-Bass, 1977.

Felson, R. B. Aggression as impression management. *Social Psychology,* 1978, *41,* 205–213.

Feuille, P., & Dworkin, J. B. Final-offer arbitration and intertemporal compromise, or it's my turn to win. *Proceedings of the thirty-first annual meeting,* Industrial Relations Research Association, 1979, 87–95.

———, & Long, G. The public administrator and final offer arbitration. *Public Administration Review,* November/December 1974, *34,* 575–583.

Filley, A. C. *Interpersonal conflict resolution.* Glenview, Ill.: Scott, Foresman, 1975.

Finkin, M. W. Collective bargaining and university government. *AAUP Bulletin,* Summer 1971.

———. The arbitration of faculty status disputes in higher education. *Southwestern Law Journal,* 1976, *30,* 389–434.

———, Goldstein, R. A., & Osborne, W. B. *A primer on collective bargaining for college and university faculty.* AAUP, 1975.

Fisher, R. Fractionating conflict. In R. Fisher (Ed.), *Interactional conflict and behavioral science: the Craigville papers.* New York: Basic Books, 1964, 91–109

Frank, J. D. *Sanity and survival: psychological aspects of war and peace.* New York: Random House, 1968.

Fuller, L. L. Mediation — its forms and functions. *Southern California Law Review,* 1971, *44,* 305–339.

Garbarino, J. W. *Faculty bargaining: change and conflict.* New York: McGraw-Hill, 1975.

————. State experience in collective bargaining. In Carnegie Council on Policy Studies, *Faculty bargaining in public higher education.* San Francisco: Jossey-Bass, 1977, 29–72.

Gee, E. G. Organizing the halls of ivy: developing a framework for viable alternatives in higher education employment. *Utah Law Review*, 1973, *233*.

Gibb, J. R. Defensive communication. *Journal of Communication*, 1961, *11*, 141–148.

Gilroy, T. P., & Lipovac, J. A. Impasse procedure utilization: year one under the Iowa statute. *Journal of Collective Negotiations*, 1977, *6*, 181–191.

Gilroy, T. P., & Sinicropi, A. V. Impasse resolution in public employment: a current assessment. *Industrial and Labor Relations Review*, July 1972, *25*, 496–511.

Golden, C. S., & Parker, V. D. (Eds.). *Causes of industrial peace under collective bargaining.* New York: Harper and Brothers, 1955.

Graham, D. L. Faculties at the bargaining table. In H. B. Means & P. W. Semas (Eds.), *Faculty collective bargaining.* Washington, D.C.: Editorial Projects for Education, 1976.

Graham, D. L., & Walters, D. E. Bargaining process. In E. D. Duryea, & R. Fisk, & Associates, *Faculty unions and collective bargaining.* San Francisco: Jossey-Bass, 1973, 44–65.

Gross, E., & Grambsch, P. V. *University goals and academic power.* Washington, D.C.: American Council on Education, 1968.

Hall, J. Decisions, decisions, decisions. *Psychology Today*, 1971, *5*, 51–58.

Haman, D. C., Brief, A. P., & Pegnetter, R. Studies in mediation and the training of public sector mediators. *Journal of Collective Negotiations*, 1978, *7*, 347–361.

Hamner, W. C., & Yukl, G. A. The effectiveness of different offer strategies in bargaining. In D. Druckman (Ed.), *Negotiations: social-psychological perspectives.* Beverly Hills, Calif.: Sage Publications, 1977, 137–160.

Hanley, D. L. Issues and models for collective bargaining in higher education. *Liberal Education*, 1971, *57*, 5–14.

Healy, J. J. (Ed.). *Creative collective bargaining.* Englewood Cliffs, N.J.: Prentice-Hall, 1965.

Hedgepeth, R. C. Consequences of collective bargaining in higher education. *The Journal of Higher Education*, December 1974, *45*, 691–705.

Helsby, R. D. *Development of professional personnel for public employment labor relations boards and commissions in state and local governments of the United States.* Association of American Colleges, February 1977.

Hermann, M. G., & Kogan, N. Effects of negotiators personalities on negotiating behavior. In D. Druckman (Ed.), *Negotiations: social-psychological perspectives.* Beverly Hills, Calif.: Sage Publications, 1977, 247–274.

Hildebrand, G. The use of neutrals in collective bargaining. In S. D. Pollard (Ed.), *Arbitration and public policy.* Washington, D.C.: Bureau of National Affairs, Inc., 1961.

Hobbs, W. C. An academic dispute-settlement commission: a proposal. *Educational Record*, Spring 1971, *52*, 181–188.

Holsti, O. R. Crisis, stress and decision-making. *International Social Science Journal*, 1971, *23*, 53–67.

Homans, G. C. *The human group*. New York: Harcourt, Brace & World, 1950.

Howe, R. A. The bloody business of bargaining. *College and University Business*, March 1970, *48*, 63–67.

Howe, R. A. The conduct of negotiations. *Community and Junior College Journal*, December-January 1974, *44*, 12–14.

Ikle, F. C. *How nations negotiate*. Millwood, N.Y.: Kraus, 1964.

Johnson, D. W. Use of role reversal in intergroup competition. *Journal of Personality and Social Psychology*, October 1967, *7*, 135–141.

Johnson, D. F., & Pruitt, D. G. Preintervention effects of mediation versus arbitration. *Journal of Applied Psychology*, 1972, *56*, 1–10.

Johnson, M. D., & Gershenfeld, W. J. State-institutional relations under faculty collective bargaining in Pennsylvania. In Mortimer, K. P. (Ed.), *Faculty bargaining, state government, and campus autonomy: the experiences of eight states*. University Park, Pa.: The Pennsylvania State University (Center for the Study of Higher Education), April 1976.

Jones, R. T. *Public sector labor relations: an evaluation of policy-related research*. Belmont, Mass.: Contract Research Corp., February 1975.

Judd, C. M. Cognitive effects of attitude conflict resolution. *Journal of Conflict Resolution*, September 1978, *22*, 483–498.

Kadish, S. H. Strike and the professionate. *AAUP Bulletin*, June 1968, *54*, 160–168.

Kagel, S., & Kagel, J. Using two new arbitration techniques. *Monthly Labor Review*, November 1972, 11–14.

Katz, D., & Kahn, R. Organizational change. In J. V. Baldridge & T. E. Deal, *Managing change in educational organizations*. Berkeley, Calif.: McCutchan, 1975.

Keaton, H. J. The realities of public employee negotiations. In H. Anderson (Ed.), *The role of the neutral in public employee disputes*. Washington, D.C.: Bureau of National Affairs, 1972, 98–106.

Kelley, H. H. Attribution theory in social psychology. *Nebraska Symposium on Motivation*, 1967, *15*, 192–238.

Kelley, H. H., & Stahelski, A. J. The inference of intentions from moves in the Prisoners' Dilemma game. *Journal of Experimental Social Psychology*, 1970.

Kelman, H. C. The problem-solving workshop in conflict resolution. In R. L. Merritt (Ed.), *Communication in international politics*. Urbana, Ill.: University of Illinois Press, 1972.

Kelman, H. C. & Cohen, S. P. The problem-solving workshop: A social-psychological contribution to the resolution of international conflicts. *Journal of Peace Research*, 1976, *13*, 79–90.

Kelley, H. H. & Stahelski, A. J. Social interaction basis of cooperators' and competitors' beliefs about others. *Journal of Personality and Social Psychology*, 1970, *16*, 66–91.

Kemerer, F. R., & Baldridge, J. V. The myth of the collegial bargaining model. *College and University Personnel Association Journal*, Winter 1977.

———. *Unions on campus*. San Francisco: Jossey-Bass, 1975.

Kerr, C. Industrial conflict and its mediation. *The American Journal of Sociology*, 1954, *60*, 230–245.

————. *The uses of the university.* New York: Harper & Row, 1963.

Kiep, R. P. A committee that actually works. *AGB Reports,* 1976, 31–34.

Klimoski, R. J. The effects of intragroup forces on intergroup conflict resolution. *Organizational Behavior and Human Performance,* 1972, *8,* 363–383.

Kochan, T. A., & Dyer, L. A model for organizational change in the context of labor-management relations. *Journal of Applied Behavioral Science,* January 1976, *12,* 59–78.

————, & Jick, T. The public sector mediation process. *Journal of Conflict Resolution.* June 1978, *22,* 209–240.

Komorita, S. S., & Brenner, A. R. Bargaining and concession making under bilateral monopoly. *Journal of Personality and Social Psychology,* 1968, *9,* 15–20.

Krauss, R. M., & Deutsch, M. Communication in interpersonal bargaining. *Journal of Personality and Social Psychology,* 1966, *4,* 572–577.

Kuhlman, D. M., & Marshello, A. F. J. Individual differences in a game motivation as moderators of preprogrammed effects in prisoners dilemma. *Journal of Personality and Social Psychology,* 1975, *39,* 922–931.

Ladd, E. C., Jr., & Lipsett, S. M. Faculty members note both positive and negative aspects of campus unions. *Chronicle of Higher Education,* February 23, 1976.

————. Faculty support for unionization: leveling off at about 75 per cent. *The Chronicle of Higher Education,* February 13, 1978.

————. *Professors, unions, and American higher education.* Washington, D.C.: American Enterprise Institute for Public Policy Research, 1973.

————. *The divided academy.* New York: W. W. Norton, 1975.

Lamm, H., & Kogan, N. Risk taking in the context of intergroup negotiation. *Journal of Experimental Social Psychology,* 1970, *6,* 351–363.

Landsberger, H. A. Interaction process analysis of professional behavior: a study of labor mediators in twelve labor-management disputes. *American Sociological Review,* 1955, *20,* 566–575.

Lavine, J. M., & Lemon, W. L. *Report of the regents task force on university governance and collective bargaining.* Washington, D.C.: American Association of Governing Boards of Universities and Colleges, 1975.

Lawrence, P. R., & Lorsch, J. W. *Developing organizations: diagnosis and action.* Reading, Mass.: Addison-Wesley, 1969.

Leache, D. W., & Satryb, R. P. Collective bargaining and the management of conflict: proposed research directions. *Journal of Higher Education.*

Lee, B. A. *Collective bargaining in four year colleges.* Washington, D.C.: American Association of Higher Education, 1978.

Lesieur, F. G., & Puckett, E. S. The Scanlon Plan has proved itself. *Harvard Business Review,* September-October 1969, *47,* 109–118.

Leslie, D. W. *Conflict and collective bargaining.* Washington, D.C.: American Association for Higher Education, 1975a.

Leslie, D. W. *Impact of collective bargaining on conflict resolution practices* (Research summary no. 2). Washington, D.C.: Academic Collective Bargaining Information Service, 1975b.

————, & Satryb, R. P. Collective bargaining and the management of conflict. *Journal of the College and University Personnel Association,* 1974, *25,* 12–22.

Levi, A. M., & Benjamin, A. Focus and flexibility in a model of conflict resolution. *Journal of Conflict Resolution,* September 1977, *21,* 405–425.

Likert, R. *New patterns of management.* New York: McGraw-Hill, 1961.

————. *The human organization: its management and value.* New York: McGraw-Hill, 1967.

Lipsky, D. B., & Barocci, T. A. Final offer arbitration and public-safety employees: the Massachusetts experience. In *Proceedings of the thirtieth annual winter meeting,* Industrial Relations Research Association, 1978.

Loewenberg, J. J. *Neutral advisors in public employee labor relations.* Philadelphia: Temple University Center for Labor and Manpower Studies (March 1975).

Loewenthal, A., & Neilson, R. Bargaining for academic democracy. Washington, D.C.: American Federation of Teachers

Long, G., & Feuille, P. Final-offer arbitration: 'sudden death' in Eugene. *Industrial and Labor Relations Review,* January 1974, *27,* 186–203.

Maier, N. R. *Problem solving and creativity in individuals and groups.* Belmont, Calif.: Brooks-Cole, 1970.

Martin, J. E. Joint labor-management meetings in the federal government: results from six sites. *Journal of Collective Negotiations,* 1977, *6,* 275–285.

McAvoy, J. Z. Binding arbitration of contract terms: a new approach to the resolution of disputes in the public sector. *Columbia Law Review,* 1972, *72,* 1192–1213.

MaCoy, R., & Morand, M. J. Establishing constructive relationships between administration and faculty unions. In G. W. Angell, E. P. Kelley, Jr., & Associates, *Handbook of faculty bargaining.* San Francisco: Jossey-Bass, 1977.

McKelvey, J. Fact finding: promise or illusion? *Industrial and Labor Relations Review,* July 1969, *22,* 528–542.

McKersie, R. B. Productivity: is it necessarily the quid pro quo for improved salaries and benefits? In H. Anderson, (Ed.), *New techniques in labor dispute resolution.* Washington, D.C.: Bureau of National Affairs, 1976, 59–73.

McMurray, R. N. War and peace in labor relations. *Harvard Business Review,* 1955, *33,* 48–60.

Megginson, L. C., & Gullett, C. R. A predictive model of union-management conflict. *Personnel Journal,* June 1970, *49,* 495–503.

Memo. American Association of State Colleges and Universities, November 28, 1977.

Metzger, W. P. A historian looks at the academic profession. Presentation to the American Association for Higher Education, Chicago, March 1976.

Milstein, M. M. Adversarial relations and organizational development: are they compatible? Paper presented at the meeting of the American Educational Research Association, April 1977.

Morris, W. C., & Sashkin, M. Phases of integrated problem solving (PIPS). In J. W. Pfeiffer & J. E. Jones (Eds.), *The 1978 annual handbook for group facilitators.* San Diego, Calif.: University Associates, 1978.

Mortimer, K. P. *Faculty bargaining, state government and campus autonomy: the experience of eight states.* University Park, Pa.: The Pennsylvania State University (Center for the Study of Higher Education), April 1976.

Mortimer, K. P., & Richardson, R. C., Jr. *Governance in institutions with faculty unions: six case studies.* University Park, Pa.: The Pennsylvania State University (Center for the Study of Higher Education), May 1977.

Nadler, D. A. Consulting with labor and management: some learnings from quality-of-work-life projects. In W. W. Burke (Ed.), *The cutting edge: current theory and practice on organization development.* La Jolla, Calif.: University Associates, 1978.

Naples, C. J. Management at the bargaining table. In H. B. Means & P. W. Semas (Eds.), *Faculty collective bargaining.* Washington, D.C.: Editorial Projects for Education, 1976.

————. Preparing to negotiate the next contract. In G. W. Angell, E. P. Kelley, Jr., & Associates, *Handbook of faculty bargaining.* San Francisco: Jossey-Bass, 1977.

————. The impact of fiscal crisis—a management view. In National Center for the Study of Collective Bargaining in Higher Education, *Collective bargaining and the future of higher education.* New York: Author, 1977.

Notes on. . . collective bargaining. *Chronicle of Higher Education,* November 26, 1979, 2.

Oberer, W. E. Faculty participation in academic decision making: as to what issues, by what forms, using what means of persuasion? In S. Elam & M. H. Moskow, *Employment relations in higher education.* Bloomington, Ind.: Phi Delta Kappa, 1969.

Orze, J. J. Faculty collective bargaining and academic decision-making. Washington, D.C.: Academic Collective Bargaining Information Service, Special Report #24, September 1975.

Osgood, C. E. An analysis of the cold war mentality. *Journal of Social Issues,* 1961, *17,* 12–19.

Patten, T. H., Jr. Collective bargaining and consensus: the potential of a laboratory training input. Management of Personnel Quarterly, Spring 1970, *9,* 29–37.

Pilisuk, M., & Skolnick, P. Inducing trust: a test of the Osgood proposal. *Journal of Personality and Social Psychology,* 1968, *8,* 121–133.

Ping, C. J. On learning to live with collective bargaining. *The Journal of Higher Education,* February 1973, *44,* 102–113.

Pisarski, R., & Landin, E. Comment. In H. J. Anderson, *New techniques in labor dispute resolution.* Washington, D.C.: Bureau of National Affairs, 1976.

Popular, J. J., II. Labor management relationships by objectives. *Industrial relations guide.* Englewood Cliffs, N.J.: Prentice-Hall, 1977.

Potter, G. E. Collective bargaining: a primer for college trustees. *AGB Reports,* September-October 1975, *17,* 21–25.

Pruitt, D. G. & Lewis, S. A. The psychology of integrative bargaining. In D. Druckman (Ed.), *Negotiations: social-psychological perspectives.* Beverly Hills, Calif.: Sage Publications, 1977.

Pruitt, D. G. & Johnson, D. F. Mediation as an aid to face saving in negotiation. *Journal of Personality and Social Psychology,* 1970, *14,* 239–246.

Rapoport, A. *Fights, games and debates* (5th Ed.). Ann Arbor: The University of Michigan Press, 1974.

Renwick, P. A. Perception and management of superior-subordinate conflict. *Organizational Behavior and Human Performance*, 1973, *13*, 444–456.

Reychler, L. The effectiveness of a pacifist strategy in conflict resolution. *Journal of Conflict Resolution*, June 1979, *23*, 228–259.

Ridgefield Park, 4 NJPER, September 11, 1978.

Rogers, C. R. Communication: its blocking and its facilitation. *ETC., A Review of General Semantics*, 1952, *9*, 83–88.

Rosenberg, S. W., & Wolfsfeld, G. International conflict and the problems of attribution. *Journal of Conflict Resolution*, March 1977, *21,* 75–103.

Rubin, J. Z. & Brown, B. R. *The social psychology of bargaining and negotiation.* New York: Academic Press, 1975.

Ruml, B., & Morrison, D. H. *Memo to a college trustee.* New York: McGraw-Hill, 1959.

Rutgers University, 2 New Jersey P.E.R.C. (1976).

Satryb, R. P. The art of settling grievances: a study in campus conflict resolution. Washington, D.C.: Academic Collective Bargaining Information Service Special Report #27, August 1976.

Schein, E. H. *Process consultation: its role in organizational development.* Reading, Mass.: Addison-Wesley, 1969.

Schelling, T. C. An essay on bargaining. *The American Economic Review,* June 1956, *46*, 281–306.

——. Bargaining, communication and limited war. *Conflict Resolution,* 1957, *1*, 19–36.

——. *The strategy of conflict.* Cambridge, Mass.: Harvard University Press, 1960.

Schmuck, R., et al. *The second handbook of organizational development in schools.* Palo Alto, Calif.: Mayfield Press, 1977.

Schwartzman, H. D. The administrators approach to collective bargaining. *Journal of College and University Law,* 1974, 351–369.

Semas, P. W. Collective bargaining and faculty governance NLRB general counsel rules that private colleges needn't negotiate over role of senates and committees. *Chronicle of Higher Education,* July 5, 1977.

Sherif, M. Intergroup relations and leadership: introductory statement. In M. Sherif (Ed.), *Intergroup relations and leadership.* New York: John Wiley, 1962, 3–21.

Shure, G. H., Meeker, R. J., & Hansford, E. A. The effectiveness of pacifist strategies in bargaining games. *The Journal of Conflict Resolution,* 1965, *9*, 106–117.

Siegel, S., & Fouraker, L. E. Bargaining and group decision making: experiments in bilateral monopoly. New York McGraw-Hill, 1960.

Sikes, W. W., Schlesinger, L. D., & Seashore, C. N. Developing change agent teams on campus. *The Journal of Higher Education,* May 1973, *44*, 399–413.

——. *Renewing Higher Education from Within.* San Francisco, Calif.: Jossey-Bass, 1974.

Simkin, W. Factfinding — its values and limitations. Government Employee Relations Report, Volume 2, 1970, 21–24.

Simkin, W. E. Mediation. In E. W. Bakke, C. Kerr & C. W. Anrod (Eds.), *Unions, management and the public* (3rd Ed.). New York: Harcourt, Brace and World, 1967.

———. *Mediation and the dynamics of collective bargaining.* Washington, D.C.: The Bureau of National Affairs, 1971.

Somers, P. C. An evaluation of final-offer arbitration in Massachusetts. *Journal of Collective Negotiations,* 1977, *6,* 193–228.

Spritzer, A. D. & Odewahn, C. A. College presidents' attitudes toward faculty collective bargaining. *Journal of Collective Negotiations,* 1978, *7,* 37–44.

Stern, I. & Pearse, R. F. Collective bargaining: a union's program for reducing conflict. *Personnel,* 1968, *45,* 61–72.

Stern, L. W., Bagozzi, R. P., & Dholakia, R. R. Mediational mechanisms in interorganizational conflict. In Druckman, D. (Ed.), *Negotiations: social-psychological perspectives.* Beverly Hills, Calif.: Sage Publications, 1977.

Stevens, C. M. Is compulsory arbitration compatible with bargaining? *Industrial Relations,* February 1966, *5,* 38–52.

———. Mediation and the role of the neutral. In J. T. Dunlap & N. W. Chamberlain (Eds.), *Frontiers of collective bargaining.* New York: Harper and Row, 1967, 271–290.

———. *Strategy and collective bargaining negotiation.* New York: McGraw-Hill, 1963.

———. The management of labor disputes in the public sector. *AAUP Bulletin,* December 1972, *58,* 399–404.

Strauss, G. The study of conflict: hope for a new synthesis between industrial relations and organizational behavior? *IRRA 29th Annual Proceedings,* 1976, 329–337.

Sturner, W. F. Struggling with the unknown: the first year of collective bargaining. *The Journal of the College and University Personnel Association,* 1976, *27,* 29–38.

Subbaro, A. V. The impact of binding interest arbitration on negotiation and process outcome. *Journal of Conflict Resolution,* March 1978, *22,* 79–103.

Summers, D. A. Conflict, compromise and belief change in a decision-making task. *Journal of Conflict Resolution,* 1968, *12,* 215–221.

Swingle, P. G. Exploitative behavior in non-zero-sum games. *Journal of Personality and Social Psychology,* 1970, *16,* 121–132.

Syracuse University, 204 NLRB No. 85, 83 LRRM 1373 (1973).

Tannenbaum, A. S. Systems of formal participation. In Strauss, *et al. Organizational behavior: research and issues.* Madison, Wisconsin: Industrial Relations Research Association, 1974, 77–105.

Tedeschi, J. T., Bonoma, T. V., & Schlenker, B. R. Influence decision and compliance. In J. T. Tedeschi (Ed.), *The social influence processes.* Chicago: Aldine-Atherton, 1972.

———, Gaes, G. G., & Rivera, A. N. Aggression and the use of coercive power. *Journal of Social Issues,* 1977, *33,* 101–125.

Thomas, K. W. Conflict and conflict management. In M. D. Dunette (Ed.), *Handbook of industrial and organizational psychology.* Chicago: Rand-McNally, 1976.

Thomas-Kilman Conflict Mode Instrument. XICOM Inc.

Tice, T. (Ed.). *Campus employment relations: readings and resources.* Ann Arbor, Michigan: The Institute of Continuing Legal Education, 1975.

U.S. mediators try a new role. *Business Week,* April 21, 1975.

Vidmar, N. Effects of representational roles and mediators on negotiation effectiveness. *Journal of Personality and Social Psychology,* 1971, *17,* 48–58.

Vladeck, J. P., & Vladeck, S. C. (Eds.). *Collective bargaining in higher education— the developing law.* New York: Practicing Law Institute, 1975.

Walker, D. E., Feldman, D., & Stone, G. Collegiality and collective bargaining: an alternative process. *Educational Record,* Spring 1976, *57,* 119–124.

Wall, J. A., Jr. Effects of constituent trust and representative bargaining orientation on intergroup bargaining. *Journal of Personality and Social Psychology,* 1975, *31,* 1004–1012.

Wall, J. A., Jr., & Adams, J. S. Some variables affecting a constituent's evaluations of and behavior toward a boundary role occupant. *Organizational Behavior and Human Performance,* 1974, *11,* 390–408.

Walters, D. F. Collective bargaining in higher education. *College Management,* 1973, *8,* 6–7.

Walton, R. E. *Interpersonal peacemaking: confrontation and third party consultation.* Reading, Mass.: Addison-Wesley, 1969.

————, & McKersie, R. B. *A behavioral theory of labor negotiations.* New York: McGraw-Hill, 1965.

————. Behavioral dilemmas in mixed-motive decision making. *Behavioral Science,* September 1966, *11,* 373–82.

Walworth, W. R., & Angell, G. W. Improving bargaining processes through self-evaluation. In G. W. Angell, E. P. Kelley, & Associates, *Handbook of faculty bargaining.* San Francisco: Jossey-Bass, 1977a.

Weimer, G. Defuse the labor bomb before it explodes. *Iron Age,* March 1977.

Weisbord, M. R. Input-versus output-focused organizations: notes on a contingency theory of practice. In W. W. Burke (Ed.), *The cutting edge: current theory and practice on organization development.* La Jolla, Calif.: University Associates, 1978.

White, R. K. Misperception and the Vietnam war. *Journal of Social Issues,* 1966, *22,* 18.

Wilson, W. Cooperation and cooperativeness of the other player. *Journal of Conflict Resolution,* 1969, *13,* 110–117.

Wollett, D. H. Some facts and fantasies about public employee bargaining. In H. J. Anderson, *The role of the neutral in public employee disputes,* Washington, D.C.: Bureau of National Affairs, 1972.

Worchel, S. et al. Determinants of the effect of intergroup cooperation on intergroup attraction. *Journal of Conflict Resolution,* September 1978, *22,* 429–439.

Yager, P. Mediation: A conflict resolution technique in the industrial community and public sectors. In H. J. Anderson, *New techniques in labor dispute resolution.* Washington, D.C.: The Bureau of National Affairs, 1976.

Index